Closson quickly corrected, "Left five-zero, drop five-zero. Fire for effect!" The fire control officer called back for verification, warning Closson that the rounds would be almost on top of our position. "Affirmative, that's where the enemy is," Closson told him. We ate dirt as we flattened ourselves into the depression that served as our NDP. We knew that final "drop five-zero" would put the next salvo just outside our claymores. And if that didn't stop them, they'd be in the perimeter with us.

Seconds passed, then we heard the deafening whoosh that accompanies a large steel projectile as it punches a hole through the sky. The incoming rounds sounded like an express train . . . with us waiting at the depot. I nearly ruptured my eyelids as I clenched my teeth and waited for the end of my life. . . .

EYES BEHIND THE LINES

Gary A. Linderer

IVY BOOKS • NEW YORK

Ivy Books
Published by Ballantine Books
Copyright © 1991 by Gary A. Linderer

Library of Congress Catalog Card Number: 91-92201

ISBN 0-8041-0819-6

Manufactured in the United States of America

First Edition: December 1991

Cover photo courtesy of:
    Sgt. Robin "KRIS" Kristiansen (Ret. Army)
    Co. L RANGER 75TH Infantry
    Republic of Vietnam 1969–70
    Rochester, WA

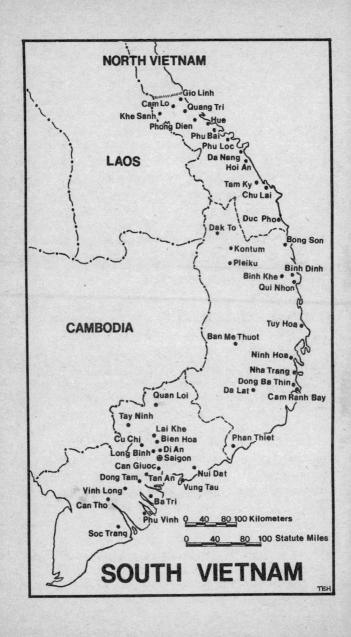

PROLOGUE

I had to smile at the irony of it all as the C-130 slammed onto the runway at the Phu Bai airstrip near the imperial city of Hue. Only seven months ago, another C-130 had delivered me to this same hot, sticky, strip of tarmac situated on the coastal plain in the northern part of the Republic of Vietnam. Back then, I had been a green twenty-one-year-old, sold on the idea that I was one of America's finest, answering my country's call. I was full of piss and vinegar and ready to take on Uncle Ho and his whole Asian horde. I had volunteered for airborne infantry, advanced individual training, and Jump School in an attempt to get into Officer Candidate School; my two years of college and ROTC had not impressed the army enough to select me as a candidate for the program. However, it did impress them enough to send me halfway around the world to attend a one-year seminar in combat survival.

I had been lucky enough to be assigned to the famous "Screaming Eagles" of the 101st Airborne Division and had opted for "fraternity life" by volunteering for special operations duty with F Company, 58th Infantry (Long Range Patrol).

The army had done an excellent job of pumping all of us full of massive doses of self-confidence. Back in the States at Fort Gordon and Fort Benning, the cadre had hot-wired my buddies and me into believing that we were indeed "the baddest motherfuckers in the valley." We developed a heightened sense of immortality and esprit that caused many of us to say a prayer each night that the war would go on long enough for us to get over there.

Some of our instructors threatened us with stories about how tough "Charlie" was and warned us that he would blow us away in a minute if he caught us "half steppin'."

1

They promised that if we fell asleep on guard, we'd wake up wearing an extra smile—one cut from ear to ear. We figured they were probably just bullshitting us. After all, we were Airborne, and the baddest motherfuckers in the valley. Airborne didn't half step, and we sure as hell didn't sleep on guard. Mr. Charles had better watch his ass when we got to the Nam.

My first seven months in country had exposed the lie. The cadre hadn't been bullshitting us, and we weren't the baddest motherfuckers in the valley, either. The damn valley was full of bad motherfuckers. Upon our arrival, we quickly discovered that we were as green as the stiff, chafing new jungle fatigues they issued us. The months of training back in the States had been woefully inadequate for what we would experience in the Nam.

The first few weeks proved to be a twenty-four-hour-a-day, seven-day-a-week cram course, "How to Stay Alive in a Hostile Environment." And no training, in any amount, could truly have prepared us for the actual trials and tribulations of combat. Combat was its own finishing school. But we learned! Slowly but surely, we became jungle-hardened LRPs.

We developed the ability to perform under adverse conditions and in situations that would have destroyed lesser men. Those who couldn't cut it were quickly and quietly weeded out of the program and sent to other units. There was no place in the Long Range Patrol for the weak, the timid, the unmotivated. In time, our "greenness" had faded, just as the color had bleached from our uniforms and the rest of our gear. The dense, mountainous jungles and the constant sun/heat, sun/rain, sun/sweat, sun/dust cycle that was Vietnam had leached the parade-ground perfection out of each of us.

Humping the steep mountains of the Annamese Cordilla with hundred-pound rucksacks on our backs had increased our endurance. We learned to stalk the thick vegetation flanking the enemy's high-speed trails with the stealth of a panther. We learned how to wait for the enemy along those trails, and to strike with the speed and deadliness of the cobra. We made an alliance with the jungle. It soon became our friend, providing us with shelter and cover as we sought out our enemies. We conquered our fear of the darkness, and learned how to use it to conceal us from the searching eyes of the NVA. We had studied the enemy at his own game. After a while, we had become its master.

For years, our six-man teams had infiltrated silently into the enemy's staging areas to gather intelligence and to find him and kill him where he thought he was secure. Swift but deadly ambushes had left numerous NVA patrols no more than fly-blown heaps of carrion along the jungle trails. Many NVA couriers and VC political officers had died while moving between the lowland villages and the distant mountain sanctuaries. Ammo caches had exploded in the faces of unsuspecting NVA soldiers attempting to resupply themselves. Base camps and supply depots had been destroyed by sudden artillery barrages and well-plotted B-52 ''Arc Light'' bombing runs. Numerous troop concentrations had been destroyed in sudden assaults by Cobra gunships or airstrikes by fast-flying U.S. fighter-bombers.

The NVA knew that this death and destruction was not the result of mere chance. Someone was out there watching them! The enemy had come to fear and hate, yet respect, the ''men with the painted faces.'' We had adopted their style of war. They had always preferred to pick the time and place to engage their enemies in combat. The men of the Long Range Patrols had taken that option away from them. They were being taught the same demoralizing lesson that they had forced our soldiers to learn: death was everywhere in Vietnam. There were no havens!

A couple of weeks before I reached the ''hump,'' the midpoint in my twelve-month tour, the NVA took back their option. It was my fourteenth mission, a twelve-man ''heavy'' team recon patrol into the Roung-Roung Valley.

Sgt. Al Contreros was the overall team leader of the two combined teams. We had inserted at dusk into an elephant grass–choked ravine next to some heavy jungle. John Sours had broken his ankles on the insertion. Not wanting to compromise the team, he had played down the extent of his injury.

We moved into the jungle at dusk and located a wide, well-used high-speed trail snaking along the base of a ridgeline. We followed it east until we heard a warning shot a couple of hundred meters to our front. We set up an L-shaped ambush at a bend in the trail and lay back to await the dawn.

During the night enemy patrols with flashlights came looking for us. They passed within ten feet of our positions. We held our fire, not wanting to initiate the ambush with so many alerted NVA soldiers in the immediate vicinity.

At dawn, we discovered that Sours's ankles were too swollen for him to function without help. The team leader made the decision to extract him from our original LZ and sent him down to the ravine with an escort of two other LRPs. As the medevac ship lifted him out, we heard another shot up the trail from our ambush site. The sound of the helicopter extracting Sours must have made the NVA think that we had all been pulled out. The second shot was probably an "all clear" signal to the NVA soldiers in the area.

An hour later, ten NVA entered our kill zone and we initiated the ambush, killing nine of them. Their point man, although wounded, escaped. We checked the bodies and discovered that among the dead were four nurses and an NVA major with a dispatch case full of maps and documents. We called for a reaction force to come in and help us secure the area. We waited for an hour before being informed that no reaction force was available. In addition, our helicopters were tied up in a brigade-size combat assault and would be unable to extract us for several hours.

Our position was precarious. We had stayed too long at the kill zone waiting for help that would not be arriving. We had violated one of the cardinal rules of long-range patrolling—never remain at an ambush site without being reinforced. The team leader informed us that we were to move out immediately and attempt to find a more defensible position on higher ground.

Jim Venable, our assistant team leader, walked out into a nearby clearing to flash our position to our company commander's circling command-and-control chopper. As he sighted through the hole in the center of the signal mirror, NVA soldiers hidden in the surrounding jungle opened up on him with automatic weapons, severely wounding him in the arm, neck, and chest. The rest of the team laid down a heavy volume of fire as two other LRPs ran out and dragged the wounded point man back into the perimeter.

Thirty or forty NVA assaulted our position from the direction of the original LZ. We beat them back, killing several of them in the process. The next few hours were hell. We drove one assault after another away from our position, directing artillery and Cobra gunships against the surrounding NVA. Our ammunition was running low, when the team leader ordered us to tighten up the perimeter so that he could direct our supporting fire in closer to us. As the remainder of the team moved to consolidate their positions, a large, command-detonated claymore mine exploded to our rear, sending thousands of deadly pellets through our ranks. When the smoke cleared, four LRPs were dead, and the remainder were wounded. Only three of us were still able to defend our perimeter.

For two hours we fought desperately to stay alive. Cobra gunships crisscrossed our perimeter in a determined effort to keep the NVA from wiping out the survivors. We brought in medevac choppers and were able to get three of the most seriously wounded out by jungle penetrator.

Just as we were about to write ourselves off, a hastily formed reaction force comprised of LRPs from our own company helicopter-assaulted into a bomb crater a hundred meters from our position and fought its way through the surrounding NVA to our perimeter. We were saved. Later, in the surgical center in Phu Bai, I was to find out how serious our losses had been. Sgt. Al Contreros, the team leader, Sgt. Mike Reiff, Sp4c. Art Heringhausen, and my best friend, Sp4c. Terry Clifton, had been killed. Sp4c. Frank Souza, Sp4c. Riley Cox, Sp4c. Jim Bacon, Sgt. Jim Venable, and Sp4c. Steve Czepurny had all been wounded so seriously that they were being shipped back to the States. Their tours were over. Only Sgt. John Sours, Sp4c. Billy Walkabout, and myself would return to duty after recovering from our wounds.

It was a heavy loss for F Company, one that would take months to recover from. I had lost a best friend on that hilltop, a loss that would cause me grief and anguish for years to follow. You see, it had been my fault that he was there that day.

I had witnessed another man's heroism that should have

won him the Medal of Honor. On three separate occasions, Billy Walkabout, although wounded in the hands, had charged unarmed up to the NVA positions to retrieve an errantly dropped jungle penetrator to medevac our wounded. I had learned of my own vulnerability. Death had been at my side that day. I had accepted it. I had made peace with my maker and then, in the next instant, had begged Him to spare me. I had even made up my mind to kill the wounded and then myself, if it appeared that we would be overrun. I would not let myself or my buddies be taken prisoner. Was I heroic, self-serving, or playing God? These were questions I could never answer.

After four weeks of convalescence at the 6th convalescent center at Cam Ranh Bay, I had conned my doctor into sending me back to my unit early. I could not bear to goldbrick in the security of a convalescent center while my comrades were still pulling missions up in I Corps. REMF (rear-echelon motherfucker) life was not for me! They cut orders shipping me back to Bien Hoa to clear the division rear before being reassigned. There was a good chance that I would be sent to another unit.

I spent a couple of days with an air force buddy from my home town at the air base at Cam Ranh Bay, then hopped a C-130 directly to Phu Bai. I decided not to report to Bien Hoa and take the chance of being shipped to another outfit. It would be good to get back. My first Christmas away from my family and fiancée would not be spent with a bunch of strangers.

December 16, 1968

The three-quarter-ton truck slid to a stop in front of the LRP compound. I gingerly lowered myself off the back and walked around to the shotgun side to thank the two engineers from the 326th for the lift. They waved and sped on up the road, leaving me standing there in a cloud of red dust. I turned to look at the large plywood sign bearing the LRP scroll of F Company, 58th Infantry (Long Range Patrol) and the "Screaming Eagle" patch of the 101st Airborne Division that stood guard over the entrance to the company area. "The Eyes Behind the Lines," painted in bold black letters under the insignia, sent a ripple of pride through me. I quickly tossed my kit bag over my shoulder and started up the road to the TOC (tactical operations center).

I felt foolish using the cane, but the wound in my right leg still caused a little discomfort when I put my full weight on it. I couldn't help but wonder what I would find when I got back to the outfit. Besides the eleven men killed or wounded on my last mission, over two dozen of the old guys had been within a couple of weeks of DEROSing (returning to the States after completing their tours in Vietnam). That had been nearly a month ago, and a lot can happen in thirty days.

As I neared the wooden steps leading up to the TOC shed, Kenn Miller came walking down the road from the supply tent. When he spotted me, he yelled, "Linderer! When did you get in?" He ran up and slapped me on the back. "Damn, Linderer, it's good to have you back, man."

I grinned back at him and said, "It's great to be back, Kenn. I had all of Cam Ranh Bay I could take."

He grabbed my bag and climbed the steps beside me.

7

"Hey, man, you're not going to believe all the cherries we got now. Shit, almost everybody's gone. It ain't the same outfit anymore. Fuck, it's good to have you back." He hesitated as he seemed to notice the cane for the first time. "Look, buddy, you go ahead and report in. I'll take your shit down to my hootch, third from the end. We got a couple of empty cots. You bunk with us until you get squared away."

I nodded my appreciation and watched as he walked away. I couldn't help but smile. I hadn't expected to see him again. He was just finishing his first six-month extension when I was hit. He must have done it again. Miller was the kind of gutsy little bastard that you knew you could rely on in a tight situation. Some guys you didn't trust, some you just wondered about. Miller was a sure bet!

I walked into the TOC and came face-to-face with the first shirt, who broke into a huge smile when he saw me. "Well, well, the prodigal son returns! Ya get tired of gold-brickin' down in REMF city?" He laughed and motioned for me to sit down as he reached for my orders. After a minute or so, he looked up from the paperwork and said, "Damn, boy, you fucked up. These orders say you were supposed to report to the division rear at Bien Hoa for assignment. Whatcha doin' here?" I had hoped that my transgression wouldn't be noticed, but obviously it was hard to put anything over on the first sergeant.

"Top, I can explain that. You see, when I got my release from the Convalescent Center I noticed that it said that I was supposed to report to Bien Hoa for reassignment. I talked to a couple of guys in the next ward that had been wounded before and had gone through the same process. They told me that half the time, they reassigned you to a new unit. I couldn't take the chance they'd do that to me, so I hopped a flight from Cam Ranh directly to Phu Bai. Hell, look at the money and time I saved the army, at the time, Top!"

It had made a lot of sense when I came up with the idea, but it sure didn't sound very convincing then. The first sergeant's eyes dropped back down to the set of orders in his hands. "Well, now that you're here, I sure as hell ain't gonna send you back down to Bien Hoa. I guess we can take care of the paperwork. What's this medical profile shit? Are they so short of beds down at the 6th that they're sendin' troops back early?''

"Let me explain that, too, Top. You see, I almost got myself killed down there in the middle of a riot at the USO show between about a thousand Koreans and twice that many GIs. If I'm going to die, it sure in the hell ain't going to be from getting myself beaten to death with my own crutches. Besides, Sarge, you don't expect me to spend Christmas with a bunch of REMF legs,* do you?''

He smiled again, "Linderer, you ought to be a lawyer or a damn used-car salesman.'' He stuck my file in a wire basket on his desk. "Go get you a bunk. We got plenty of empty ones. We'll find you something to do until you're ready to go out again. Anyway, son, it's good to have you back again.''

Captain Eklund, the CO, and Lieutenant Williams, the XO, walked in as I turned to leave. The CO grabbed my hand and pumped it warmly. "I was wondering how long you'd ghost on us down at Cam Ranh. I'm glad you're back. Go get your shit squared away, then come back and see me. You still know how to play bridge?''

I nodded and said, "Well enough, sir. And it's good to be back.'' I stepped back and saluted, then turned and pushed my way through the door.

Miller was waiting for me. "C'mon, fuckhead, show me around,'' I whispered as we walked down past the row of hootches.

We passed several LRPs, none of whom I recognized. Miller saw my puzzled expression and stated, "See, I told you. There are only a couple of dozen guys here now that were here when you got hit last month. This is a different outfit. It's going to take some rebuilding to get this unit back in shape again. They've even got me, a spec four, as an acting platoon sergeant! I'm about the only one who knows everybody. The company can't get division to shake loose any promotions.''

I shook my head in disbelief. "Are Sours and Walkabout back yet?''

"No,'' he answered. "Sours is at Camp Zama in Japan and isn't supposed to return until February, and Walk-

---

* Non-Airborne Infantrymen.

about went home a week ago on a thirty-day-extension leave. None of the others are coming back. They were all hit hard. We haven't gotten any of the details yet, but we heard that Venable, Cox, and Souza really got shot up bad. You're the first to return.''

He found me a bunk at the end of his hootch and was helping me get my gear stowed, when John Looney, J. B. Bielesch, John Mezaros, Boom Boom Evans, Larry Chambers, Mother Rucker, Claymore Owens, and Ray Zoschak all crowded into the barracks to welcome me back. God, it was great to see those guys again. There weren't many of the old vets left, but the ones still around were good enough to provide a nucleus for several new teams.

After I got settled in, we all headed down to the Ranger lounge to tip a few brewskies. I went to see Captain Eklund after evening mess. He wasted little time offering me the job of company clerk. He had read my file and knew that I could type. I politely refused, telling him that I would like to get back on a team as soon as possible. He seemed pleased at my response and told me to help around the orderly room until my leg recovered, then he'd see what he could do about getting me back on the team. He said that he doubted we would be pulling very many missions for a while because there weren't enough experienced men in the company to field more than three to four operational patrols. The rest of December and part of January would be spent breaking in and training replacements for the LRPs we had lost over the past month.

We talked about the last mission, comparing notes on what had happened. I could tell that he was shouldering a lot of the responsibility for the men we had lost. The CO had served his first tour as a platoon leader with the 1st Brigade of the 101st back in '65 and '66 and had not lost a man. The four LRPs who had died on the November 20 mission into the Roung-Roung had been his first losses as commander of F Company, and he was having a difficult time with it. My heart went out to him. I tried to assure him that no one blamed him. That day, too many factors had contributed to our predicament. He had done everything he could have done. It just hadn't been in the cards for us. The fact that we had killed over two hundred NVA, including the executive officer of the NVA 5th Regiment did not lesson his grief.

I considered telling him about Terry Clifton, the source of my own guilt, but decided that it was something I would have to bear alone. When we had finished, I excused myself and returned to my hootch. It had been a long day, and I was still under the euphoria of my return to the LRPs.

December 17, 1968

My first full day back with F Company was occupied with replacing the weapon and all the gear and equipment I had lost November 20. I had to start from scratch replacing my LBE (load-bearing equipment) and my rucksack and pack frame. Then I went down to the ammo bunker and picked up a couple of bandoliers of M-16 ammo and fourteen empty magazines. It felt good to be armed again. Believe me, bouncing around Vietnam with only a cane for protection left a lot to be desired.

I had reported to the 2/17th Cav's dispensary after breakfast to have my wounds checked. The medic told me that the wound in my left thigh seemed to be draining all right, but he was concerned about an abscess forming after the wound itself closed over. He wanted to take the plastic drain out and start packing it so that it would heal from the inside out. Oh, boy, that's all I wanted to hear. I could still remember the screaming pain from the raw nerve endings in my right thigh when they changed the packing in that wound.

December 18, 1968

I put in some time typing day-reports in the orderly room. Tim Long, the company clerk, seemed relieved to have someone to share his boredom with. It didn't take me long to realize that there had to be a better use of the time it would take for me to work off the remainder of my profile. The doctor back at Cam Ranh Bay told me that it would be two to three months before I made a full recovery.

The CO came in and told me not to make any plans for the evening. With Sours, Souza, and myself away for the past month, and Schwartz off at Recondo School in Nha Trang, he hadn't been able to put together a foursome for bridge. One of the new "shake 'n' bakes," Sgt. Bill Marcy, played a mean game of bridge. Lieutenant Williams, the CO, and I made four. I told him that I would be happy to play if he could find some duty for me a little more exciting than flogging a Remington typewriter to death. The captain said that he'd see what he could do. Marcy and I lost four games in a row to the F Company officer corps, but the bottle of Dewar's Scotch that we disposed of somewhat mitigated the pain of defeat.

December 19, 1968

The CO called me down to the TOC and told me that, if I thought I could handle it, he would let me fly belly-man on some of the overflights and insertions coming up. In addition, I could ride along in that capacity on his next hunting expedition over the A Shau Valley. Captain Eklund occasionally sought a little additional excitement by going out in an LOH scout chopper or a Huey slick when one was available to see what he could scare up in the valley. Once in a while, he'd come across an NVA truck park or a bunker complex back under the trees and fire them up. If there was a Cav "pink" team in the area, he'd soon have a couple of Cobra gunships blowing the hell out of the area with 40mm cannons and aerial rockets. It was great sport and very effective. The rides would give me a chance to feel useful again and give me a few hours to log for an Air Medal.

December 20, 1968

Captain Eklund selected me to go before the 2/17th Cav Soldier of the Month board. I didn't know whether to feel honored or abused. We had been attached to the Cav back in August and were expected to furnish a soldier for the competition each month. The winner represented the Cav in the competition for the division Soldier of the Month. I finally decided that it was my availability and not my ability that had won for me the dubious opportunity.

The Cav really didn't have a lot of use for LRPs, and we reciprocated their feelings, especially after their reaction team's heroic actions November 20 (when they cowered on the LZ while our fellow LRPs charged to our rescue). Since the competition had started, I couldn't recall one LRP winning at the Cav level. Of course, none of our participants had expected to win, so they probably hadn't tried very hard.

The first sergeant told me to bone up on military regs, general orders, map reading, communication procedures, and general knowledge of U.S. small arms. I would be expected to show up in my best set of starched ''cammies'' with all the appropriate patches and insignia in the correct places. He informed me that he didn't expect me to make a career out of the preparation, but since I had to go through the motions, he would sure appreciate it if I would try to make a better showing than our usual entrant. The standard run-of-the-mill LRP was not a slouch, a sluggard, or a sleaze-bag. No, sir, there wasn't a drop of air force blood in any of us. But we didn't mix very well with others. LRPs had a natural tendency to do the unexpected, to try the unconventional, to play the nonconformist. It wasn't that we didn't care—hell, caring's what kept us alive out in the bush. So I promised the first sergeant that I would give it my best shot. I didn't have anything else going on anyway.

The trips to the dispensary every day were becoming a drag. The medic would push and probe a little at the wounds, remark about how well I was coming along, give me a few strengthening exercises to do, and then curl the hairs on my ass changing the packing in the wound. I just knew that if I could persuade him to let me hold his balls in my hand while he worked, I could convince him to be a little more gentle in his approach. Damn, I couldn't wait to shake the medical profile and get back to a team.

December 22, 1968

I went before the Soldier of the Month selection board at 1000 hours on the morning of the twenty-second. There were four other guys ahead of me, one each from A Troop, B Troop, and C Troop, and one from headquarters. They all seemed pretty sharp. I wondered if any of them had ever been outside the perimeter wire. We waited outside the briefing room in the Quonset-type headquarters building over at the Cav compound. The others all seemed nervous. They must have planned on winning. I just wanted to avoid embarrassing the company. I must admit that I looked pretty damn sharp in my heavily starched cammies. The Koreans at the laundry had outdone themselves at my request. My newly issued jungle boots had really taken a spit shine. New patches and insignia were freshly sewn and in the right locations on my shirt. If they were going to pick us for our looks, I was the sure winner.

When it was my turn, I was amazed at the thoroughness of the questions. By some quirk of nature, every question they asked me happened to be one of the items I had paid special attention to during my studying. I answered everything—correctly. The final question required me to go over to a table containing a topo map, a compass, a straight-edge, and a pencil, and, given two known points and the compass heading to each, compute my present location and the distance between my present location and point A: Hey, no sweat! In two minutes I had determined the back azimuths and had run my lines back to the point of intersection and then amazed the five-man selection board by estimating 1,350 meters as the distance from point A to my present location. I hit the distance right on the money. I knew from the way that they looked at each other that I had impressed them.

I went back to the company and told the first sergeant that I thought that I had done pretty well but the competition had looked awfully sharp.

I started getting my mail again. I had received a lot of letters and packages from people I had never heard of before while I was recovering in the hospital. You know, friends of friends, distant relatives, local people who had read about it in the paper. I felt honored at all the attention. To date I had received bundles of letters from eighty-six different people. I had made up my mind that if all those people could take the time to write to me, I would find the time to answer every letter.

Writing to that many people was going to be tough, but it felt good to know that there were still a few people who cared about us. We were only over there trying to do our duty as we saw it. Maybe there was hope for us yet. Like our forefathers, we had answered our country's call. It was not our privilege to justify the reason. When the day comes that the American soldier reserves the arbitrary right to decide if he will or will not fight, then that will be the day that our great nation becomes a third-rate power.

Our service in Vietnam did not mean that we individually agreed with American foreign policy, or that we condoned the way that the war was being waged. It only expressed the love of freedom and the patriotism that we, as U.S. military men, felt. History would judge our actions and justify our participation. Those who called us baby killers, who maligned and defiled us, would be shown for the cowards and traitors that they were.

December 24, 1968

I received forty-two more letters and twelve packages at mail call on the morning of the twenty-fourth. Nine of the letters were from strangers. I had to borrow stationery from several of my friends to answer my mail. I had yet to receive one letter condemning the war or my participation in it. Where did all of the protestors that we constantly heard about come from? It sure in the hell wasn't from my hometown.

All of the mail and packages, and the fact that I was able to rejoin my comrades, had combined to make the Christmas holiday one of the happiest and most memorable of my life. Only the absence of Barbara, my fiancée, and my family had prevented my joy from being total.

Tim Long walked into my hootch and informed me that Top had just gotten a call from the 2/17th Cav informing him that F Company's representative had been selected as the Cav's Soldier of the Month. Top told him to congratulate me and then to break the news that I had five days to prepare to go before the selection board for division Soldier of the Month. What a royal pain in the ass!

December 25, 1968

Christmas day arrived with all the joy and happiness of the day before and probably the day after. The expected snowfall missed us by about 1600 miles. Armed Forces Radio good-naturedly announced that Santa Claus reportedly had been hit by a SAM battery crossing the DMZ, and had last been seen going down in flames north of Dong Ho. SAR (search and air rescue) had failed to find the wreckage.

It really didn't seem any different from any other day. A last minute flurry of letters and packages resulted in a bumper-crop mail call, and a few of the hootches sported toy Christmas trees sent from home. Judging by their condition, they had been brought via Tibet by camel caravan. AF Radio played carols and holiday music all day, but it just didn't seem like Christmas.

Word was out that a major holiday cease-fire was in
effect, but no one really expected the NVA or the VC to
honor it. Tet of '68 was still too fresh in everyone's memory. At our morning formation, the first shirt told us that
the cooks over at the mess hall had prepared a special meal
in the holiday spirit. He encouraged us all to go over and
partake of the feast. It was a well-known fact that LRPs
never passed up a chance for good chow.

The mess hall was packed when we arrived. The fan-
tastic aromas wafting through the building made the half-
hour wait in the long line worth the effort. When we finally
reached the serving line, we were shocked to find that the
cooks and their assistants where actually smiling and making a concerted effort to be friendly. We shuffled along the
line as they heaped mounds of mashed potatoes, sweet
potatoes, cranberry sauce, green beans, and dressing on
our trays. Just when we thought that we couldn't carry any
more food, the final three servers forked thick slabs of
turkey breast over the top of the pile and then tried to cover
it all up with steaming slices of pink ham. A couple of
large, freshly baked biscuits were added for balance.

We staggered away from the serving line to the nearest
tables with empty seats, and passed by the beaming Puerto
Rican mess sergeant. I swear, not one insult or obscenity
blasted us as we moved by him. In fact, he shocked us all
by saying, ''Ju men enjoy jour food now. Cum back and
take all ju can eat. We don want dos dinks down by da
dump to hab a feast now, do we?''

Well, buenos fuckin' noches, Sarge! We didn't know
you even gave a shit! The chow was unbelievable. We ate
until we couldn't walk. If the NVA had decided to pick
that very moment to launch 122s at us, we wouldn't have
had time to waddle to the bunkers.

On the way back to the LRP compound, Chambers the-
orized, ''You know, if those bastards can put out a feed
like that at Christmas, what in the hell do they do back in
the kitchen the other 364 days of the year?''

About 1400 hours, one of our slicks landed down on the
chopper pad. A couple of LRPs who had been out on
an overflight jumped out and motioned for us to come on
down. We were standing around the Ranger lounge down-

ing a few beers in an attempt to stimulate our digestive process, so we stumbled down to see what they wanted.

When we arrived, the two LRPs reached inside and slid the carcass of a large tiger out on the asphalt pad. They told us that they had been on their way back in when the pilot had spotted the cat out in the open south of Firebase Birmingham. A tight 180-degree turn had put them alongside the running tiger, who dodged and twisted but couldn't evade the marksmanship of the two LRPs and one of the door gunners. They had landed and retrieved their prize. It was a beautiful specimen, but seemed to be only half grown.

We skinned it out for the pilot, who said that he would try to find a taxidermist in Saigon to tan it so he could send it home.

Early that evening, and after quite a few beers, John Looney, Larry Chambers, John Mezaros, and I decided to put on a little entertainment for the company—sort of a mini Bob Hope Special. In the spirit of the season, we decided to dress up like Christmas characters and go through the company area caroling. Looney returned from his hootch dressed as a Roman centurion. He wore leather sandals, a tunic fashioned from a sleeveless black T-shirt and a black towel, a survival blanket draped from one shoulder, and a jungle machete tied to his waist. To top it off, he had made a Roman helmet from a steel pot with a scrub brush attached to its crown for a crest. It wouldn't win any prizes for authenticity, but it had to rank high for originality.

Chambers was breathtaking as the Blessed Virgin. His realistic approximation of the Judean veil and gown worn by the Hebrew women of Our Lord's era was indeed something to behold. Although jungle camouflage was probably not in vogue two thousand years ago, the final impression was definitely one of Mary—as a commando.

Mezaros showed up in his hand-fashioned burnoose and robe of a Nazarean shepherd, again in camouflage. But the costume and the staff he carried did lend a good deal of credibility to our Christmas troupe.

Obviously not as inventive as my cohorts, I reported back without costume. A twenty-minute scavenger hunt through every footlocker in my hootch yielded *nada*. There was a limit to what you could do with a survival blanket. After a short discussion, we all decided that, to complete the program, what we really needed was a Christ child. In unison, we all shouted "Miller!" Our delegation of four soon cornered him in his hootch and proposed our offer. He really got pissed! Short guys must be light on holiday spirit. You would have thought he'd be honored! Penchansky was mentioned as a possible alternative, but he was Jewish and wouldn't go for it. Besides, Penchansky looked more like Howdy Doody with bifocals than he did baby Jesus.

We found ourselves running out of time, so Mezaros came right out and nominated me for the role. Now I've been a lot of things in my life, but at six feet, one inch, and 195 pounds, I sure in hell wasn't going to be baby Jesus. Inspired, I decided to go dressed as Easter Jesus. Hopefully none of the other LRPs would notice the difference. I quickly limped back to my hootch and stripped down to a pair of shower shoes. After putting on a swimming suit, I wrapped a black towel around my waist. A dose of Kiwi shoe polish provided a pretty realistic beard, and a piece of black gauzy fabric torn from a "good" VC's black pajamas and draped over my head provided the hairdo. I confiscated someone's Christmas wreath for a crown of thorns. Somebody fashioned a cross for me out of a couple of 1×4s, and we were in business.

Soon the F Company Touring Troupe was moving from hootch to hootch belting out one Christmas carol after another. A problem developed immediately when we discovered that none of us knew all the words to any of the carols. We'd begin booming out the first verse or two, then one or two of us would either fade out or ad lib words that rhymed but didn't make sense. A sharp ear could definitely distinguish the alien words in our rendition of "Come All Ye Wasteful" and "Jungle Balls."

The participation from each hootch varied, but most of the guys showed enough compassion to join in and help us cover up our mistakes. By the time we reached the last hootch, we had gathered quite a following (Jesus would have been proud!).

We drifted down toward the club. Singing does parch the throat, so our shepherd, Mezaros, suggested that we all adjourn to the "inn" to refresh ourselves before continuing on. The entire entourage, numbering somewhere in the neighborhood of forty disciples, took heart from these words and began to mill about in search of libation. The festivities lasted late into the night, with much singing and merriment. Many onlookers arrived and were baptized into the faith. Later, when the supply of beer began to run low, someone suggested that I repeat the miracle of the wedding feast at Cana and turn some water into wine. I refused on the grounds that that particular miracle had come much later in the life of Christ and I just really wasn't up to it.

The party broke up around 2300 hours when Kenn Miller, obviously unimpressed with the deeply religious spirit of the day, tried to molest our blessed virgin and got punched out for his troubles. (Actually, I think Chambers rather appreciated the pass!)

December 26, 1968

Don't ever put Kiwi shoe polish on your face. I looked like Aunt Jemimah for a week.

The first sergeant announced at morning formation that, beginning on the twenty-seventh, we would begin conducting classes for all the replacements. The platoon sergeants and the more experienced LRPs would provide the instructions. The goal was to be able to field twelve operational teams by the middle of January. It was obvious that to achieve that goal, no team would have more than two experienced members. The very thought of that possibility unnerved me. Most of the guys that I came incountry with did not yet see themselves as experienced as the Old Foul Dudes were. They were long gone. Now we were being called upon to provide leadership and backbone for these new teams. It would be tough!

Top told me after formation that he wanted me to give classes on map reading and to assist Zoschak in teaching immediate-action drills and patrolling techniques. Besides the two of us, ten of the other senior team members would be conducting classes on other components of long-range patrolling. We would probably not be pulling very many missions until the cherries were broken in.

As in the past, part of the training would consist of numerous ambush missions outside the perimeter wire. They were seldom very successful, but they did provide a suitable laboratory for refining skills learned inside the classroom.

I received word that I was to be awarded the Bronze Star for valor for the Nui Ke mission back on November 4. This came as a complete surprise to me. Zoschak was awarded the Silver Star and the chopper pilots received Distinguished Flying Crosses. Everybody, including the company commander, should have been decorated for that mission. I was told that the award would be given out at the next awards ceremony. I was really feeling high. The Bronze Star would look good between my Silver Star and my Purple Hearts. I knew that my fiancée and my family would be proud when I got off the plane with my ribbons on my chest.

December 27, 1968

It was Barb's birthday. God, I wished that I could share it with her! She had turned twenty-one and was already quite a lady. I really admired the way she had held up under the pressure of my being in Vietnam. I knew that it was tougher on her than it was on me. I was aware of my situation at all times, while she was forced to rely on in formation that was always a week old by the time she got it.

She wrote and told me that she was fully aware that it was possible for her to receive a letter from me saying that I was safe and sound, while at that very moment I could be lying in the jungle dead or wounded. I prayed that her job as a nurse and the planning of our wedding in June would keep her mind occupied. I wrote her every chance I got, telling her about what was happening in my life. I knew just how important letters were. I was definitely a lucky guy to have such a wonderful lady.

That knowledge gave my presence in Nam a purpose and meaning far greater than anything else. It was my primary motivation for enduring the anxiety and suffering that all of us went through during our tours. My family ties and patriotism fed my sense of survival, but it was Barb that kept me going when I didn't think I had anything left. I really felt sorry for the guys who didn't have anyone waiting back home. I felt even worse for the poor bastards who got the Dear Johns. I saw how it destroyed their attitudes and affected their performance in the field.

In Vietnam, distractions were deadly, and there doesn't come any bigger distraction than a Dear John. If the young ladies back home could only have seen the effects of such letters, I doubt that very many would have been written. It was a gut-wrenching, mind-numbing experience to watch a buddy's heart torn out and dropped in his lap. There wasn't much you could do for a friend in that situation. Dear John letters killed their share of American fighting men, of that there can be little doubt.

I was still trying to keep up with all the mail from the States. I wrote about eight to ten letters a day but didn't seem to be gaining much ground. I was lucky that my medical profile afforded me the time to respond at all.

December 29, 1968

Chambers and I walked outside the wire around 0930 hours to detain a Vietnamese who had been spotted digging behind one of the graves about seventy-five meters from our perimeter. When we got to him, we discovered that he had a U.S.-issue smoke grenade and a trip-flare in his possession. He seemed quite nervous and became visibly terrified when the Cav chopper landed a few feet away. His eyes rolled back in his head as the helicopter took off with him on board. They would take him to division and drop him off for interrogation. If the ARVNs (Army of the Republic of Vietnam) got him, he would be in big trouble. I was only glad I wasn't in his sandals.

The medic at the dispensary was really pleased with my recovery. The drain had been taken out and the wound had closed over. He told me to try some jogging and stretching exercises to get my muscles back in condition.

That afternoon, I got involved in a pass-and-tag football game down on the chopper pad. I knew that I was probably overdoing it a little, but it looked like so much fun that I had to join in. Big John Burford promptly knocked me on my ass a couple of times for my trouble. The exercise felt good, but I paid dearly that night when my right hamstring went into spasm on me.

Later in the day, I went before the review board for division Soldier of the Month. The competition was a lot tougher than when I went before the Cav's board. I hadn't studied as much as I had the last time. I felt that I did pretty well but didn't really expect to win. After all, these guys were professional lifer-type REMFs.

General Zais, the commanding general of the 101st, was there. He remembered me from the surgical hospital at Phu Bai back in November. I must admit that this man really impressed me.

24

January 1, 1968

Well, a new year had arrived. It was the year that I would return home. The year that I would marry Barbara. It was undoubtedly the most important year of my life. All that I had to worry about was that I would still be around when it came to an end. I found myself thinking about that a lot, maybe more than I should have. I fully realized how lucky I had been back on November fourth and again on the twentieth. I had survived two missions over a sixteen-day period that should have, by all rights, resulted in the untimely deaths of eighteen LRPs. We had escaped annihilation on both occasions by the narrowest of margins. I had always been pragmatic and believed that you made your own luck. But those two missions had convinced me that something—call it fate, or the divine hand of God—had interceded to save our lives. No rivers had parted, no bushes had spontaneously ignited, no enemy soldiers had been struck down by lightning. But dammit, when everyone around you is dead or wounded, you're almost out of ammo, and outnumbered twenty to one, something more powerful than "luck" has to be around to save your ass.

There were many variables that influenced our survival on those two missions. Weather, terrain, artillery and helicopter gunship support, TAC Air, reaction forces, extraction choppers, the enemy's ability and perception of the situation, our own ability and perception of the situation. All contributed to the odds of survival.

Yet, after weighing those odds, it was very difficult to understand how we had survived. Sure, we had an influence on the odds, but we sure in hell didn't control them. The only conclusion that I could draw from either experience was that a little luck is fine, but it sure didn't hurt

25

none to know how to pray. I only hoped that God wasn't
Buddhist.

I sensed a danger in philosophical and rational thought.
Soldiers were taught to follow orders and to leave the
thinking to their superiors. That eliminated a lot of self-
doubt and apprehension. During the first part of my tour,
I had been able to follow that pattern. But a few brushes
with death had thrown me off on a tangent.

I began to see that combat was actually a game of
chance. Everything relied on the odds—the percentages.
My destiny was not really in my hands. I had sensed that
this line of thought was dangerous and made up my mind
to work it out before I got back on a team. I couldn't afford
a case of the jitters.

Tim Long stopped by my hootch and told me that I had
come in runner-up in the competition for division Soldier
of the Month. I had surprised myself by coming that close.
But close only counts in horseshoes and hand grenades.
(Whoever had coined that phrase had never witnessed an
Arc Light.) I was glad it was over!

For participating in the competition, I received a "nifty"
Storm King cigarette lighter with the Screaming Eagle patch
on one side and an outline of Vietnam on the other (they
couldn't even give us a Zippo!), a full case of good old Coca-
Cola, a Parker pen and pencil set, and a letter of commendation for my file. The Cav awarded me an engraved statue
of a paratrooper. Believe me, I would have traded it all for a
chance to get back out with a team.

We had put on a big party at the Ranger lounge New
Year's Eve. All of the cherries had really gone out of their
way to make us few surviving vets feel important. Damn,
it was hard to believe that the two dozen of us who were
left were the old guys. Does seven months in-country do
that for you? The Old Foul Dudes were the old guys. In
our eyes, they always would be. But they were gone, and
the rest of us wondered if we would be able to fill their
boots. They had been so good in the bush. They had been
unshakable. They had brought out the best in us. Now that
they were no longer with us, would we still be able to
function the same way?

Maybe it was just an attitude adjustment that we each
had to go through, but something told me that we had a

long way to go before we could achieve their abilities. There were a lot of new men in the company who would be relying on our skill, our experience, and our leadership. I just prayed that we would not be found wanting when the real test came.

I looked at my short-timers calendar and discovered that I was down to 155 days and a wake-up. Although I was still not a true short-timer, or even a double-digit midget, I was shocked to realize that I had already been in Nam for 209 days. The time had really gone by quickly, and yet it seemed as if I had been born there. I wasn't really "short," but I was a lot shorter than 75 percent of the LRPs in the company. I couldn't even imagine having 364 and a wake-up. Yes, my time had passed very quickly, but then, one year was really not very long.

It had become glaringly obvious that the one-year-tour policy of our government was a tragic mistake. I knew that it had been created to keep the American public from rejecting our participation in the Vietnam conflict. A year was an acceptable period of time to keep an eighteen- to nineteen-year-old from his family and his future. Committing him to battle for a longer period or for the duration would have caused immediate public outcry back in America. Vietnam was not World War II. We hadn't been attacked, and the security of our nation was not at risk. The one-year combat tour fit in nicely with the two-year draft.

The problem that it caused was that it took six months for the typical American recruit just to attain the level of confidence and proficiency necessary to make him an effective combat soldier. Just when he had reached this highly tuned degree of efficiency, he went "over the hump." He found himself on the back side of his tour. He could see daylight for the first time and actually began to believe that he could survive his tour—if he didn't take any unnecessary risks. No longer was he concentrating on defeating the enemy. No longer was he anxious to engage him in mortal combat. He was only trying to stay alive, to survive the end of his tour and go home. When he had finally attained the skills and had acquired the experience to get the job done, the motivation was gone.

I am not saying that he didn't continue to perform or to do his job. It was just that the fine edge was no longer there. His mission had changed to pure survival. In my opinion, the combat tour should have been extended to two years. Many Vietnam vets extended their tours for six to twelve months anyway. Some because they liked it, some because their Nam time would give them an early out and would cancel any Stateside duty still due on their enlistments. The one-year tour resulted in a loss of experience and talent that was not passed down to new arrivals. We paid for this mistake with mounting casualties and, often, substandard performance from our soldiers. We were in a war we couldn't win, fighting under silly rules made by career-building officers to satisfy a misinformed government that was hiding the truth from an irrational media that was trying to incite an uncaring American public. We were dying for nothing.

January 3, 1969

It began raining again on the third. The monsoons had more or less called a halt to the fighting since I had returned from the hospital. They had come with a vengeance in '68–'69. The training had to be postponed until the weather cleared.

Jim Schwartz returned from MACV Recondo School in Nha Trang. It was good to see him again. We were supposed to have attended the school together, but our departure, scheduled for November 27, was interrupted by the Roung-Roung mission on the twentieth.

January 5, 1969

The continuing rain forced us to move the classes inside the hootches. The forecast called for several more days of rain before we could expect a break. The classes were kept small for lack of space and so that the instructors could give some personal attention to their students. Immediate-action drills and patrolling techniques were taught but could not be demonstrated.

Mother Rucker and John Looney explained radio-communication procedures. They did an excellent job on a very difficult subject. I, too, learned a lot from them. I had been a wee bit weak in technique on adjusting artillery fire missions and calling in gunships. One had to be proficient at all the skills of long-range patrolling to lead a team.

My specialty was the map and compass. I was good. I had a sixth sense in the field that enabled me to orient myself with a map to the terrain I was in. Zoschak told me that I had the "feel" for it. I could study a topo map before a mission and then feel my way through the area of operations as if I had been there before. The contour lines on a topo map provided a three-dimensional image in my mind. Usually, when we got on the ground, the terrain looked familiar to me. It wasn't anything I had learned in the army. I had been able to do it back in my Boy Scouting days and, later, when I roamed the Ozarks in pursuit of whitetail deer.

January 6, 1969

The temperatures began dropping during the night of the sixth, reaching the low 40s. We were freezing to death and nobody seemed to give a shit. The hot Vietnam weather had not conditioned us for such an extreme temperature shift. We huddled in our hootches around five-gallon metal paint buckets quarter-filled with sand. Anything dry enough to burn was broken up and fed into the buckets. Strips of wood from ammo crates, pallets, shelves, and old foot-lockers were tossed into the flames. When they were used up, old newspapers, magazines, letters from home, card-board, anything that would burn was added to fuel the fires. Even the precious heat tabs we used for cooking and chunks of C-4 explosives were offered up in our quest for warmth.

The penetrating dampness caused by days of monsoon rains made the cold even worse. None of us realized the threat of hypothermia. Those of us who were vaguely fa-miliar with the word didn't know for sure if it was the medical term for rabies or the vacuum-sealed bottle be-longing to a large, aquatic African animal.

The condition itself was not well known during the Vietnam era. We spent a miserable day trying to stay warm while the wind gusted and the rain poured. Only the knowledge that in Vietnam such weather couldn't last sus-tained us.

January 7, 1969

More of the same weather. Someone brought up the possibility of being asphyxiated by the fumes from the fires raging within our hootches. We panicked momentarily, then realized that the 25-mph winds gusting through the screened windows undoubtedly removed any noxious gases—along with the heat. We kept canteen cups of water boiling over the fires. Coffee, mocha, and hot chocolate kept our pilot lights going while we waited out the tropical "blizzard."

January 8, 1969

Our platoon sergeant stopped by to tell us that the army would be flying in field jackets and blankets from Korea. They promised to have them here as soon as the weather broke. But when the weather broke, we wouldn't need them anymore.

January 9, 1969

We burned the rear steps from our hootch in our fire buckets. Tomorrow, we vowed that we would draw lots to see who would ignite the phoo-gas barrel along the perimeter wire while the rest of us sat on it. Death by conflagration was beginning to look appealing. Highs in the low 60s, lows in the low 40s. We couldn't store enough warmth during the day to sleep through the night. The only protection was damp survival blankets and poncho liners.

January 10, 1969

The rain stopped. The wind abated. The temperature rose into the high 90s by midday. Our fatigues dried out just in time to soak up the sweat that poured from our bodies. Crazy!

Training was to start up again on the eleventh. They told us that missions would begin again around the sixteenth. The teams would be ready. I almost killed myself stepping out the back door to go to the piss tube. Some idiot son of a bitch had swiped our rear steps.

January 11, 1969

About 2200 hours, two heavy explosions shook our hootch. They seemed to come from a couple hundred meters outside the perimeter. The cherries in the hootch panicked, not knowing what was happening or what to do. Playing the veteran, I calmly stepped into the aisle and announced, "Those were rockets, let's get to the bunkers." I was nearly trampled in the ensuing stampede as the occupants of my barracks blew past me on the way to the bunker located between the hootches.

Expecting the attack to be over by then, I calmly walked out the front door and looked up just in time to see another 122mm rocket explode one hundred meters outside our wire. To the west I saw two more streaks of white light pushing hardware toward our perimeter. I noticed a reddish glow off in the distance between Nui Ke and Banana mountains as another rocket rose from the jungle to join its comrades. It was enough for me! I dove into the bunker as two more explosions erupted, one just outside our perimeter bunker, the other among the revetments guarding the Cav's Cobra gunships on the opposite hillside. They weren't after us, they were after the choppers.

We stayed in the bunker until the attack was over. Ten rockets had been launched from the vicinity of Nui Ke Mountain before patrolling gunships had reached the area and discouraged further attack. The first four had hit outside Camp Eagle. Another had impacted in the Cav compound but had caused little damage. The last five had failed to explode. We had been lucky for a change.

January 12, 1969

Billy Walkabout returned to the company from a thirty-day extension leave. He was about six days late, but no one said anything about it. All of the veteran LRPs turned out to welcome him back to the unit. I was really glad to see him. He was the only other survivor of the Roung-Roung mission, besides myself, to have returned to the company. But I was surprised by his attitude. He seemed changed—totally different from the comical, fun-loving kid I had known two months before. One minute he would seem distant, almost unreachable, then the next minute he would swing into a different mood that bordered on the obnoxious. He was loud and boisterous, saying things that were designed to provoke rather than patronize, to shock rather than soothe. I tried to get close to him. After what we had been through together, I had felt a special survivor's bond had formed between us. But he seemed to ignore my friendship, not wanting to share the experience or resurrect its memories.

I was hurt by his rejection but soon realized that Billy had been wounded on that mission, perhaps more deeply than anyone had even realized.

After evening mess, I went down to the CO's quarters to have a chat with him. I had been doing a lot of thinking since rejoining the unit, and it was becoming apparent that I had developed some serious doubts about my self-confidence and my ability to function on a team. These feelings hadn't popped up overnight. They had grown over the past couple of weeks from a small seed of doubt planted a month earlier when I was recovering from my wounds back at Cam Ranh Bay. My vulnerability had been revealed to me for the very first time.

The LRPs had not lost a man or had one seriously

wounded in the seven months since I had joined the company. The teams had been through a number of close calls but had survived each unscathed. On November 20, our immortality had been stripped from us. I learned the hard way that LRPs bled, LRPs suffered pain, and LRPs died. It scared the shit out of me! For the very first time, I realized that my life could come to a sudden and tragic end in the lush, endless jungles of Vietnam. I could easily wind up like Reiff, Heringhausen, Contreros, or my friend Terry Clifton.

I dreamed about their shattered bodies lying where they had fallen amid the devastation of combat. I had witnessed the instantaneous metamorphosis of four strong, healthy young bodies into four lifeless mounds of torn flesh and fractured bone, watching helplessly as their blood and bodily fluids drained from them to nourish the fertile jungle floor. My friends and comrades, in a millisecond of time, in the blink of an eye, in the flash of an explosion, had simply ceased to exist. Life was too fragile for war! Death was too final for life! I had begun to see myself in my dreams, lying among the dead back on that hilltop. There, I, too, was one of the lifeless mounds of torn flesh and fractured bone. I no longer felt pain, discomfort, loneliness, comradeship, or love. I didn't feel anything. I would think to myself that if this was death, then it really wasn't that bad. Except for the sad condition of my body lying there on the jungle floor, nothing had really changed.

In my dream, I would tell myself that it was time to leave that place of death and destruction and go back home to my loved ones. There were places I had to go and things I had to do, time was wasting. Then I would realize that I couldn't leave that hilltop without my body. I would will it to get up and come with me, but it ignored my pleas, satisfied to remain there with its comrades for eternity. There was no place for the dead among the living, except in their memories.

I would wake up in a cold sweat, clutching the sides of my cot and hoping that the men around me had not witnessed the nightmare that had shattered my sleep. The dreams had begun to come more frequently and more vividly. They were eroding my self-confidence and creating an apprehension about going back out in the field. I knew that my only salvation was to get back on a team before the dreams became an obsession.

I told Captain Eklund that I thought I was ready to go out again and asked him if he could get me reassigned to a team. He told me he appreciated my spirit, but he wasn't going to send me back out until the doctor removed my profile. The CO wouldn't be responsible for me until I was 100 percent. He said he needed experienced LRPs, but he wouldn't assign me back to an operational team until I was ready—both physically and mentally.

I was shocked. He seemed to sense the battle that was building up inside me. Then he smiled and said, "All of your wounds have got to heal before you go back out in the field again. Only you will know when you're really ready. You come and tell me when you think you are." I walked slowly back to my hootch, aware that my commanding officer had known more than he had let on. He had to have known the confusion and doubt that I was going through! I would take his advice. I had to face up to my problem myself. Until I could handle it, I wouldn't be fit to fill a slot on one of the teams. And only I would know when that day arrived.

January 13, 1969

I made the decision to take my R & R in late April. I had originally decided to do without one, wanting to save the money for life after Nam. But I found myself calculating that I could probably get out of the field by the end of April if I took my R & R then. By the time I returned and spent a couple of days fucking around down at Bien Hoa, I would be too short to go out on any more missions. Two months before, I would never have thought about ways to keep from going out. What was happening to me? What had changed me? Was fear getting the best of me? Walk-about wasn't the only one suffering hidden wounds!

January 18, 1969

The company held a memorial service for the four LRPs killed November 20. The entire unit stood in formation down on the chopper pad as the division chaplain read the eulogy for our fallen comrades.

As I stood facing the four inverted rifles planted firmly in the ground by their fixed bayonets, I eyed the empty boots in front of each weapon. My gaze moved to the four helmets adorning the memorial altar behind the rifles. I stared unblinkingly as the chaplain's words struggled to penetrate my daze: "... brave ... heroic ... valorous ... noble ... glory ... duty ... the supreme sacrifice ... a grateful nation ... a heavenly reward."

Then suddenly, it hit me that it was all bullshit—pure, unadulterated bullshit. They were dead! I had been there! I had seen them die ... and the way they died. There hadn't been anything glorious or noble about it. Dying is not a glorious or noble act. Oh, they had been brave, all right. The poor bastards wouldn't have been there if they hadn't been brave.

Heroic and valorous? What determines heroism and valor? I witnessed an act of heroism and valor that day, the kind that Medals of Honor were awarded for. I had seen Billy Walkabout charge repeatedly into an enemy position to retrieve a jungle penetrator, even though he was wounded and weaponless. He didn't do it because he wanted to be a hero or because it was a valorous thing to do. He did it because his buddies were lying wounded around him and that penetrator was their only hope of rescue. Love and devotion had inspired him.

Riley Cox had fought the enemy with a grin plastered

across his face. His right forearm had been broken and was dangling down from above his wrist. Somehow or another, he had tied it back out of his way using his other hand and his teeth. He had then shoved a towel into the hole in his abdomen to keep his intestines from spilling out into his lap. In spite of his severe wounds, he had fought on for over three hours, pumping round after round from his 12-gauge shotgun into the enemy positions. Did he do it for glory? Hell no, he did it because his comrades could no longer defend themselves and somebody had to do it. Love and devotion had inspired him.

And then there was Jim Bacon, our radio operator. I had seen him ignore the pain caused by a fist-size chunk of meat blown from above his right knee. He continued to brief the company commander flying above us in his C&C chopper, then he called for medevac helicopters to extract our wounded. The entire time, he had battled shock from loss of blood. Did he do this because it was his duty? Negative! Love and devotion had inspired him.

No, padre, don't preach of supreme sacrifice to us. A sacrifice is an intentional surrender of something dear for a greater good. Those men didn't sacrifice their lives intentionally. They were taken from them! They hadn't wanted to die. I'm quite sure that it had come as a complete surprise to all of them. Call it what it was, chaplain. They had paid the maximum price. They had gotten their tickets punched. They had bought the farm. But please don't stand there and tell us they made the supreme sacrifice. If there was a sacrifice involved, it was because some insensitive, incompetent brigade commander had made the decision that a surrounded twelve-man heavy LRP team, twenty miles out in the jungle, could wait a few hours for rescue. He was the son of a bitch who "made" the sacrifice.

A grateful nation? C'mon now! We read the papers. We knew what our nation thought of us. Our nation hadn't shown gratitude for its soldiers since 1945. Oh, sure, the entire country didn't feel that way. Some of them had loved ones in Vietnam. But the rest of them were just too damn apathetic to give a bloody shit. They were just thankful that it wasn't them doing the fighting and dying. I guess wars without causes just weren't very popular.

And please, chaplain, a heavenly reward? Does that mean that God was on our side and, somehow or another, had given us His blessing for the death and destruction we had wrought—sort of a supreme seal of approval? He may accept war as one of the necessary evils that overshadows mankind, but surely He doesn't condone it!

Must we believe the Muslim doctrine that heaven is the assured reward for those who have died in battle? Wouldn't it be wonderful if it were true! But what if it is not? What if only cold, dark, empty, lonely, everlasting absence of life is a soldier's reward for death on the battlefield? Do you have to make a religious experience out of it so that the survivors are inspired to embrace it openly and without fear? "So, Padre, just finish your service and let us get back to our work. We've got some friends who need avenging."

January 20, 1969

I decided I would go to the dispensary in the next day or two and get my damned profile removed. The memorial service a couple of days earlier had helped me to come to grips with my fears. I had rationalized that if it was my time to go, then it was my time to go, and there was damn little I or anybody else could do about it. I was back in control and maybe a little wiser. Fearing death and then suffering guilt for that fear was a personal conflict in which there could be no winner.

January 24, 1969

Great news! I went to the medics after breakfast and let them probe my wounds for a few minutes. Satisfied with the way they had healed, they watched as I ran in place and climbed up and down a series of steps. When I finished, they signed a medical form, removing my profile. I was to be a soldier again.

I returned to the company area and turned in a copy of my release to the first sergeant. He looked at it and smiled before saying, "Good timing, young man! You've got a mission tomorrow. You'll be going out as Sergeant Closson's assistant team leader (ATL). Keep an eye on him, it's only his second mission as a TL (team leader)."

I returned to my hootch, wondering if I had been too hasty in getting released from my profile. Closson was a shake 'n' bake (graduate of the noncommissioned-officer course) and hadn't had a lot of experience LRPing, let alone leading a team. I knew I needed a sort of reorientation mission, without any additional pressures, to make sure I still had what it took. Going out as Closson's ATL was forcing the issue. At least Mother Rucker and Jim Schwartz would be going along as the senior RTO and point man!

Closson and I took off for the overflight at about 1400 hours. The AO (area of operation) was along the Perfume River, just north of Leech Island. We would be reconning a four-square-klick area on the west side of the river. The terrain consisted of low, rolling hills covered in thick single-canopy jungle interspersed with elephant grass and bamboo thickets. I knew from past experience that the going would be slow and tough.

We spotted several trails from the two passes we made over the area. From an altitude of one thousand feet, it was difficult to tell if they had been used recently. That was why we were going in. All of the trails seemed to drop down toward the river from the mountains to the west. Obviously, they had been used by the NVA at one time or another to move from their jungle sanctuaries to the lowlands around the cities of Hue and Phu Bai.

We returned to the company area, where we briefed the rest of the team. Our operation order had stipulated that the mission was purely reconnaissance. We were not to set up an ambush along any of the trails. A couple of cherries would be going out with us. Groff was a timid kid from central Pennsylvania. But he had shown in training that he was capable of learning and following orders. The other one was a short, chubby soldier named Kilburn who Closson picked to hump the artillery radio. He seemed a little slow in adapting and would bear watching on the mission. I had to go down to supply and draw an entire new issue of combat patrol gear. All of my old gear had been lost when I had been wounded back in November. I had already drawn a new pack and frame and replaced my LBE, but I had put off replacing all of the miscellaneous equipment that enabled a LRP to survive in the field while accomplishing his mission: Penflaires, compass, poncho liner, D-ring, rope, K-bar, albumin, medical supplies, flash panels, signal mirror, etc. The list was endless. Two hours later, I was looking at a cot full of enough military paraphernalia to open up my own army surplus store.

I was pleased to discover that all of the old skills in packing the rucksack and sound-proofing my gear had come back to me. I hoped my prowess in the field would do the same. I spent a restless night searching my soul for the courage and self-confidence I would need the next day. A lot would be riding on my attitude. I realized that if I couldn't recover what I had before I had been wounded, then I was done as a LRP. No one would need to tell me. I would pull myself off the team.

January 25, 1969

We inserted by helicopter about two hours before dark. Momentary panic set in as I dropped five feet to the ground from the right side of the chopper and headed for a dense stand of bamboo twenty feet away. I looked back over my shoulder: Schwartz and Kilburn were right on my heels. The team leader and the other two men were to my left and a little ahead of me, running for the same cover.

We dove into the middle of the bamboo thicket and set up in the usual wagon-wheel defensive position, as we had trained to do. The panic began to subside as the initial excitement receded. I noticed that everyone seemed to be performing as a well-oiled machine—even the cherries. We "laid dog" for perhaps fifteen minutes, silent and motionless, before Closson signaled for Rucker to try to establish radio contact with our relay team on Firebase Brick. Mother nodded that he had them "lima-charlie" (loud and clear) and proceeded to give them our sitrep (situation report).

After radio contact was broken off, Closson motioned for Schwartz to lead the team off to the south. The team leader moved up to walk "slack" for the point man, as Rucker fell in behind him. I nodded for Groff and Kilburn to take up their positions in the patrol formation and then moved in behind them to provide rear security. We moved out slowly, easing through fields of razor-sharp elephant grass and crossing narrow stands of thick brush.

The heat was intense, and soon we were drenched in perspiration. We had to cover a couple of hundred meters to reach our RZ (recon zone) before dark. It didn't take me long to realize that I had really gotten out of shape during my two months of convalescence. My right leg was already in spasm and the seventy-five-pound rucksack on my back felt like it had doubled in weight.

Suddenly, Schwartz held up his hand and then slowly lowered it, palm down, to indicate that the team should stop—he had found the first trail. We set up line security, each man in file alternately covering a flank. I covered our back-trail as Closson and Schwartz moved up to check the path for sign of recent activity. Minutes later, they returned. Closson looked back at me and shook his head. The trail had been cold. It was too close to darkness to try to move on and locate another trail, so, being careful not to leave tracks, we crossed the first one and moved down toward the river to set up an NDP (night defense position). If we couldn't watch an active trail, then at least we would be able to monitor sampan traffic on the river. Closson was thinking! He was showing all the characteristics of a good team leader.

Schwartz located a dense copse of bamboo on a high bank just above the water. He, too, knew his shit. It was an excellent site, offering good concealment and possessing a slight rise to our west that would provide excellent cover should we get hit during the night. We waited until dark, then Schwartz and I crawled out and set up four claymore mines to guard the land approaches to our position. It felt good to be back on patrol. At least, I hadn't forgotten how to function.

We took turns eating in twos. The cold, dehydrated chicken-and-rice LRP ration tasted delicious. Adrenaline must feed the appetite! I couldn't help but notice that Schwartz, Rucker, and I were the only ones on the team who had prepared our first meal of the patrol back at Camp Eagle. We had removed the heavy foil cover from our rations and added water to them before we boarded the insertion ship. It was a trick we had learned from the old guys. Cold water took a long time to re-hydrate the freeze-dried rations. If you mixed your first meal before you inserted, then taped the plastic bag shut and stuck it inside your front pocket, not only was it warm when you were ready to eat it, but it was also soft and palatable. In addition, you didn't have to worry about tearing off or disposing of the brown foil outer bag. When we finished our meal, we took out our next meal, untaped the clear plastic bag, added cold water, then resealed it. The morning's meal would be ready when we were.

Closson assigned guard watches of one and a half hours each, with the cherries pulling the first and second watches. I had drawn the last watch, 0400 to 0530. I approved of his assignments but, personally, did not care for one and a half hour stints. It was too hard to lay there awake and alert for that long. I preferred breaking each watch into forty-five-minute periods, with each man pulling two separate watches. But it was his team, and I wasn't going to challenge his preference.

As darkness set in, and our night vision adjusted, I was once again amazed at the period of total silence that occurred before the night creatures began their incessant chirps, clicks, and hums. They always started up on cue, as if some superintelligent critter among them gave a sign with a director's baton. Once the din began, it would lapse into a reassuring chatter of activity that would continue until someone or something trespassed into the immediate vicinity. Then, as quickly as it had begun, the jungle sounds would cease, as if someone had thrown a switch, silencing all activity. Nature's alarm system! It was our signal that something or someone alien was out there.

It must have been close to midnight before I finally pulled my poncho liner over my head and settled into its womblike security. The two cherries had not been alone on guard. I had been their silent backup. Closson must have realized this when he had assigned them their slots.

January 26, 1969

Four hours later, Rucker's hand on my arm alerted me to the fact that it was my turn to provide security for my sleeping comrades. I sat up, wrapping my dew-dampened poncho liner around me. A distant sliver of moon, just setting over the mountains to the west, cast a pale illumination over the river below. A dense layer of mist rose from the surface, concealing anything that might be moving over the water. An hour later, I noticed the black had begun fading to gray along the eastern horizon as the morning sun began to push the darkness ahead of it. The noises of the night diminished as if the conductor had decided it was time to turn down the volume.

In the predawn light, I began to wake the rest of the team. It was time to eat the first of our two daily meals. As the men stirred around me, I pulled out my two-quart collapsible canteen and took a couple of swigs of the lukewarm water. I stuck the trigger finger of my right hand into my mouth and attempted to rub a night's worth of caked-on saliva from my teeth. It would never replace a toothbrush!

Rucker and I downed our morning ration while the rest of the team maintained security. When I had finished, I moved out to the front of our perimeter to pull in two of the claymores while Schwartz went for the others. While I was out there, a sharp cramp told me I had better take the opportunity to empty my bowels. I had become accustomed to mess hall food again, and the dehydrated supper of the night before had decided that it was time to seek the freedom of the great outdoors. I quickly scooped a cat hole in the soft, black soil, off to the side of the little nob we had spent the night on. When it was deep enough to hide its contents from marauding animals or NVA soldiers, I quickly dropped my pants and emptied the contents of my bowels into the hole, sacrificing accuracy for speed. I hurriedly pushed the fresh earth back into the hole, carefully concealing any sign of my overnight deposit. Wild bears were not the only creatures who shit in the woods! I just wondered if they felt as vulnerable as I had when they were locked in that position. My God, what a horrible time to have the enemy walk up on you! Should one complete his mission or E & E (escape and evade)? I would imagine that the sight of a camouflaged recon man sprinting through the jungle with his pants around his ankles would momentarily render the surprised enemy unable to give chase. Of course, at the first opportunity, something would have to be done to cover up the scent trail.

I returned to the perimeter just as Mother was calling in the morning sitrep. I had everyone police up their sleeping positions before we moved out. I remained behind to provide the finishing touches to restoring our NDP to its original, undisturbed condition. After I was satisfied that no enemy soldier would be able to discover our presence, I moved out and caught up with the rest of the team. We continued upriver, hoping to locate the next trail before the sun rose in the sky. We had to be very careful, because it was at that time of the day that Mr. Charles and his boys were the most active. We inched through the mixture of dense single-canopy forest and elephant grass. Schwartz stopped the team every ten to fifteen meters to listen. He was being extra cautious, but none of us seemed to mind. If the NVA were in the immediate vicinity, we would hear them long before they heard us.

Two hundred meters away, we encountered another trail. This one, too, showed no sign of recent passage. We stepped over it and gingerly proceeded upstream.

Late in the afternoon, we located a third trail. It showed signs of three to four individuals having used it within the past forty-eight hours. The ground was still damp from all the rain we had had the previous week, and the faint outlines of tracks made by Ho Chi Minh sandals showed clearly. The tracks were heading east, away from the mountains. We moved away from the river, staying parallel to the trail, and crossed the single-canopy cover to the base of the mountains a klick away.

As we moved cautiously into double-canopy jungle, we suddenly found ourselves in the middle of a bunker complex. We froze in place as Schwartz moved up to check out the first two bunkers. They appeared to be old and to have been unused for several months. They had been dug about a meter deep into the jungle floor and then covered over with a roof of teak logs, leaving a six-inch firing slit across the front and access from the rear. Dirt had been spread across the log roofs and shaped so that, to the unsuspecting intruder, they appeared to be just another couple of the ever-present termite mounds. They were large enough to accommodate three to four men and their weapons. Moss had grown over the tops of the mounds, adding to the natural camouflage effect. If they had been occupied, we would have been up Shit Creek without a paddle. We were only five meters away when we first spotted them.

A search of the area revealed three more in the same general condition. The five bunkers were only fifteen meters off the trail we had been flanking. We decided not to stay in the immediate vicinity of the bunkers, so we moved another fifty meters up the trail, crossed it, and set up our NDP where we could observe any movement on it during the night.

January 27, 1969

The second night proved uneventful. No one used the trail under the cover of darkness. I felt my self-confidence returning as each hour passed. I was proud of my own ability and also of the performance of my comrades. No one had become complacent or bored even though the AO was beginning to appear cold.

We decided to move back down to the river and spend our last night monitoring the Perfume. We knew from past experience that the thirty-meter-wide river was often used by the NVA to move supplies and personnel between the populated areas to the east and the enemy base camps to the west. "Our teams had interdicted their attempts on many occasions."

January 28, 1969

Around 0200 hours, Schwartz shook me awake. His hand over my mouth told me there was danger in the air. I sat up and slowly reached for the CAR-15 on my right and the claymore detonator on my left. Seconds passed before I could hear the muted sounds of an engine moving down the river in the direction of Hue. It appeared to be moving slowly and staying in midstream.

We were in a free-fire zone and could initiate an ambush on the boat and its occupants. I realized we had screwed up by not setting up any of our claymores facing the river.

Closson eased up next to me and whispered in my ear that he felt we should let them pass. Visibility was less than ten meters, and the mist hanging over the river made a sighting totally impossible. It also served to muffle the sounds of the sampan, making it difficult to get an accurate fix from the engine noise. We let it move on past us in the darkness, then Rucker contacted our relay team on Firebase Brick and reported the sighting. They radioed back that we should call in a fire mission if another one should try to pass our position.

We went to full alert just to be on the safe side, but the remainder of the night proved to be uneventful. As dawn approached, we broke camp, again making sure that the NDP had been restored as close to its natural condition as possible. Our extraction sight was a clearing a few hundred meters south of our present location and a hundred meters back from the river. We had to reach it by 0930 hours. Rucker radioed our relay team that we were moving out to our PZ (pickup zone) and would inform them when we reached it.

It took us the better part of two hours to reach the clearing. The vegetation was dense single-canopy and saw grass choked with a variety of "wait-a-minute" vines. We were forced to move in spurts, covering ten meters at a time. It was difficult for our point man to break through the cover without making a great deal of noise. We changed point position three times, just to keep the lead man from wearing out.

The heat was unbearable in the thick cover. No breeze arose to cool us off, and the humidity in the moist vegetation must have been close to 100 percent. When we neared the clearing, the brush began to thin out, making the going a little easier. We made it with ten minutes to spare.

Rucker reported that we had reached our PZ. He was informed that our extraction ship was already inbound and less than five minutes out. We set up a circular perimeter in a clump of waist-high grass and sat back to await our bird. Seconds later, we could hear it coming down the river. It was low and hard to pinpoint, but the unmistakable sound a chopper makes flying close to water reverberated down the valley.

Lieutenant Williams was flying C & C and broke in to tell us to pop smoke. Closson liberated the pin on a purple smoke grenade and tossed it downwind from the clearing. I finally sighted the Huey as it flared up over the trees to our east, and I stepped into the PZ and guided the ship in with hand signals. The pilot set the Huey down forty feet to my front. It wasn't often we had the opportunity for an extraction from a set-down PZ.

As soon as the ship touched down, the six of us were up and running. We on-loaded in the reverse order of our insertion. Timing was everything during an insertion or an extraction. These were the most critical times of a mission. We were good at it, seldom keeping the chopper on the ground over seven seconds.

I gave the thumbs up to the crew chief, and he relayed to the pilot that we were on board. Mr. Poley, the AC (aircraft commander), pulled back on the stick, and we were up and out of the clearing in seconds. I sat back and enjoyed the ten-minute flight back to our compound. The throbbing of the Huey's powerful turbine made conversation below a scream impossible. The air blowing back through the open doors of the cabin cooled us and made us temporarily forget the midmorning heat that had already reached into the high 90s. We came in low over the rolling, grass-covered hills to the north of F Company's chopper pad and eased in for a gentle landing on the tarmac. As we climbed out of the crowded cabin, we all turned and waved our thanks to Mr. Poley and his flight crew. They were among the best in the aviation battalion that supported the LRPs. We appreciated the risks those men took to get us in and back out again without regard for the peril they often faced. Many of us owed our lives to the daring and flying ability of those pilots and their crews.

We plodded uphill to the hootch to drop our gear before proceeding down to the TOC for debriefing. We had covered our entire recon zone in the four days we had spent out in the bush. There had been no current enemy activity in the four-square-klick AO. However, the NVA were still using the river at night to move supplies and personnel through the area.

After the debriefing, Sergeant Burnell, my platoon sergeant, informed me that I would be going out again on the 30th as Zoschak's ATL. I was delighted! In my opinion, Zo was the best TL in the company. The old enthusiasm had returned, and I knew I had licked my problem. A mission with Zo and his "Howling Commandos" would be icing on the cake. He had been on some of the hairiest missions that our outfit had pulled and had always come out smelling like a rose. He had been the TL on the double mission back on November 4 when we had been shot out of two AOs in a matter of twelve hours. The NVA had mortared us and then come after us with whistles blowing and bugles blaring, but Zo had gotten us all out safely both times. No, the tough little NCO from Worcester, Massachusetts, knew his shit and managed to keep his cool under the most stressful of situations. It was hard to panic when Zo was standing there with a big grin on his face.

January 29, 1969

Zo and I took off at 1300 hours for an overflight of our AO. We would be going in at first light on the thirtieth in the double-canopy jungle north of Nui Ke Mountain. Same old shit—find the rocket sites that had been hitting Eagle.

The AO was full of bomb craters left over from several B-52 Arc Lights, so the selection of an LZ was simply a matter of picking a hole in the jungle. Zo decided on one that was located about halfway down a finger coming off the dominant ridgeline bordering the west edge of our recon zone. It looked like an excellent choice. The finger ran another two hundred meters toward the center of our AO and then began to drop gently down into the major terrain feature in our RZ—a huge bowl-shaped valley bisected by a three-meter-wide jungle stream. We quickly located an alternative LZ four hundred meters to the north at the base of a lesser finger ridge and then marked primary and alternative PZs on the east side of valley as our extraction points. All four sites were deep bomb craters. The extraction ships would have to be rigged with forty-foot ladders.

The east edge of our AO ran up to the west face of Bald Mountain, which was in the immediate area of the launch sites of the last rockets that had hit Camp Eagle back on the eleventh of January.

January 30, 1969

The sky behind us was just beginning to get light when the insertion ship lifted from our chopper pad and headed west toward Nui Ke Mountain. Looking past the pilot's head, I could just see the outline of the massive landmark on the horizon. Our ship soon picked up the C & C chopper and our two Cobra escorts. When we neared the Perfume River, the four-ship formation swung north toward Bald Mountain. Our approach would take us around the north side of Old Baldy to the north-south ridgeline behind it, and then down the face of the ridge to our LZ. We had timed the insertion so that the LZ would still be in the shadow cast by Bald Mountain.

I felt my stomach move up against my Adam's apple as the pilot pulled the plug on us, letting the Huey drop out of formation and descend into the valley below. We flew south, just below the crest of the dominant ridgeline, looking for the finger that harbored our LZ. Suddenly, I heard the Huey's turbine change pitch as Mr. Poley sideslipped to the left and then flared up over the crest of the finger. Our bomb crater was right below us as he brought the chopper into a drifting hover. I took one look below me, not sure if the ground was five feet or fifteen feet away, and jumped. It wasn't five feet. I hit on all fours in soft, red earth on the side of the crater. I was vaguely aware of other LRPs landing all around me. A couple landed higher up on the lip of the crater after a short drop of a few feet. I spotted Zo in the bottom of the crater on his back. His drop would have qualified for a free-fall. Surprisingly, he had not been injured on landing.

The four of us in the crater spent several uncomfortable seconds trying to reach the top, but the loose soil on the sides made climbing almost impossible. The rucksacks we carried threatened to pull us over backward and send us sliding down to the bottom of the pit again. But we finally managed to claw our way to the top and join our two comrades, who were pulling security for us. We moved away from the crater about fifty meters east, staying on top of the finger, until our point man cut to the right and pulled up in a spray of jungle ferns growing from a cluster of large mahogany trees.

We laid dog for fifteen minutes to catch our breath and to listen for sounds of pursuit. Finally, Zo signaled for us to prepare to move out. He wanted to get off the ridge and down into the valley while we were still in shadow of Bald Mountain. We dropped off the ridge, not straight over the side, but on an angling, lateral descent. It took us nearly an hour to cover three hundred meters. Finally, we reached a stand of dense brush twenty-five meters above the floor of the valley. We could hear a stream gurgling and splashing as it dropped down over the rocks fifty meters away.

Just below us was a well-used high-speed trail that hugged the base of the ridge we had just come down. It was little more than a meter wide, but the total lack of vegetation on it indicated that it had seen a lot of heavy foot traffic in recent times. It didn't take the jungle long to heal the wounds inflicted on it by mankind.

Zo wanted to spend a little time monitoring the trail before we moved out into the valley. The enemy traveled a lot in the early hours of the morning, and we were in an excellent position to spot him if he used this particular trail. So Zo signaled that we would remain where we were for an hour or more. I could tell by the way that he kept looking uphill in the direction we had come from that he was uncomfortable setting up so close to the insertion point, but it was the only place we could monitor the trail from a position of high ground without backtracking and moving back up the ridge. We actually stayed there, hidden among the ferns, for three hours before Zo motioned us to prepare to move out. We took our time edging down toward the trail. When we reached it, we crossed it, one at a time, and moved into the heavy brush between the trail and the stream.

I couldn't help but notice the footprints in the damp compacted soil on the trail as I gingerly stepped over it. There were many, going both ways. They hadn't been made by Ho Chi Minh sandals; they showed the unmistakable cleat marks of the canvas tennis shoe-type combat boots worn by the NVA. Some of the tracks appeared to be less than forty-eight hours old. We dropped into a wagon-wheel defense perimeter and lay motionless as Zo took the handset from the RTO and radioed in our observations. We were in the middle of a lot of NVA and we knew it. The relay team radioed back that our "Six" (company commander's designation) wanted us to remain in the immediate vicinity for the next twenty-four hours to monitor the trail. Zo "rogered" the instructions and then motioned for us to set up where we were.

We were about fifteen meters from the trail and nearly the same distance to the stream. We couldn't see the trail itself, but if anyone came up or down it, we would have little trouble spotting him through the vegetation. The noise made by the river would disguise any sounds we might make, but would also drown out any commotion made by approaching enemy troops. We would have to be extra cautious, and keep our fingers crossed that we hadn't been observed inserting. The point man and I crawled out and set up five claymore mines. We set up two facing the trail to our front. I placed the next two to our rear, crisscrossing each other's line of fire and guarding the approaches to our position from the stream. I preferred setting them that way whenever I could. Mike Tonini, a previous team leader, taught me that if you set the claymores perpendicular to your position and then ran the electrical wire straight back to your perimeter, a prowling NVA sapper could guess where you were by the direction the claymore faced and the wire ran. Besides knowing your location, he could also turn the claymore around, aiming it in the direction of the wire. Then he would move back, make a little noise, and as soon as you detonate the mine, *BLAM*, you're history.

By setting your claymores facing away from your perimeter, on forty-five-degree angles, and running the wires straight back from the mine a few meters, then turning the wires back toward your position, one could delude the enemy into believing that the direction of your perimeter was forty-five degrees off from its actual location. If he moved back to the rear of the claymore he had turned around, he would move right into the kill zone of the one set up with crisscrossing fire. The claymore that had been turned around would not be aimed at its owners, and the backup claymore would still take out the sapper.

While I was engaged in setting up my surprise, the point man set up the fifth claymore to the east of our NDP. It would be used to clear a path through any encircling NVA soldiers to our designated rendezvous point across the valley on the crest of Banana Mountain, in case we had to E & E during the night. We rejoined the team when we had completed our work. There were still three hours of daylight before darkness arrived.

Mr. Charles liked to travel in the waning hours of the day almost as much as he favored the two or three hours after sunrise. We quickly downed our evening rations and disposed of the litter. We removed the rocks and sticks around our positions so that we would be comfortable during the night. Shifting positions at night created too much noise.

January 31, 1969

The night was uneventful. The jungle was pitch black, making visual observation on the trail impossible. The sounds of running water to our rear intensified in the tomblike silence of the night, muting any noises made by passing NVA. There was little chance of them marching a military band through the valley, and anything less would have passed unnoticed.

Zo decided to stay in place during the daylight hours of the 31st, monitoring the trail. If we saw nothing by the end of the day, we would cross the stream at dusk and set up a new NDP on the other side. That would give us the final two days of our mission to check out the rest of the valley.

Time passed slowly. Nothing was as tedious as trail-watching. By the end of the second day, my thoughts had shifted toward a good game of bridge.

Just before dusk, Zo signaled for everyone to ruck up and prepare to move out. Minutes later, we were up to our knees in the cool water of the stream, slowly wading to the opposite shore. We weren't thirty meters into the trees on the other side when we ran smack dab into another trail that was the twin of the one we had been baby-sitting before.

The point man froze when he reached it and waved the team back on our tracks. We found a clump of large boulders a few meters upstream from where we had crossed and set up another NDP. We were only ten meters from the new trail, but our cover and concealment were excellent. We set out four claymores in a tight circle around our position, against the outside of the largest boulders that ringed our perimeter. We wouldn't suffer from the backblast if we had to blow our claymores during the night.

We were very close to the trail, almost too close. We would have to be extra careful with our noise and movement discipline. For the second night in a row, our proximity to a well-used high-speed trail would prevent us from applying insect repellant to keep the mosquitoes away. The numerous leeches that we had picked up crossing the stream were allowed to fatten up and drop off when they were finished dining. We couldn't use the aromatic bug juice or a lighted cigarette to remove them, and pulling them off was an invitation to infection. Chow was on us that nigh

February 1, 1969

Twice during the early hours of morning we thought we had movement out on the trail to our front, but we couldn't be sure. It could have been animals. We had heard monkeys howling off in the distance the morning we inserted. If the movement had been enemy troops, they would have probably used flashlights or some other form of illumination in the total darkness of the night. The NVA were good, but their night vision was no better than our own, and we were unable to see across our little ten-foot-diameter perimeter.

A few minutes past 0800, Zo snapped his fingers lightly to get our attention. He then gave the sign for silence and held up four fingers, pointing up the trail to the west. The entire team readied weapons, then froze as a single NVA soldier stepped into view twenty meters up the trail. Right behind him came three more, all clothed alike in fresh khaki uniforms. None of them were humping rucksacks, and only two were armed, both with AK-47s. They didn't appear to be overly cautious, so we were shocked when they stopped out on the trail to our front, a mere twenty feet away.

I tried to become a bush and felt the skin on my back try to crawl down the crack of my ass. I held my breath as I waited for one of them to look over at the mound of boulders we lay hidden in. The two in the front began arguing over something. One of them began gesturing and pointing down the trail to the front, chattering loudly and shaking his head. The second and third NVA seemed to be in total disagreement with him, but he continued yammering about something, obviously trying to make a point. The fourth one appeared to ignore what was going on, preferring not to give a shit about anything.

Finally, the leader won out. The others shrugged their shoulders and followed him as he led them on down the trail.

56

We all looked at each other, and I almost broke into laughter
as Zo flashed us a big shit-eating grin and made the one-
fingered circular sign at the side of his head that stood for
"beaucoup dinki dau." Most definitely! Either they were all
crazy as hell, or they had gotten themselves lost in the jungle.

It was a shame we were after the 122mm rocket sites.
We had just passed up an excellent chance to get a body
count and a couple of prisoners. We could have easily
killed the two with weapons and shot the other two in the
legs and gotten to an extraction point in ten minutes. There
just hadn't been enough time to weigh the alternatives and
make any plans. But we had ascertained that the NVA
were in the area and that they probably had come from a
base camp nearby. Otherwise, they would have been wearing rucksacks along with their web gear, and their uniforms wouldn't have been so clean.

These four NVA were either new to the area, or we had
just witnessed the passage of four enemy REMFs trying to
find their way to the latrine. REMFs acted the same no matter which side they were on! I wondered what they would
have thought if they knew that they had been standing there
arguing with six weapons trained on them with the safeties
off. They would have never made it to the latrine.

We radioed in our sighting and decided to stay where
we were until the next day. Our extraction was set for 0900
the next morning. We weren't comfortable staying in the
same place two nights in a row, but it was likely that the
enemy had no idea we were in the area. It would probably
have been more dangerous to move around trying to find
a new NDP with enemy troops in the vicinity. At least we
had cover and concealment where we were.

Sometime around 2230 hours, six rockets were launched
from four hundred meters east of our NDP. We could see the
red glow against the night sky as they set off from their launch
points, heading toward Camp Eagle. They were close enough
that we could actually hear them as they rose above the jungle.
The launch area was within one hundred meters from one of
our preplotted artillery coordinates, and Zo responded immediately by calling for a fire mission, estimating the exact
location and making the adjustmen for the first volley.

Within seconds, 155-mm rounds from Firebase Bastogne were screaming in from the north to impact almost

dead on target. Zo worked them back and forth over the suspected location of the NVA rockets for nearly five minutes before radioing for a cease-fire. No additional rockets had been launched during the shelling. From all outward appearance, the enemy had been taught a valuable lesson that night. You don't hang around a launch site after you have expended your ordnance. He would think twice about hitting Camp Eagle for a while.

The excitement of the fire mission quickly wore off. We decided to go on two-man watches for two hours each to give everyone a chance to get a little shut-eye.

February 2, 1969

Around 0300, I heard Zo waking the rest of the team. I had developed the habit of getting by on four hours sleep or less when we were out in the field, so I was still awake. When everyone else was awake and alert, Zo whispered in the ear of the man to his right, who in turn passed the message on to the man next to him until it had traveled all the way around to me. Zo thought that he had heard two separate groups of enemy soldiers pass our NDP in the past hour. His position was nearest the trail, so if anyone would have detected movement, it would have been Zo.

Zo put everyone on full alert. The two NVA units had been moving quietly and without any type of illumination. It was obvious that they had been sweeping the jungles for whoever had called the artillery in on their positions. The speed and accuracy of our response had alerted them to our presence. Chances were that they wouldn't stumble over us in the dark, but come daylight, that would be a different matter altogether.

As dawn approached, the CO radioed that he was in the air and inbound with our extraction ship and a pair of "Snakes" (Cobra gunships). He told us to break camp and move to our nearest PZ. We were to be extracted two hours ahead of schedule. Captain Eklund didn't want to give the NVA time to set up reception committees on the area's probable LZs.

We picked up our claymores and moved out quickly to the south toward a cluster of three bomb craters in the middle of a field full of elephant grass that we had spotted on the overflight. They were nearly three hundred meters away and offered the best chance for a quick and safe extraction. We had to cross the trail we had observed all the activity on, and it seemed like it had grown to the width of an eight-lane divided highway since the night before.

Finally, we were all safely across and heading toward the PZ. We moved quickly but stopped every twenty to thirty meters to listen. We were making more noise than normal, and we wanted to make sure we weren't walking into a hasty ambush of the sort the NVA might improvise if they heard us coming. Schwartz was our point, with Zo backing him up at slack. I noticed that Rucker was in constant commo with the CO's C & C ship and was warning him to stay off until we reached the PZ.

It took us over a half hour to cover the three hundred meters, but finally we broke out of the eight-foot-high elephant grass and ran right into the cluster of bomb craters we had been looking for. Zo formed the team up in a tight perimeter just back away from the first crater and motioned for me to do a circular recon of the immediate vicinity. I grabbed Calhoun and we moved out into the grass to scout the area around the craters.

We patrolled a fifty-meter radius around our perimeter and found nothing until we reached the west side of the craters. I broke through the tall grass and stepped into a small fresh trail heading in toward the PZ. It was only fifty meters away from the team's present position and heading in its general direction. The grass in the trail, still wet from the morning dew, had not yet popped back up; someone had come through in the past fifteen minutes. There could only have been one or two men, probably LZ watchers, but somebody was trespassing in the neighborhood.

Calhoun and I completed our circle, cutting no other sign in the elephant grass. I grabbed the handset from him and radioed Rucker that we were coming in from their north. I also warned them that we had an unfriendly or two in the immediate vicinity.

When we joined back up with the team, I related our observation to Zo. The son of a bitch only grinned! He got on the radio and told the CO to send in the pickup ship, he would not be popping smoke. He would signal the ship by mirror and then guide it in by flashing a red panel. Smoke would only give our position away. We had gooks in the immediate area, numbers unknown. Zo requested that the escorting Cobras circle the PZ as the extraction ship came in. If a pair of Cobras couldn't keep the NVA's heads down, nothing could! He directed the Cobras to fire up the grass to our "november-whiskey" (northwest) and to our "sierra-echo" (southeast) as the bird maneuvered in over us.

Not wanting to expose the team during extraction by having us move out into one of the bomb craters, Zo ordered us to fan out and knock down as much of the elephant grass as we could. We would make our own LZ in the middle of all the cover. Within minutes, we had stomped down a circular clearing in the grass fifty feet in diameter. Zo moved into the center of the clearing and began signaling with his mirror. As soon as the circling extraction ship spotted us, it radioed in to confirm his signal. I whipped out a flash panel and began popping it as I backed up to the west side of the clearing to guide in the extraction ship.

Within seconds, the Huey was over us, dropping slowly down into the man-made clearing. The prop wash from the chopper whipped the still-standing elephant grass around us to a frenzy, making it appear that five thousand NVA were attempting to break through its cover and reach us before we could board. As it touched down, the six of us piled into the cabin in record time. WO (warrant officer) W. T. Grant, the pilot, along with Mr. Poley and Captain Meacham were, the best in the business. Grant looked over his shoulder at us and gave a thumbs up, then pulled back on the cyclic and began lifting up and away from the PZ. It was only then that I could hear the steady drone of the Cobras' miniguns as they harvested the remainder of the elephant grass. As far as I could tell, we had taken no fire.

Soon the jungle and Bald Mountain were dropping behind us in the distance, as the Huey beat a path through the thick early-morning air back toward Camp Eagle. I looked out the left side of the chopper to see Firebase Birmingham passing by to the north. We had chalked up another successful mission.

February 4, 1969

I woke up to realize that it was my twenty-second birthday. Funny! I felt as if I had aged ten years since the last one. At least I was satisfied that I was performing as I had hoped I would when I had returned to the unit. I guessed that I was probably just physically tired. Vietnam had a way of just taking from you and never leaving anything of equal or greater value in its place.

I received a package from my fiancée (unbelievable timing!). I opened it to find two large, hard salamis, twenty packs of Kool-Aid, four black Fruit of the Loom T-shirts, twelve cans of peaches, and a couple of bags of pretzels. For some reason, the salamis were covered in green mold. We scraped the mold off and ate them anyway. They were excellent.

Billy Walkabout's team called for an emergency extraction the morning after it had been inserted. They had not been compromised or made contact. Billy had just freaked out on them and exposed their position during the night. It had been his first mission since returning to the company from his extension leave. The pressure had been too much for him. It was a goddamned shame. It was apparent that the tough little LRP had suffered more than physical wounds back on November 20.

Captain Eklund decided to send him down to SERTS (Screaming Eagle Replacement Training School) at Bien Hoa. Billy's combat days were over. He had been a good one, a true hero, but his nerves were shot. It was hard for me to accept. The last time I had been with him in the bush, he had had enough nerve for an entire company. I could empathize with him, though. I, too, had ''seen the elephant.'' It had weakened my resolve and eroded my self-confidence.

It began to rain again. Damn, just when we were getting used to being dry! The rain brought the cold back. It got down to 39 degrees that night. I would rather have seen it 120 degrees. Burnell told me that I would be going back out again as soon as the weather broke. I would be leaving Zo's Howlers and going back to Closson's team.

February 6, 1969

We were enjoying our third consecutive day of rain and cold weather, and my body had responded by catching some sort of bug. I took it over to sick call with me and was happy to discover that the medics concurred with my preliminary diagnosis—I had some kinda bug. Whatever it was, I was running a 102-degree temperature and was passing blood in my shit. It took a temperature of 103 degrees to get you admitted, so they sent me back to my unit with a cold-pack. As far as the blood in my stool, the medic said not to worry about it, it just added color.

He gave me a slip putting me on restricted duty for a week and told me to try and stay out of the rain. Yeah! Like where in the fuck was I supposed to go? He also gave me a couple of different kinds of pills to take but didn't really know if they would help or not. I guess it was something I had eaten—or maybe something that had eaten me.

February 10, 1969

I was still extremely sick, too sick to go back on sick call. So I just stayed in my cot and tried to keep warm. I just couldn't seem to shake the fucking thing. I had gotten all stopped up and was still running a fever. I was sure the rain and cold weather were playing a role in my inability to recover. I discovered I was not the only LRP to come down with it.

John Sours returned from Camp Zama, Japan. He came in and told me that I was also in bed the last time he had seen me. He thought I must be getting lazy. I reminded him that he, too, had been in bed and had ridden his profile pony for over two months. He looked good, and it was great to have him back. He was sure to get his own team, and with Zo getting short, I wanted to go out as John's ATL. The company desperately needed another team leader with his experience. While he was there, I asked him to be a groomsman at my wedding in June. He thanked me and said that he would be honored.

Closson's team went out early in the morning even though it was still drizzling. Sgt. Bill Marcy took my place on the team. Zo came into my hootch about 1400 hours and told me that the team had taken a prisoner, but they had gooks around their position. Zo was taking out a heavy team to secure an LZ for them and to act as a reaction force if they couldn't break contact. Both teams were safely extracted around 1730 hours.

Closson's Team 22 had captured an NVA NCO while he was out looking for a place to shit. What a time to get snatched!

February 11, 1969

Well, my fever finally broke. When I woke up around 0700, it was just gone. My congestion broke loose, too. I no longer felt ill, but I had developed a pretty good idea of how Johnny Quick had felt when he had been shot out of a McGuire rig eighty feet up. I felt like I had been dropped that far and had landed on my head. I was weak and hurt all over. I probably just needed to get some good old cold LRRP rations in me and I would be as good as new.

I received word that Team 22 would be going out along the Song Bo River on the 12th to plant some sensors along the trails bordering the river. Burnell told me that he was sending Sours in my place. My "pussy ass" would probably need another day to recover from that little "touch" of the flu I had.

Captain Eklund was relieved of command of F Company in the afternoon. It seemed as if the army policy of rotating its officers from field commands to staff positions every six months had caught up with him. General Zais, the division commander, personally wanted him up in G-3 assisting in operations. The CO called us to formation and told us that it had been his honor to lead us for the past six months. We were the finest group of soldiers he had ever commanded. He invited us to come up to division and visit him anytime. It was obvious that his reassignment had not been considered a promotion by him. He would have preferred to stay in command of the LRPs. We would miss him. I pitied the officer who had to replace him. He would be hard-pressed to fill Captain Eklund's boots.

At the end of the formation, the first sergeant informed us that we were no longer F Company, 58th Infantry (LRP). By some divine military madness, F Company had been officially deactivated. We had been immediately reactivated L Company 75th Infantry (Ranger). All of the LRP companies in Nam had gone through the same metamorphosis effective February 1. Our unit: lineage was now part of the old Merrill's Marauders who had fought so valiantly against the Japanese in Burma in World War II.

None of us knew whether this change in unit designation would change our overall mission, which had primarily been reconnaissance. Several of the older LRPs predicted that we would probably be seeing some really deep-penetration, commando-type raids. I wondered if the army would give us some special training this time or just let us pick it up during OJT. Only time would tell. I had to admit that the prospect of a bit of offensive initiative was appealing. You get a little paranoid hiding all the time.

February 13, 1969

I had been awaiting orders for an appointment to OCS after my tour was complete. It had been four months and I hadn't heard a damn thing. I couldn't understand why I couldn't get an appointment. I had run into too many officers without any college whatsoever who couldn't lead a land leech to an open sore. How had they gotten into OCS? Here I was with two years of college, two years of ROTC, two Purple Hearts, a Silver Star and a Bronze Star with V, and a true desire to be a career man, and I couldn't even get the Department of the Army to answer my application for appointment. Maybe a lobotomy would improve my chances!

I was pleasantly surprised to find out that Captain Eklund's final act as F Company commander had been to recommend myself and Phil Myers, a buck sergeant from the first platoon, for direct field commissions to second lieutenant. With my previous track record, I doubted seriously if my chances of being commissioned would be improved through this channel. The first sergeant told me to write home and have my college transcripts sent over as quickly as possible. The division needed all pertinent information to consider me for a direct commission. Top also let me know that, if Meyers and I received our commissions, we would be transferred to another division in Vietnam for the commissioning—army SOP. That was the only part of the process that bothered me. I would hate to leave F Company, er, I should say, L Company.

February 16, 1969

I was put back on Team 22 with Closson on the fifteenth. We inserted at first light on the morning of the sixteenth on the north side of the Song Bo a few klicks east of LZ Sally and northwest of Hue. I wasn't at all happy with the LZ. It was on a barren ridgeline that commanded the entire AO. To make matters worse, the pilot, who was flying his first CRP insertion, had circled out over the RZ before coming in to drop us off. I didn't understand why he hadn't just gone in a day early and dropped leaflets announcing our arrival time and coordinates.

It took us a half hour to reach cover. We were so exposed we didn't even bother to lay dog. When we finally got into some single-canopy, it appeared that every line company in Vietnam had trained in the area. We must have run across four platoon-size NDPs within one hundred meters. The place looked like a garbage dump. Old jungle fatigues, empty C ration cans, grenade canisters, plastic spoons, moldy cardboard, and even a few corroded 7.62 rounds were scattered about in the brush. We LRPs were fanatical housekeepers compared to the shabby sloppiness of line units. When they broke trail, it stayed broken.

Nothing happened the first day out. For some unknown

reason the NVA left us alone. They must have figured that we were all crazy coming in the way we did. Maybe they had a superstitious respect for the "touched" that caused them to lose face and suffer eternal damnation if they harmed us. Whatever the reason, they left us alone. We located a stand of bamboo on a steep side of a ridge and crawled into it to set up an NDP. There was little cover.

I dropped my ruck and sat down against it while Rucker got on the radio to call in our position. I thought I felt something move under me but ignored it, until I saw Mother's eyes go wide in alarm. I looked to my left just in time to see the green head of a bamboo viper squirm out from under my buttock. Only the pull of gravity kept me from achieving orbit as I executed a world-record sitting high jump. I landed on my feet, shaking so badly that the shit running down my leg didn't know which way to go.

Rucker, realizing I hadn't been bitten, was trying to shove his boonie towel down his throat to keep his laughter from compromising our position. The rest of the team hadn't actually witnessed the event and stared blankly at me as if I had finally gone all the way off the deep end.

When Rucker finally got control of himself, he quietly told them what had happened. The smiles on their faces reflected their concern for my mental well-being. I looked around for the snake but couldn't find it. Rucker motioned that he had seen it crawl off downhill. He was still holding the towel over his beaming face. I spent the entire night awake, wishing I had brought along a hammock to sleep in.

February 17, 1969

The next morning, the team moved off the ridge and continued patrolling west. We found some good cover on a secondary ridgeline a klick west of our LZ. The ridge ran south toward the Song Bo and was choked with elephant grass and dense scrub brush. We followed it north for a hundred meters, zigzagging back and forth to confuse anyone tracking us, then doubled back toward the river when we thought we had left enough false trails. We ran out of ridgeline when we reached the Song Bo, but found a choice site to establish an OP (observation post) overlooking the river.

The ridge came to an abrupt end twenty feet above the water. The very tip of the ridge was covered with thick stands of bamboo. Just behind the screen of bamboo was a natural ditch about three feet deep that ran about fifteen feet across the crest of the ridge. It was almost as if someone had carved it out years before for the very purpose we were now using it.

To our backs was the densely covered ridgeline we had just descended. Anyone coming after us would have to make as much noise as we had getting there. We set claymores facing out into the elephant grass to our rear. Rucker discovered a four-by-eight foot level spot between two clusters of bamboo on the river side of our NDP where a single Ranger, lying prone, had a commanding view of the river for over two hundred meters, both upstream and down. We had found a home for the next couple of days. It was a choice location, but I was bothered a little by the fact that our escape options had been cut exactly in half by the river to our front.

February 18, 1969

A full moon provided enough illumination through the night and early morning hours so we could see up and down the river for a hundred meters. We had observed no boat traffic on the Song Bo, but on a couple of occasions had heard something or someone moving through the grass to our rear. Whatever it was never came close enough to justify blowing the claymores.

We stayed put during the day, relaxing and trying to find some way to pass the time. The temperature neared 100 degrees, but the low humidity and a breeze kept us relatively comfortable. We lost radio contact after our morning sitrep and didn't get it back again until just before dark. Our relay team on Firebase Rakkassan had really been nervous. At about 2300 hours that night, we picked up a radio transmission between Team 21 and the relay team. Snuffy Smith, who had taken over until Gregory returned from R & R, was the team leader of 21 and was reporting movement around his NDP. He reported his co-ordinates and set up an artillery fire mission. He told them to remain on standby to fire only on his command. The enemy soldiers were too close for artillery to do any good. Rucker, Closson, and I got under a poncho liner and pulled out our map to see if we were close enough to move to their aid if they were hit. Their position was about six klicks south-southeast of us and north of Firebase Birmingham. We would have to cross the river and a major ridgeline to get to them. Team 21 had gone in a day after us and consisted of Smith, Sours as ATL, Jackson, Doc Glasser, and two cherries. Our company commander was dropping teams all along the edge of the mountain range from Leech Island north to Camp Evans in an effort to monitor NVA infiltration from the Roung-Roung and A

Shau valleys toward the cities of Hue and Phu Bai and the military bases in the immediate vicinity. Tet '69 was upon us and no one wanted a repeat of Tet '68.

Thirty minutes later, we heard Snuffy whisper into his handset that he had heavy movement to his front and feared that two of his claymores had been turned around on the team. Seconds later, he radioed that someone was throwing sticks into the Rangers' perimeter. Nothing happened for several more minutes, and then Smith reported he had one man WIA and another out of action. I could tell by the tone of his voice that he was under major stress. The relay team asked him if he was under attack. He radioed back that he was not, but that an attack appeared imminent. None of us could understand how he had a WIA and another man incapacitated if he hadn't been hit. Our question was answered when he radioed back and phonetically spelled out the names of the WIA and the other Ranger, and said he had been forced to disarm the second individual. Jackson had been hit, and the other man, who was one of the cherries, had "lost it."

Smith came back on the horn a short time later and reported that the medic had dressed the WIA's wounds and that they would require a medevac and a reaction force at first light. They could not initiate escape and evasion, and the enemy was too close for an attempted medevac at that time. They must have really been in a tight situation. Things remained quiet until around 0400, when the enemy began to maneuver in toward the Ranger team's position again. Smith had been forced to disarm the young Ranger after he had freaked out and sprayed his M-16 across the perimeter in the direction of the movement. Snuffy had just cautioned them about blowing their claymores and discharging their weapons. He told them that they should throw grenades to avoid giving away their position. Now that the NVA were again trying to penetrate the perimeter, Smith had been forced to return the kid's weapon to him. Suddenly, the cherry opened up again, hitting Jackson a second time, wounding Doc Glasser in the foot, and shredding Sours's rucksack.

The commotion must have frightened off the enemy, for they never bothered the team again. As the sun came up, the team medevaced Jackson. They sent the cherry out on a second chopper. Glasser refused to be extracted, deciding to stay in until the mission was over. When we called in our morning sitrep, our relay team informed us that a lot of U.S. military bases had gotten hit during the night . . . not as bad as last year during Tet, but bad enough to make one wonder if it was starting all over again.

The episode with Team 21 had kept us awake and alert all night and hadn't done much to improve our spirits. Jackson was one of the few blacks who had volunteered for duty with our company, and he had been a good trooper. He had done an excellent job in the field and never had a bad word to say about anybody. I recalled that he always walked around with a big stogie stuck in the corner of his mouth.

None of us had really gotten to know the cherry. He had joined the unit back in December when I was at the 6th Convalescent Center. He had come in with Kilburn, Anderson, Groff, Thomas, Krahl, and Croker. I remembered him as a little on the smart-ass side of sarcastic. He had seemed all right in training and especially eager to learn. He liked to cut up a lot—but hell, we all did.

The relay team reported that the kid had taken too many Dexedrine tablets in an attempt to stay awake. That could have been the reason he freaked. I was only glad that I wasn't in his boots. The guilt would have killed me.

Later in the morning, things quieted down and got back to normal. We spent the remainder of the day lazing around and trying to catch up on some sleep. It was difficult to get any shut-eye for an extended period of time because of the heat. But I did manage to chalk up about two or three hours before giving it up as a lost cause.

About noon, I crawled off a few meters into the grass and relieved myself. While I was straddling the cat hole I had scooped out of the dry, sandy soil, I thought I heard something scurrying quickly away from me up the side of the ridge. It hadn't sounded like a man so I didn't give it a lot of thought.

At dusk, we finished our second meal of the day and got ready to spend our second night in the OP along the river. In spite of our excellent location, we were a little nervous about staying too long in the same spot. We had been taught to stay on the move and change our NDPs each night.

About 2115 hours, Rucker hissed, then held his finger up to his lips, pointing back over his shoulder at the elephant grass–covered ridgeline to our rear. He had heard something moving out in the brush. We froze . . . listening for what we hoped was only the breeze blowing through the vegetation. But there wasn't any breeze. I cupped my hands behind my ears to amplify any sounds coming from the elephant grass. Yes, I heard it, too! It sounded like two, maybe three people, moving through the brush behind us. They were trying to avoid making any noise, but silence was impossible in the dry cover.

I nodded in agreement to Closson and Rucker as the skin on my back began to crawl. The enemy had either spotted us or had tracked us to our NDP, and were probably moving into position to cut off any escape routes when they hit us before dawn.

Rucker was already calling in a sitrep to our relay team, informing them that we had movement around us less than fifty meters away. Closson got on the artillery net and called Firebase Jack's 155 battery, requesting a fire mission on the preplotted coordinates we had set one hundred meters up the ridge to our rear. We had little time to waste before the NVA moved in too close for artillery support to do any good. They had us trapped with our backs to the river. They would most likely have ambushes set upstream and downstream from our position in case we tried to break out and follow the river one way or the other.

Trying to break through their maneuver element hiding in the tall grass on the ridge to our front would be suicidal. Closson called for a WP (white phosphorus) spotter round directly on the preset coordinate and alerted the fire control officer that we would adjust fire, all subsequent rounds to be HE (high explosive).

Closson turned and motioned for everyone to get down as the spotter round roared in from the east. We heard the dull *krmpppf* and saw the bright flash up the ridge from us as the round impacted about 100 to 120 meters away. Closson, on one knee, whispered, "Drop five-zero, fire for effect."

He dropped flat on the ground and told us to stay down as the first salvo of 155mm HE rounds roared over and impacted about seventy meters away. The ground shook as the shock waves rippled down the ridgeline. We hugged the ground as the team leader requested a second salvo, "Right five-zero." I cringed as Closson whispered into the handset. The 155s had a much greater kill radius than the 105s that usually fired for us. Rounds were hitting close to our position.

Closson requested a cease-fire after the second salvo. We froze, listening for movement out in the grass. It wasn't long before we heard it, the sounds of men scurrying through the brush. We couldn't tell how many there were, but we knew there had been enough to get the job done. The 155s had hit behind them, forcing them toward us to avoid the flying, white-hot shrapnel.

Closson quickly corrected, "Left five-zero, drop five-zero. Fire for effect!" The fire control officer called back for verification, warning Closson that the rounds would be almost on top of our position. The team leader gave him an affirmative and told him, "That's where the enemy is!" We ate dirt as we flattened ourselves into the hollow depression that served as our NDP. We knew that final "drop five-zero" would put the next salvo just outside our claymores. And if that didn't stop them, they'd be in our perimeter with us.

Closson, his face pressed to the ground, mumbled, "Shot out!" Seconds passed, then we heard the deafening *whoosh* that accompanies a large steel projectile as it punches a hole through the sky, displacing the air that had previously filled it. The incoming rounds sounded like an express train . . . with us waiting at the depot. I nearly ruptured my eyelids as I clenched my teeth and waited for the monstrous projectiles to end my life.

The concussion was devastating. It lifted me bodily from the ground. I seemed to hang there, momentarily suspended, before the earth rose back up and slapped me hard as it convulsed from the impact of the rounds. Dirt and debris showered back over us.

I heard Closson yell that he was hit. I was momentarily powerless to do anything about it. Another salvo followed, repeating the episode of mass trauma we had just survived. How could anyone out in that grass live through this? My mind and body were numb, my ears ringing like a Chinese gong. I heard Closson shouting, "Cease-fire! Cease-fire!" into his handset.

The ensuing silence was more frightening than the exploding confusion of the artillery barrage. We gasped, trying to draw breath back into our lungs. One of the new guys was whimpering, and, from the smell, someone had messed his pants. Rucker and I crawled over to Closson. He was checking himself for wounds.

He mumbled, more to himself than to us, "Jesus Christ, I know I'm hit, I felt it!" as he ran his hands up and down his legs. Rucker grabbed him and said, "Look, Closson, your heel's gone!" Sure enough the hard-rubber heel of his left jungle boot had been slicked off as cleanly as if a surgeon had performed the amputation. Closson had just missed losing a foot.

As the ringing in our ears receded, we heard a low moaning sound out in the grass. Somebody was lying out there wounded, suffering from the terrible destruction wrought by the 155s. The artillery had done its job. No one could have lived through that barrage and still had enough left to come after us.

Closson called for H & I (harassment and interdiction) fire throughout the rest of the night. He gave preplots for a spot about 150 meters up the ridge from our position, and a couple of points along the riverbank both upstream and downstream. A reaction force would be inserted at first light to sweep the ridge for enemy wounded and dead.

We spent the rest of the night on full alert. We didn't think they would be back, but you could never be sure.

February 19, 1969

At 0600 we got word there would be no reaction force. Marcy's team, with Miller as ATL, had found a large number of NVA in a wide valley behind Nui Ke Mountain.

Our reaction force was standing by in case they got hit or were compromised. We were told to sit tight and wait for an extraction.

We ate our morning chow, two men at a time, as we waited for word on our exfiltration. One of the cherries slipped off down to a stagnant pool of water next to the river to rinse out his pants. The rest of us stayed on alert. We really didn't think the enemy would move back on us in broad daylight, but felt they would be waiting if we tried to leave the vicinity of the river.

We decided our extraction would take place twenty meters out in the grass where the 155s had leveled several LZs large enough for a Huey. About 0930 it was my turn to move back to the observation point in the bamboo to watch the river and its opposite bank. Just as I got into position to relieve Gilette, I spotted a man wearing an OD (olive drab) uniform walking up the gravel bar on the other side of the river and about 150 meters upstream.

He didn't seem to be alarmed or to be looking for anything in particular, nor did he appear to be carrying any type of weapon. I sent Gilette back to get Closson. While I was waiting for the team to arrive, I considered taking a long shot at the enemy soldier, but my CAR-15 had only been sighted in at fifty meters, and I didn't trust it's accuracy that far out. Suddenly, the Vietnamese turned and stepped into the jungle bordering the river and disappeared from view.

I sensed Closson at my side and, without turning, said, "We've got company upstream on the opposite shore. One gook . . . doesn't seem to know we're around."

Closson answered, "Good, let's not alert him. I think we've got enough of them pissed off at us on this side of the river." That was okay by me. With no place to go and time on our hands, I was more than content not to rock the boat.

An hour later, I happened to look back upstream. I saw a single Vietnamese in a sampan, making his way toward our position. This one was dressed in black and seemed to be in no great hurry to get down the river. This was crazy! Didn't those people have radios? Surely word had gotten out that a Ranger team was in the vicinity! I slipped back and told Closson what I had seen. The two of us moved back to the OP just as the Vietnamese was passing our position.

Closson decided to call in artillery on the sampan and its occupant. He didn't want to bring further attention to our location by having the team initiate fire. There were just too many unfriendlies in the area for us to go around acting like the bully on the block. He called for a single HE round, an airburst at a height of ten meters, and timed it so that the round would catch the Vietnamese just as he reached the point of our downstream midcurrent preplot.

We rubbernecked to witness the explosion as the single shell screamed in from Firebase Jack. It was beautiful! The 155 round was right on the money. The poor Vietnamese sat frozen as the shell screamed in. At the last minute, he must have realized he was a dead man. I unconsciously cringed as the projectile exploded just above the sampan. *POP!* I couldn't believe my eyes! The goddamned thing was only a marker round . . . nothing but white smoke.

We sat there totally dumbfounded, unable to do a thing. By the time we recovered our senses, the Vietnamese had recognized his good fortune and was frantically paddling his sampan toward the far shore, two hundred meters downstream from us. He pulled the wooden craft up into the trees and quickly disappeared into the jungle.

Closson was pissed. He called the fire control officer back at Firebase Jack and thanked him, on behalf of the North Vietnamese Army, for the timely warning they had just given one of its soldiers. Mistakes happened, but that kind was totally unnecessary. We didn't wait for a response because the other radio had suddenly crackled to life. It was Captain Cardona, our new CO, flying C & C on his way out to extract us. The two slicks and their escorting Cobra gunships were five minutes out and coming up the Song Bo.

We didn't have time to pull in our claymores, so the team leader instructed us to wait until we could hear the choppers, then blow them in place. If nothing else, they would help clear a PZ for the choppers to land in.

Two minutes later, the *whopp . . . whopp . . . whopp* of Hueys reverberated off the sides of the narrow river valley. Closson bellowed, "Blow 'em!" The four simultaneous explosions tore the elephant grass apart, finishing off what the artillery had started. Suddenly a Huey was over us, circling around to come into the purple smoke Closson had tossed out onto the crest of the ridge. Another Huey and two Cobras moved into orbit around three hundred meters above us, flying cover over the extraction ship as it settled into the smoking grass to our front.

I had just finished coiling the remainder of the claymore wire and shoved it and the detonator device into one of the cargo pockets on my pants. The six of us ran fifteen meters into the clearing and jumped aboard the Huey as the pilot lifted the slick off the ridge, then nosed to the left and followed the river downstream to where it broke from the mountains onto the rolling countryside northwest of LZ Sally.

Something told me I was getting too short for this kind of shit! I was down to 105 days and a wake-up.

February 20, 1969

We received a warning order for a mission at first light on the twenty-second. We were going back in on the Song Bo, this time on the south side of the river. Intelligence wanted us to verify enemy activity in the area.

My God, I thought we had just done that! Either they wanted another confirmation or they just didn't believe us the first time. I vowed never to complain about a lack of missions again. We were barely getting two days turnaround time before going back out again. And none of us had earned a trip down to Coco Beach in two months.

Somebody must have been bucking for career points, and we suspected our new CO. He never appeared to be around the company area unless we had teams in the field. He was definitely not the officer Captain Eklund had been. We picked up a new first sergeant. His name was Car-

din. No one knew much about him, but he supposedly had
come to us by way of Special Forces and had seen some
combat. He appeared to be a cocky, by-the-book lifer,
suffering a bad case of Little Man Syndrome. We nick-
named him Cubby.

I got a letter from home along with a monthly bulletin
from my Knights of Columbus council back in Missouri.
It appeared that my brother Knights had voted me the
Knight of the Month for the month of February. I felt
honored, yet somewhat baffled. I had joined the council
after I graduated from high school but had not been able
to attend any meetings. College and the army had kept me
away from home for the past four years.

We got word that Jackson was on his way back to the
States. His wounds were serious and there was a good
possibility that if he survived, he would be paralyzed. One
of the rounds had hit him in the head and had caused some
brain damage. The cherry who had freaked out on Dex
had been transferred out of the company to a line unit
within a day of returning from the mission. It was just as
well. No one would have gone out with the kid again. That
kind of fuck up just wasn't tolerated in the unit.

The mission had left Sours blaming himself even more.
The talented Ranger team leader was building up one over-
size guilt complex that was going to be tough to live with.
The bitch of it was that none of it was deserved.

February 21, 1969

The mission for the twenty-second was postponed for
twenty-four hours due to inclement weather. Dense fog
had moved in among the mountain valleys where we had
been operating. Flying conditions had become dangerous
or, in many cases, impossible.

I couldn't say that I didn't appreciate the stand-down.

Most of the Rangers needed a break. We had been going at it hot and heavy for over a month, and the stress was beginning to show. Besides, I wasn't nearly as confident of Captain Cardona's resolve to get us out of a tight one as I had been of Captain Eklund's.

It makes a big difference when you're out in the bush with your shit flappin' in the wind, and you know your CO will move mountains, if necessary, to get you out. Maybe I wasn't being fair to the new CO, but I wasn't the only one in the company who felt that way. Only time would prove me wrong.

February 22, 1969

The mission was rescheduled for the twenty-third at 0900, in hopes that the fog would burn off by then. Four teams would be going in, deeper into the mountains than we felt was advisable. If fog was going to be a problem, the teams could be in real jeopardy inserting that far back.

February 23, 1969

The mission was scrapped again, but not because of the fog. Over a hundred U.S. and ARVN bases were hit during the night of the twenty-second. All military installations were on red alert until the threat ended. We were really surprised at the news, since Camp Eagle had not been touched. Were the NVA afraid of us, or were they saving us for something special?

February 25, 1969

A stiff breeze blew in from the sea early in the morning and drove the cloud bank back into Laos. It left us with some of the nicest weather I had seen since arriving in-country. The temperature was in the high 80s, but the humidity was below 50 percent for a change.

The CO decided to take advantage of the break in the weather and insert four teams early in the afternoon. It didn't take us long to get ready, as our gear had been packed for the past three days. We boarded slicks at 1320 hours for the long ride out to our AOs. We would be inserting on the three points of an imaginary triangle spanning the Song Bo River.

The XO would insert Gregory's team, Team 21, into the exact same AO we had patrolled on our last mission. He would then fly eight klicks upstream and put Marcy's team, Team 11, in along the river at the mouth of a wide valley. Simultaneously, Captain Cardona would insert the other two teams, Closson's Team 22 and Reynolds's Team 12, into a large bomb crater on the south side of the river, halfway up the crest of a long ridgeline.

We would be at the point of the triangle. Reynolds's team was to move west toward the A Shau while we were to work east by southeast back toward Firebase Veghel. Our mission was to locate the 5th NVA Regiment. The division was giving us all the firepower we needed to wipe it out. Artillery had been laid on from five different fire-bases: Eagle's Nest, Jack, Veghel, Bastogne, and Bir-mingham. A squadron of Cobra gunships and two flights of air force F-4 Phantoms would be on standby.

I remembered the 5th. That was the same NVA regi-

ment my team had tangled with back on November 4 and
again on the twentieth. I recalled that they weren't afraid
to stand up and do battle, and they always had their shit
together. I was torn by the desire to be on the team that
found them, and by the fear of what might happen once
we did.

We flew over Firebase Birmingham on the way out. The
cool wind blowing in through the open cabin was refresh-
ing. It was too nice a day to die! We leapfrogged over a
couple of mountain ranges before sighting the Song Bo to
our right. The first slick went in low, directly below our
circling Huey. I looked down and watched the first chopper move in over the bomb crater and drop off Reynolds's
team. I could see the ant-size Rangers as they ran from
the crater and into the jungle to the west to make room
for our team.

Our slick went into a tight turn and headed for the same
LZ. I stepped out onto the skid, held back only by the
centrifugal force of our spiraling descent. Suddenly, I
could see Reynolds's team running back toward the bomb
crater. Something had gone wrong. From my bird's-eye
view, I noticed puffs of smoke and tiny lights blinking off
and on from the edge of the jungle surrounding the LZ.
My God, it was an ambush! I looked back over my shoulder and screamed, "It's hot, it's hot, the LZ's hot!" I
peered down again just in time to see green tracers flying
past our Huey.

The pilot jerked back on the collective and began a wide,
climbing turn to the right as I nearly tumbled off the skid
and out into space. Only my grip on the seat-brace at my
side and someone's hold on my rucksack kept me from
pitching forward and plunging to my death in the jungle
below. Strong hands pulled me back inside the cabin as
the pilot continued to climb away from the ambush.

I heard *ping . . . ping* sounds as rounds hit our chopper.
In seconds we were out of range, circling the area in a
high orbit. We would stay on station until Reynolds's team
got out. Rucker gave me the handset to his radio for a
moment. Team 12 was surrounded and already had one
WIA, their senior RTO. They asked for the gunships to
work over the jungle around their perimeter and requested
a "dust off" for their wounded man. For the moment, they

were holding their own, but getting them out of that hornet's nest was going to be next to impossible.

As Reynolds's team put out an ammunition-eating base of fire, the two Cobras came in ''hot'' and turned the jungle into a junkyard, shredding the vegetation around the edge of the bomb crater with cannon and minigun fire. After their third run, Reynolds's reported that the enemy fire had fallen off.

Suddenly Mr. Poley, the pilot who had inserted Team 12, brought his slick back into the LZ and hovered just above the lip of the bomb crater. His blades chopped leaves from the trees as Reynolds and his ATL on-loaded the wounded RTO, and then climbed in behind him with the rest of their team. The Huey lifted drunkenly toward us as the NVA gunners opened up again, trying to knock it out of the sky.

The Cobras were still plastering the vicinity of the crater as we joined the C & C ship and Mr. Poley's chopper for the flight back to Camp Eagle. When we landed, we discovered that our slick had taken six hits in the tail boom. Mr. Poley's chopper had sustained over twenty hits. Even the Cobras had suffered damage. But we had lucked out again. The NVA had blown their ambush too soon. If they would have held their fire for just sixty more seconds, they could have annihilated both teams.

The other two teams, inserted to the north of the river by Lieutenant Williams, were also shot out within minutes. They had suffered no casualties. Four teams shot out of three LZs within twenty minutes had to be a new company record. The 5th NVA Regiment was back. They had been bloodied too many times by our LRP teams back in '68. This time, they had apparently made up their minds that they weren't going to let us infiltrate their sanctuaries, no matter what the cost.

February 26, 1969

The weather turned sour again. We were overjoyed that the enemy had taken the time and trouble to prevent us from successfully inserting into their neighborhood the previous day. We would have been in *big* trouble if we had gotten hit in the middle of the heavy fog that had settled over the area during the night of the twenty-fifth.

In the past couple of weeks, several of our teams had been forced to extend missions without resupply. Some had to stay in for as much as a week beyond their designated time. All of the teams have gone to carrying extra rations and spare radio batteries. Being stuck twenty klicks out in the jungle without food or commo was a terrifying experience that no one wanted to go through a second time.

I became a double-digit midget on the twenty-sixth. Just ninety-nine days and a wake-up and my ass would be back in the USA. I was officially *short!*

February 27–March 1, 1969

My platoon sergeant informed me that he thought I was ready to take out my own team. I was surprised. I had been expecting my promotion to E-5 to come through any day, and had thought that once I had gotten the rank, I might stand a good chance of getting my own team. There hadn't been very many spec fours who had taken out their own team. The only ones I could recall were Tonini, Sours, and Miller. I didn't know whether to feel honored for being selected to run a team or ashamed because I hadn't been promoted yet.

I was getting Team 22. Closson was taking over Team 23. Our call sign would be Lynwood Team 22. I got Jim Schwartz as my ATL and Ken Munoz as senior RTO. Hillman, Groff, and Kilburn, all cherries, would fill the remaining slots on the team.

I had always wondered if I had the right stuff to be a team leader. I had served in many positions of leadership in civilian life and even in basic training. I had never had any problems that would cause me to question my ability to lead others. Yet, some of the attributes and qualities that I had observed among the men leading the LRP and Ranger teams went beyond the normal qualities of leadership. Some possessed all the classic characteristics: strength, endurance, command presence, self-control, intelligence, motivation, training, goal orientation, spirit, and the ability to bring out those traits in the men they commanded. Yet others had little more going for them than guts, common sense, and an unquenchable instinct to survive.

Bill Marcy, John Sours, Lou Ondrus, Ron Reynolds, Joe Gregory, and Al Contreros were all perfect examples of the former—the classic leader. Richard Burnell, Big John Burford, Mike Tonini, and especially Zo and Ray Martinez were prime examples of the latter.

The classic leader's authority was established by his rank and maintained by his performance. If he knew his job and did it well, his men would obey and follow him because he was their leader. The other type, let's call it charismatic leadership, established authority and maintained it by sheer presence of personality. Rank was not necessary to establish authority. Men just naturally followed that type of leader because they sensed he would get the job done and look out for his men at the same time. Soldiers obeyed this type of leader, not because they had to, but because they wanted to. The charismatic leader wore his rank on his back and not on his sleeve.

Don't misunderstand me. The classic team leaders I

named above were all top-notch team leaders. I would have followed them anywhere. The real difference was that those men were made team leaders because of rank, experience, and performance. The others would have been selected to serve in that capacity by the men on their teams regardless of rank, experience, or performance.

I didn't have any idea what kind of combat leader I could be. I wasn't even sure that I was ready for it. I knew that a lot of responsibility went along with the position—maybe more than I wanted. I would be responsible for the lives of five other men. It would be my job to inspire them with self-confidence and confidence in the team as a whole. I would have to assess the individual talents of each man and utilize them so that their interaction as a team sufficed to accomplish the mission. It would be up to me to inspire peak performance by each man at all times, and to maintain that level of proficiency myself.

If I couldn't set and maintain standards of the highest order, then I could not expect those intrusted to my care to do the same. I felt that most leaders were motivated more by fear of failure than by gain and glory. My only desire was to perform my duty to the best of my ability and to care for the health and well-being of my men. Recognition and achievement should always be a result of leadership ability and not the reason for it.

Schwartz and I went to the TOC for a premission briefing on our mission. The XO conducted the briefing and, for my benefit, kept it short and simple. We would be inserted at dusk along the Perfume River, just north of Leech Island. I had pulled a mission in that same area just a month before, but this time we would be operating on the east side of the river. The terrain was predominantly flat to rolling, with heavy vegetation in the form of bamboo, single-canopy jungle, and patches of elephant grass along the river. Low, grass-covered hills began about a hundred meters back from the river and ran all the way back to Camp Eagle.

Our mission was reconnaissance. We were to scout the shoreline for river crossings, rest areas, and small caches. At night, we were to set up along the water and monitor the river for boat traffic. We could count on support from Firebase Brick in the form of a 105mm battery, and the

2/17th Cav's platoon of "Blues" would serve as a reaction force if we got into trouble.

The mission didn't sound impressive. I remembered that most of the trails we had found on the west side of the river had been old. We had heard a sampan move upstream one night but had been prevented from doing anything about it because of dense fog. Fields of elephant grass ran along the opposite shoreline, giving way to double-canopy jungle two hundred meters back from the river where the mountains began.

One thing was certain, we would have to do our best to stay in what cover was available when we moved. Our entire RZ would be exposed to any NVA spotters monitoring the river from the mountains to our west.

The overflight reaffirmed what I had already guessed. There was indeed little cover in our AO. It was not the ideal situation for a reconnaissance mission. I made up my mind that we would move only at night if we had to move. I would not risk the team's safety by parading up and down the sparsely timbered riverbank during daylight hours. At least we wouldn't have to cross the Perfume if we were forced to E & E. We would only have to cover about eight klicks of low hills with all the concealment of a freshly mowed football field to reach Camp Eagle.

The mission looked like a typical humbug, the type that made you wonder who in his right mind had ever come up with the idea. Unfortunately, past experience had proven that more men were killed or wounded on the humbugs than on the tougher, riskier missions we pulled. I guess there was just a natural tendency to let your guard down when there appeared to be little danger of contact.

I decided we would not get caught with our pants down. Intelligence gave us a 35mm camera and asked us to take pictures of trails, river crossings, or any other enemy signs we found. I was surprised by this. I had often wondered why cameras were not made part of a team's basic equipment. How did the old saying go—"A picture is worth a thousand words." I recalled all the debriefings I had sat on where the Intelligence personnel had acted like we were full of shit when we described what we had found. By God, they wouldn't have doubted a photograph!

I usually carried my Penn double-E 35mm camera when

I went on patrol. However, the pictures I took were personal and contained little that would interest the boys in Intelligence. Besides, I doubt if they would have replaced the film. I asked for permission to take along a starlight scope. I thought the night-vision device would be a big help in monitoring the river, and for scouting our RZ if we moved at night like I planned. Permission was refused. The army valued those damned scopes more than they did us.

Schwartz and I returned to our hootch to brief the rest of the team. They had already packed their rucks while Jim and I were on the overflight. It would only be a two-day mission, so I cautioned everybody to travel light. We could get water from the river, and if we ate before we went in, we would be able to get by on two meals, since we were to come out at 0900 on the third day.

I did recommend taking along a couple of extra claymores and an M-79 grenade launcher with twenty-four HE rounds and six CS gas rounds. In the type of terrain where we would be operating, a "thumper" could prove invaluable.

We checked our gear a couple of hours before we were to be inserted. I wasn't surprised to find that two of the new men rattled. Schwartz and I applied the usual dose of green duct tape, and the problems were cured. I wrote a short letter to my fiancée and another to my parents, telling them I was about to lead my first mission. I tried not to sound too full of my own self-importance, but I failed miserably. After all, becoming a team leader was the ultimate goal of any good Ranger.

When the time finally arrived, the six of us walked down to the chopper pad to board the insertion slick. Captain Cardona's C & C ship was parked just to the front of our Huey. The CO walked by, nodded without saying anything, and boarded his chopper. Sergeant Burnell flipped us a "V" and climbed into our ship. He would be flying belly-man on our insertion.

The turbines on the two Hueys started to whine as the powerful engines roared to life. It was our signal to get aboard. I made sure everyone got on in proper order before backing myself in and sitting on the cabin floor with my feet dangling down toward the skid. I would be the first to un-ass the ship on the port side, with Munoz and Groff close behind. Schwartz would precede Kilburn and Hillman out the starboard side.

I nodded to Burnell, who said something into his helmet-mike, and we were airborne. We were only seven minutes out from our AO, and the terrain was wide open all the way in. Mr. Grant, our AC kept the Huey "on the deck" as he flew "nap of the earth" all the way to the Perfume River. Once over the water, he swung south and headed upstream barely fifty feet above the surface of the water.

When we were three minutes out, he flared over the west bank and hovered just off the ground for several seconds. The false insertion was designed to fool the enemy as to where we actually inserted. I noticed the C & C ship had leapfrogged us and was in the process of doing another false insertion two hundred meters upstream on the opposite shore. The CO's ship flared out and up as we shot in below it for the actual insertion. With luck, any NVA in the area were busy watching that chopper as it climbed away from the river, and overlooked us as we approached our LZ.

I jumped for the ground while the Huey was still six feet above it, and noticed out of the corner of my eye that the rest of the team was right behind me. I hit the ground running and headed for a small clump of trees twenty meters away. As I dove into the thick cover, I was vaguely aware of the two Cobra gunships roaring past us on either side of the river.

I turned to make sure that everyone had made it, when I saw Kilburn trying to struggle to his feet. Munoz ran over to him, grabbing him by the arm, and got him back up and on his way into the cover.

We fanned out in a circle, each man providing security in a sixty-degree arc while we listened for sounds of enemy movement. A surge of adrenaline had us all panting like terminal asthmatics. When we finally got ourselves under control, we lay silently for a good twenty minutes listening to the sounds of the river twenty feet away. We could still hear the choppers off in the distance, but for the most part the sound of running water filled our ears.

I signaled for Munoz to get a commo check with our company rear. We were close enough that we didn't require a relay team on this mission. He signed that we had them loud and clear. I pulled my map and compass out, orienting the map to true north. I shot an azimuth to a known mountain peak northwest of our location. It was 326 degrees. The back azimuth was 146 degrees. I then shot another azimuth to another peak three hundred meters south-southwest. It was 230 degrees. The back azimuth was 50 degrees. I took a straightedge and drew the lines with a grease pencil across the acetate cover of my map. The point of intersection was just over a hundred meters north of where we were supposed to have gone in. Not a major crisis, but enough to piss me off. How anybody could miss an LZ in this type of terrain was beyond me. Mr. Grant was going to have to buy everyone on the team a round of beer for screwing up. He didn't often make that kind of mistake.

We would have to move and move quickly. I wanted to be a couple of hundred meters into our AO before it got too dark to take stock of our surroundings. We had over three hundred meters to cover in less than thirty minutes. I motioned for Schwartz to move out on point, knowing that he would try to stay in the cover and move as fast as noise discipline would permit.

He maneuvered through the single-canopy trees and the stands of bamboo in fifteen- to twenty-meter spurts, stopping every few minutes to listen. Good, he was not sacrificing caution for speed. He covered nearly two hundred meters before darkness caught us.

Schwartz held up his hand to stop the team. I moved up past Groff to the point man's side. It was too dark to go any farther without making noise. We would not be able to see what kind of cover we were in, and setting up an NDP without knowing what was around you was an invitation to an ambush at dawn. Jim pointed to the east. The moon would be up in a few minutes and we would be able to see well enough to cover the final hundred meters and find a decent spot to set up an NDP/OP along the river.

Fifteen minutes later, we were moving again. The pale illumination from the moon cast eerie shadows across our path but provided just enough light to distinguish the vegetation to our front. We moved into a dense bamboo thicket that I thought I recognized from the overflight. If it was the right one, there would be a river crossing just to the right of us, and probably a trail leading away from the river.

Schwartz stopped the team and signaled me up. He was standing on the edge of a narrow trail that ran from left to right across his front. The surface of the trail shone gray in the moonlight. Brush and bamboo thickets lined both sides of it. I motioned for the team to watch our flanks and indicated that I was going to check out the situation to our front. I turned to the right, flanking the trail by a meter or two, and followed it twenty meters to the west where it dropped down into a low spot in the bank to the river below. In the glow of the rising moon, I could see the dark tracks where several people had come out of the water and moved up the trail. I could only tell that they had been made in the past two or three days.

I backtracked to rejoin the team, making sure that they heard me coming in. I didn't want to be mistaken for a gook and shot by one of my own men. I whispered in Schwartz's ear, telling him what I had found, then motioned for the team to follow us as we moved toward the high bank just north of the crossing.

We discovered a dense cluster of bamboo only fifteen meters away from the trail and silently crawled into it. We lay motionless for twenty minutes, listening. I signaled for Hillman and Kilburn to drop their rucks and set five claymores in a semicircle around us, leaving the eight-foot-high riverbank unguarded. We weren't there to blow an ambush. Schwartz wanted to go out with them to make sure they didn't line up our NDP in the back-blasts from the claymores. I nodded in agreement. He motioned me closer and whispered in my ear, "I checked the trail out to the left while you were scouting the right. It only goes about ten more meters, then forks. One branch goes off to the north about five meters inside the tree line, the other takes off across that open country to our east." I nodded again. We had been lucky. We had paralleled that damned trail for three hundred meters as we moved into position, and it had been less than ten meters away. If a platoon of NVA had been moving toward us in the dark, we could have really gotten ourselves in a bind.

We were pretty sure that we were sitting on an active

river crossing, so the only thing to do was to wait and see if our friends from the North were going to use it that night. When the three Rangers returned from setting out the claymores, I passed out the guard shifts—full alert until 0100, then 50 percent alert, two-and-a-half-hour shifts until dawn. Everyone was pretty fresh, so I didn't feel the longer shifts would kill anybody.

It was close to 2200 hours before we finally settled in. I hated moving around in our RZ and setting up an NDP in the dark without fully scouting the surrounding terrain, but we didn't have any other choice.

Kilburn, Hillman, and I took the first split-shift from 0100 to 0330 hours. I had Kilburn watch the jungle to the southeast and Hillman keep track on the cover to the northeast. I crawled out to the edge of the river to monitor any boat traffic that might try to sneak by in the darkness.

It was close to 0230 when we heard the sounds of a motor coming downstream. The small combustion engine had to be pushing a motorized sampan down the river. I crawled back to wake up Munoz and Groff. Schwartz was already awake. The engine seemed to be a good hundred meters upstream, but appeared to be moving steadily toward our position. I held my finger up to my lips as a sign for everyone to remain motionless and to keep silent.

Suddenly, the sampan idled down and pulled into shore on our side of the river about thirty or forty meters upstream. The engine was switched off before the boat reached the bank. We froze, listening for any sound that would indicate what the enemy was up to. A half hour later, we had still heard nothing. It was as if the river had just swallowed them up. Did they know we were there? What was going on? They couldn't have gotten past us. I had been watching the river.

I whispered to Munoz to contact Firebase Brick and have the 105s stand by for a fire mission. When we requested it, I wanted the first round a "willie pete" (white phosphorus) fifty meters to our south in the middle of the river. If we got hit in this narrow stretch of cover, I wouldn't have a hell of a lot of time to adjust fire. He also called the radio watch back at the TOC and gave them a report on our current situation. The entire team stayed on full alert the remainder of the night. Nothing happened,

nor did we ever hear the sampan depart. My gut feeling
was that the occupants had probably pulled it up on the
shore and then had moved out on foot, either across the
open country to the east or back down along the tree line
to the south. They sure in hell never passed our position
on the river or the trail.

We had to find out for sure what they had done, so when
the sun finally came up, I passed it around the perimeter
that we would have to move out on line and check the
cover across the trail from our NDP. We pulled in our
claymores and cleaned up our campsite, restoring everything to its natural condition. Then we got on line, three
meters apart, with Schwartz anchoring the left flank and
myself anchoring the river side. We moved slowly up to
the trail before stopping to listen. Nothing. Dead silence.
We waited five minutes before stepping cautiously over the
narrow trail and moving on into the tree line. The sampan,
if it was there, could only be twenty to thirty meters ahead.
We moved up another ten meters before I signaled for the
team to hold up.

I motioned for Schwartz to remain behind with Groff,
Hillman, and Kilburn, while Munoz and I went slowly
forward to scout the jungle. Ten meters ahead, we discovered a natural trough running parallel to the river toward
the south. I had never seen anything like it in Vietnam,
but it reminded me of an old sunken wagon road like the
ones I had often encountered deer hunting on abandoned
farms back in Missouri. It was about three meters wide
and about a meter deeper than its heavily wooded sides.

I backed off a few feet realizing that it was an ideal
place for an ambush. I reached out and took the handset
from Munoz and called back to Schwartz on Kilburn's
radio. I whispered for him to bring up the rest of the team
and told him to flank the roadbed on the left while Munoz
and I flanked it on the right. I advised him to break squelch
two times when they were in position. Five minutes later,
he signaled that they were ready. Munoz and I swung to
our right and moved slowly up the back side of the cover
lining the trough.

Twice we were forced to cross open areas right up
against the riverbank. If anyone was observing from across
the river, they couldn't have missed seeing us. Schwartz

broke squelch and whispered that they had found a large bunker and a newly constructed lean-to behind the wall of cover on the left. I told him to sit tight while we crossed over and swung back to him. We would be approaching them from the south. I cautioned him to make sure the rest of the team knew from which direction we would be coming.

Munoz and I continued along the hedge of bamboo and single-canopy vegetation. I happened to look over the riverbank and saw a little spit of sand running out five or six feet into the water. I could see where someone had run a small boat up onto it and had then stepped out into the soft sand. The tracks didn't lead to the shore. Whoever had pulled into the bank there had changed his mind and pushed back out into the river again. How had they gotten back upstream without our hearing them?

Thirty meters on, the roadbed petered out. It quickly narrowed to a point where the vegetation ended. Munoz and I swung around it and started moving back to the north, careful to contact Schwartz and tell him we were coming in.

My ATL showed me the bunker and the lean-to after we reached his position. The six-by-ten-foot bunker had not been designed as a fighting position, but seemed to have been constructed for the purpose of protecting the occupants from being spotted from above. The lean-to was made of bamboo and crudely thrown together. It appeared to have been erected within the past week or two. Its open side faced the cover lining the roadbed.

Both structures were empty even though they showed signs of recent occupancy. We took photos with the camera provided by Intelligence. It was their film and we thought we might as well give them something to look at. I told the rest of the team to stay put near the bunker while Schwartz and I moved back to get a picture of the trail and the river crossing.

When we rejoined the team, we moved south through the trees toward the location of another crossing we had spotted on the overflight. It took us six hours, using every spot of cover we could find, to travel the 1200 meters to the site. It was nearly 1600 hours when we finally reached it.

The trail coming up out of the river was old and over-grown. I considered moving the team back to the first crossing and sitting on it during the last night of our mission, but I decided that would be foolhardy. Munoz and I had gotten too close to the edge of the river and could very well have compromised the team. If the NVA had spotted us, they might come looking for us that night. There wasn't much cover for us to hide in anywhere among the trees along the river.

I thought about moving back to the bunker and setting up an NDP in it. They wouldn't expect us to do that, and at least we would have some cover if they hit us. I asked myself what I would do if I were an NVA platoon leader and had observed an American Ranger team patrolling through that narrow strip of jungle across the river from me. I decided that I would probably wait until dark and slip most of my platoon across the river at the northern crossing. Then I would send a squad across at the old southern crossing as a blocking force. When everyone was in place, I'd put the first group on line and sweep south through the tree line until I made contact with the Yankee dogs or flushed them into my blocking force. Either way, I'd probably bag an entire American Ranger team.

The more I thought about it, the more apprehensive I became. We had accomplished our mission. The enemy was using the northern crossing. The southern crossing had been abandoned. We had discovered what appeared to be an overnight squad-size rest area, and we had pictures of everything. We even ascertained that some phantom gook was out running up and down the river in a sampan in the middle of the night. There was no good reason to stay another night.

I decided to radio the rear and request an extraction at last light. Spending a second night in the same tree line would be counterproductive and exceptionally risky. Captain Eklund had always left it up to the team leaders to decide when, in their judgment, they were in jeopardy of being compromised. When I radioed for the extraction, the new CO wanted to know why. When I told him, he responded that my reason was unacceptable and that we should continue our mission. We would be extracted at 0900 hours in the morning, as planned.

Bullshit! Fuck a bunch of REMFs. That ain't the way it works in L Company, sir. We're down here where the nut cuttin' is done, and these kind of decisions get made right here. That's what I should have told the man, but I opted for a bit of diplomacy and kept my thoughts to myself. I pulled the team back away from the river into the thickest cover we could find, which in a pinch would probably not have kept the sun off a piss ant.

We set out three claymores and sat back to wait for darkness to set in. It arrived on the scene the way it always does in the jungle—a brief twilight as the sun drops below the horizon and then an overdose of pitch black. I knew we had about an hour to do something before the moon came up and exposed us again. I instructed the new men to pull in their claymores. When they were secured, I moved the team across the open terrain east of the tree line. I didn't know where we were headed or what we would run into, but at the moment, anything was better than that narrow strip of jungle.

A hundred meters away, we stumbled into what, in the darkness, appeared to be a gigantic female breast. Upon closer inspection, we discovered that it was one of the numerous barren hills that dotted the Vietnam countryside between the Perfume River and the coastline. The knoll rose about ten to fifteen feet above the surrounding terrain. It would have to do. The moon was rising to the east. I stopped the team and moved them around to the back of the knoll. We weren't in the shadow of the hill, but I wanted to put it between us and the river. We set up a tight little NDP, setting out all eight claymores.

The hill offered some protection from the tree line and gave us a heightened sense of security we hadn't felt in two days. If the NVA came at us from the river, at least we would have something in front of us. If they decided to hit us from the rear, they would be more exposed than we were. I posted a guard on top of the knoll facing the river and instructed him to stay prone to avoid standing out against the skyline.

A couple of hours later, I put a second man on top facing east. I signaled that I would spell them about midnight. I didn't like leaving anyone on watch that long, but it would minimize movement. I figured two men lying side by side should be able to keep each other awake for a couple of hours.

It was nearly 0230 when Kilburn slipped down off the knoll and woke me. When I asked him what was wrong, he told me he was positive he had seen a light in the tree line where we had first set up, earlier in the evening. He wasn't sure, but he thought that it had either been a match or a cigarette lighter. It lasted too long to be a lightning bug.

I asked him if Jim had seen it, too, but he said no, he didn't think so, because he was looking the other way. I told him to wake the rest of the team and tell them that everyone was to stay on full alert for the rest of the night.

While he was following my instructions, I crawled up next to Schwartz and asked him if he had seen anything. He said, ''No, I've been watching the spot where he said he saw it, but I haven't seen a thing.'' I told him to stay alert just in case and crawled back down to the rest of the team.

''Kilburn, go on back up. Keep your eyes open. If you get tired or sleepy, come down and get someone to replace you.'' Had he seen something, or was it just his imagination? It had happened before to guys who weren't as green as Kilburn. Had the NVA come looking for us under the cover of darkness? Had one of them lit up a cigarette in disgust when they discovered that we were long gone? If we had stayed in that last NDP, would we all be lying there dead in the tree line right now? They were questions that would never be answered.

We weren't budging until the extraction ship came for us at 0900. The sun rose, revealing no movement or any sign of anybody having been in the tree line during the night. We would leave it at that. None of us required any proof. We were alive! That was all that mattered. I thought about taking one of the men and going back in, just to make certain, but the new possibility of walking into an ambush or a booby trap, just to satisfy my curiosity, wasn't worth the risk.

The CO radioed at 0850 to tell us he was five minutes out. We gave him our coordinates and waited until we heard the popping sound of the two Hueys rushing up the Perfume in our direction.

Schwartz popped a green smoke grenade when we spotted the choppers two hundred meters downstream and closing. They seemed to hesitate momentarily, then veered over the tree line to circle our position. The C & C ship climbed over us and went into a covering orbit at about five hundred feet while the extraction ship slipped in on the north side of our little hill and touched down. I yelled, "Go, go, go," and the six of us were up and running for the safety of the chopper.

After we landed at the company area, all of us headed for the TOC shed to be debriefed. The first question from the CO was, "What were you doing away from the water? You were supposed to be monitoring the river."

I had anticipated his reaction and had prepared a story that I hoped would satisfy him. "Sir, we were waiting in our NDP for the pickup ship, when the breeze kicked up a little. I thought it would be easier on the pilots if we moved out into the open to await an extraction rather than expect them to set down anywhere near those trees."

He reflected momentarily over my words and decided he really couldn't find fault with my excuse. He moved quickly on into the debriefing itself. While Schwartz was answering some questions about the trail we had spotted and the tracks we had discovered coming up from the river, I made the decision to omit any explanation about the light Kilburn had spotted the night before, or what I had suspected had gone on in the tree line.

It wouldn't have taken him long to realize that my first story had been a fabrication. When the debriefing ended, I went back to my hootch, kicking myself in the ass for having lied in the first place and then leaving out what could have been an important piece of intelligence information to continue the cover-up. If Captain Eklund had been the CO, there would never have been a problem. His policy had always been to leave the ground decisions up to the discretion of the team leader. The new CO was a different story altogether. He tried to run the teams from the company area, approving or disapproving the team leader's decisions without the benefit of being on the scene. At the rate he was going, it would only be a matter of time before one or more of us paid the price for his lack of judgment.

March 1, 1969

I sat in the Ranger lounge downing a few cold Pepsis (Schlitz and Ballantine had been put off limits until after 1800 hours) and telling myself what an outrageously "bad" motherfucker I had become—after all, had I not taken out my own team as a spec four? And by God, I hadn't been to MACV Recondo School, either.

When I heard the plywood door open and then slam shut, I looked up to see Tim Long, the company clerk, standing there with about eight sheets of paper in his hand. He smiled and stepped over to me, handing me what proved to be a set of orders promoting me and seven other spec fours in L Company to the rank of sergeant E-5. I completely forgot about my self-edification of a few minutes before. I was finally an NCO, a buck sergeant. Seventeen months in the army and I could finally feel like I was more than just a name on somebody's fucking roster. No more KP, no more degrading shit-burning details. I could finally get a beer in an NCO club. I quickly forgot about the status of my application for OCS. At that moment, being an NCO seemed to satisfy my every ambition.

We had received word we would begin training a group of combat engineers in the art of rappeling from the skid of a Huey helicopter. Some higher-up over at division had decided that our boys could build firebases much more quickly and efficiently if a platoon of combat engineers, with all their equipment, could be inserted by helicopter right onto the summit of a tree-covered mountain out in the middle of Indian country.

In a matter of three or four hours, the engineers, with their chainsaws and explosive charges, would be able to cut and blast a clearing large enough to handle a CH-47 Chinook transport helicopter. Within twenty-four hours, the poor saps could be well into completing bunkers, fighting trenches, PSP helipad, mortar and howitzer pits, and even an outer perimeter of tanglefoot and concertina wire. Then, after a night's sleep, they could go outside the wire and shove the jungle back for fifty to a hundred meters to create fire lanes for the infantry and artillerymen who would be occupying the firebase.

In the past, the engineers had to either climb up to the peaks with the infantry or hope there was a big enough bomb crater in the vicinity of the summit to land a Huey. Climbing was always risky, tiring, and time-consuming. And going into an existing clearing, whether natural or man-made, often resulted in the engineers being met by a contingent of life members from the local North Vietnamese Welcome Wagon chapter. It was very difficult to extricate oneself from a well-planned ambush when armed with only a chainsaw.

The training had already begun when I finally decided to leave the lounge and walk down to the chopper pad to catch the rest of the show. A Huey was just lifting from the chopper pad and was moving toward a hover directly over the tarmac. I could see Sergeant Burnell backed up to the cabin door on the right side of the helicopter.

Fifty or sixty Rangers and probably that many more combat engineers encircled the pad to watch the demonstration. I didn't observe any ropes dangling from the hovering chopper, so I assumed that Burnell was going for the shock effect of performing a "slack jump" in front of the unsuspecting engineers. Now even a standard rappel from a helicopter hovering at 120 feet is a pretty exciting demonstration. The students would have been duly impressed just witnessing the old master performing one. But you had to know Sergeant Burnell to understand what he was up to. He was about to demonstrate the Ranger method of rappeling from a hovering chopper.

The similarity between a standard rappel and a slack jump is akin to that between a static-line parachute jump and a free-fall sky dive—from just over a thousand feet up. When you rappel from a helicopter in a standard rappel, you must first attach the rappel rope, secured to the anchor rig on the floor of the chopper, to the D-ring connected to the "Swiss" seat harness worn around your waist and down through your crotch. The rappel rope is then looped back again through the D-ring. This creates just enough friction to keep you from receiving the full effect of the law of gravity upon your body and smashing you into the ground at an approximate speed of 120 mph.

The D-ring loop by itself will reduce your airspeed by approximately 50 percent. But unfortunately, the human body was not designed to weather an impact with a solid object at that speed, either. So, some enterprising young adventurer discovered that if you were to take your free hand and clasp the trailing rope securely to the center of your lower back, the additional drag created would act as an emergency brake, further controlling your descent in direct proportion to the amount of pressure exerted by the gloved hand. Combining the two techniques can enable you to descend from a hovering helicopter at a rapid but controlled rate of speed and then brake just prior to landing at an impact that is comfortable enough to insure your survival without risk of bodily injury.

However, the possibility still existed that you could be vulnerable to enemy small-arms fire while dropping fully exposed from a hovering helicopter. If this did occur, the probability was that the injury caused by your subsequent uncontrolled impact with the earth would not be nearly as damaging as the prior penetration of your body by a lethal swarm of steel-jacketed AK-47 rounds.

Once this theorem had been proven in the field, it became apparent that an alternative solution was needed. As luck would have it, our elite Special Forces quickly solved the problem and came up with the answer—slack jumping. Very simply put, slack jumping is not unlike executing a standard rappel, with one minor variance. Instead of the rappel rope being connected to your D-ring a few feet down the rope from where it is attached to the anchor rig on the floor of the helicopter, it is connected to your D-ring seventy-five to eighty feet further down your rope.

The beauty of this innovation is that you are actually free-falling until the entire length of the slack has played out of the rope. It is easy to assume that at the distance of seventy-five to eighty feet, you have probably accelerated, with the aid of gravity, to an airspeed of about 75 mph. When the slack has been evenly distributed between the anchor rig on the floor of the helicopter and the D-ring located just below your navel, you may experience a sudden, massive—but momentary—jolt to your entire anatomy, centering primarily in the shoulder joint of your brake arm.

Now, if you had paid attention during the demonstration of the slack jumping technique, you would obviously realize that, as long as you permitted the loop in the rope running through your D-ring to take the bulk of the initial shock and then slowly absorbed the balance through the firm but gradual application of the brake, then chances were fair to good that you would not even hear the popping sound or experience the excruciating pain caused by your shoulder being dislocated.

This phenomenon is commonly caused by the slack jumper's braking too hard and too quickly, which causes the brake arm to immediately cease its descent, but has little effect on slowing down the rest of the body.

Well, getting back to Sergeant Burnell, when I saw that he was standing in the open door with his back to us and no rope lead was dangling from the Huey, I knew immediately that he was about to execute a slack jump. I was also aware that the Rangers were supposed to be teaching the engineers how to rappel—not slack jump. So, I figured that old Bernie was simply about to set the standard by which Rangers were judged by their peers. He was going to show those engineers that what they would soon be learning was pussy stuff when compared to what we did—routinely.

I was somewhat surprised when he stepped off the skid while the chopper was only about seventy-five feet above the ground. Usually, we jumped from an altitude of 100–120 feet. You see, you were supposed to run out of slack line about 20–40 feet before you ran out of altitude. Well something had gone wrong here! Bernie executed a beautiful slack jump. His exit was tight and upright. He maintained the position until a split second before he hit the tarmac chopper pad. It must have been about the same time that he realized that he had too much slack (or not enough altitude—depending on how you looked at it).

The platoon sergeant demonstrated that he was indeed a professional. As he hit the ground, he executed one of the most classic PLFs (parachute landing fall) that I had ever seen. He landed on the balls of his feet, shifted his weight to his right leg, and then rolled to his right hip and side as he distributed the force of the impact over his entire body. The move saved his life!

There were already four others bending over him as I reached his side. Doc Proctor, one of the company medics, was there, trying to keep the badly injured platoon sergeant immobilized until a medevac chopper could reach the scene. It was obvious that Bernie was in tremendous pain. Doc told us to hold the struggling NCO down. There was little doubt that, from the appearance of his legs and hips, the stocky platoon sergeant had suffered some radical damage to his lower extremities and probably his pelvis.

It must have taken fifteen minutes for the medevac ship to arrive. Bernie was injected with morphine to ease the pain, then strapped to a wooden back-board for the flight to the surgical hospital at Phu Bai. We didn't know if he would make it or not. At the very best, it appeared that his military career was over. The army didn't employ hopeless cripples. But then again, if anyone could come back from those kinds of injuries, it would be Burnell. After all, how many times had I sat in the lounge and watched Burnell and Johnny Quick eat razor blades, drinking glasses, and sixty-watt light bulbs. Burnell had teased us about how he had used to eat only hundred-watt bulbs, but was now cutting back because he was trying to watch his weight.

After he was gone, the engineers, who had stood back in shock after viewing the tragic accident, decided it was getting too late in the day to conduct any more training. I couldn't blame them. For all they knew, they had just witnessed a demonstration of rappeling, Ranger style. If I had been in their boots, and thought that was how I was supposed to learn to rappel, all of the NVA in South Vietnam couldn't have gotten me onto that helicopter.

Captain Eklund dropped by the company area that evening just to say hello. While he was there he asked me if I'd be interested in joining him up at Division G-3 as an operations NCO. Boy, it was tempting, but I couldn't picture myself functioning as an REMF.

March 2, 1969

We received word at morning formation that Sp4c. Jackson was in a hospital at Camp Zama, Japan. He had gone into a coma after being wounded by the freaked-out cherry on Sours's team a few weeks before. Surgery had kept him alive but had not repaired the damage. If he lived, he would be paralyzed from the waist down. Almost everyone in the formation bowed his head and offered a prayer for our wounded comrade.

I went out as belly-man with a Cav "pink team" early in the afternoon. Pink teams were helicopter hunter-killer teams specializing in locating and destroying enemy camps, bunkers, transportation, food supplies, and commo centers. The team was made up of one or two LOH scout choppers, a Huey slick rigged with a coiled rope ladder and McGuire rigs, and a pair of Cobra gunships.

The slick and the two gunships would hover at five thousand to seven thousand feet while the fast-moving LOH scouts flitted across the treetops looking for anything that wasn't natural. If they discovered something, they would usually bring it under M-60 fire or drop a WP grenade on it. If it was too big for them to handle, they would mark the site with a smoke or WP grenade and then back off while the Cobras came in and destroyed whatever had frightened their little brothers.

The slick remained in orbit, joining the fray only to rescue the crew of one of the other choppers if it went down. I had flown on a couple of pink teams with Captain Eklund and S.Sgt. "Contact" Johnson. They both enjoyed the excitement, and Bill Marcy, Ron Rucker, or I usually went along as belly-man. I never had the opportunity to do anything, but Rucker had gone out with the CO once when they had discovered and destroyed an NVA five-ton truck hidden in some trees in the A Shau Valley. Later they had gotten lost and ended up somewhere in Laos over the Plain of Jars.

This mission had turned out to be a little exciting. We had been out in the "game preserve" for about an hour, and I was watching the two LOHs zigzagging back and forth over the treetops down on the jungle floor below me. Suddenly, I saw the LOH on the left stand on its nose as the crewman poked the sling-mounted machine gun out the open side and began firing at something on the ground. The other LOH quickly moved in and dropped three WPs. Then one of the pilots radioed in that they had spotted four bunkers and a cluster of huts back in the trees. When they had moved in to take a closer look, a gook, dressed in black pajamas, had popped up out of a nearby "spider hole" and had opened up on them with some kind of old semiautomatic carbine.

We watched as the two LOHs spent ten minutes trying to take out the single NVA. They would take turns hovering directly over his hole trying to put the machine gun fire directly into it. Then they would drop a couple of grenades before moving off to the side to let the other one have a try. Each time they pulled out, the plucky little Vietnamese would jump up and pop off a couple of more rounds at them. Finally, they ran out of ammo and grenades. So one of the LOH pilots brought his ship back in and dropped a red smoke grenade on the spider hole from a height of about ten feet. Sure enough, as he spun away from the hole, the gook popped back up and let go with a couple more shots.

The two Cobras rolled in on the red smoke and blasted the area with rockets. After six separate rocket runs, they rolled in again and tore the jungle apart with automatic cannon fire. When they had exhausted their ammo, they made a couple of final passes over the area with miniguns blazing. They radioed my pilot that they were low on fuel and had exhausted their ordnance and were returning to base. We "rogered" the transmission and affirmed that we would all head back in.

As we swung over the jungle to head back in the direction of Camp Eagle, the same enemy soldier popped back out and fired three or four more shots at our departing helicopters. I was amazed. We must have spent close to twenty thousand dollars trying to put our little friend on General Westmoreland's tote board. Somehow or another, he had survived, still trying to put us on General Giap's tote board. You had to admire somebody with balls that big! We should have just given him the money we wasted on him and told him to go home and retire. You know, that's not a bad idea! Twenty thousand dollars U.S. would buy one hell of a lot of rice and *nuoc mam* sauce. Hell, five thousand dollars U.S. would buy a lot of rice and fish sauce! Throw in a couple of cases of good old Ba Muoi Ba beer, a couple of pounds of opium, a bundle of joss sticks, and a black-toothed mama san, and he would be humping back up the Ho Chi Minh Trail.

We could drop flyers all over the jungle, just like with the Chieu Hoi program: SEND FOR YOUR FAMILIES, TURN IN YOUR WEAPONS, AND THE U.S. GOVERNMENT WILL SET UP A BANK ACCOUNT IN YOUR NAME IN THE AMOUNT OF $5,000. WE'LL GIVE YOU ALL THESE OTHER THINGS TOO AND EVEN BOOK PASSAGE FOR YOU AND YOUR LOVED ONES TO ANY THIRD WORLD COUNTRY ON EARTH. YOU CAN ALL LIVE LIKE KINGS FOR THE REST OF YOUR LIVES! With the kind of money we spent in Vietnam each year, we could have bought victory in thirty days.

Let's see. If we spent $5 billion a year—at $5,000 per NVA, that would have removed a million of them a year. Hell, let's be generous and give each family $15,000 a year. After all, we're Americans, aren't we? Well, that's just wishful thinking! Even if it did make sense. The other side of the coin would be to get the South Vietnamese Army to show half that much spunk in combat, and we could all go home and let them win the war.

A side benefit from the extra flying time was that I had been able to log enough hours to qualify for an Air Medal and was only twelve more hours away from a second one.

March 3, 1969

Someone had scrounged up some really "bad" X-rated
skin flicks, and word had gotten out that they were going
to be shown in Miller's hootch later in the evening. Forty
of us must have been crowded among the four cots at the
end of the building. The pornography was as raw as it was
bad. In one particularly revealing episode, an overweight,
excessively heavy-chested bleach-blond stripper was giving head to a skinny little shit with no chin who's only
redeeming characteristic was that he had a pecker that
looked like a 60mm mortar.

Everyone was laughing and making lewd comments
about "Blond Bertha" eating a mortar round, when a lifer
staff sergeant who had only been in the company a couple
of months, walked in and said, "Motherfuck! I'd be
damned if I'd ever make love to a woman who had put
somethin' like that in her mouth!"

Somebody quipped up from the front, "Shit, Sarge, how
long have you been in-country?"

The PX finally got in a stock of the new "L Co, 75th
Inf. RANGER" tabs. They were black and red and really
looked sharp. It was hard to take off those old black and
yellow LRP tabs. A lot of pride had gone into them. I put
the LRP tabs in an envelope and sent them home to Barb.

We had a new ID and a new reputation to establish.
Like our black hats, none of the tabs had been authorized
by the Department of the Army. Not that it made a lot of
difference. Most of the guys purchased black berets to wear
home when they DEROSed. They weren't authorized, either, but all the Ranger companies were going to them.

March 4, 1969

About forty of us went down to the MACV SOG compound just north of Phu Bai for some rappeling practice off their sixty-foot towers. The camp was better known as FOB 1 (Forward Observation Base One). It sat on the east side of Highway 1 just north of the Phu Bai Airport. We never saw many of the Americans stationed there, but there was always a contingent of grinning, overfriendly Vietnamese lounging around in their gun emplacements and bunkers.

The place was a veritable fortress. I would have hated to be an NVA sapper assigned to infiltrate the base. I always enjoyed rappeling off FOB 1's towers. One side was open, which simulated rappeling from a helicopter. The other side was covered with PSP panels that the SOG personnel had liberated from the nearby airbase. It provided an outstanding platform to simulate rappeling from a building or down the side of a cliff.

March 6, 1969

We received an unexpected treat in the afternoon. The first sergeant passed the word out that a couple of Red Cross "Donut Dollies" would be arriving in the company area in an hour. We were to be on our best behavior. Anyone caught attempting to fraternize, fondle, frag, fricassee, fry, franchise, or do or attempt to do any other inappropriate f-word action-verb to either of the girls would be cremated, court-martialed, crapped on, canceled, corked, cauterized, clobbered, creamed, and carbonized. That is, of course, unless he had previously been canonized, castrated, commissioned, or Congressionally Medaled, then he was exempt.

Expecting the worst from my hard-core, sex-starved, uncouth fellow Rangers, I was totally shocked to see them turn into a courteous, mannerly, polite formation of gentlemen. We all sat obediently around the supply tent playing games like find-a-word, scrambled letters, and twenty questions. They had us too embarrassed playing those stupid games to protest. No one wanted to be the first one to disrupt the proceedings. So, good-naturedly, we all just stood there lusting as the two girls commented about what a nice bunch of guys we were. If the enemy ever found out about this, our reputations wouldn't be worth a shit.

Word came down that a Special Forces camp in the Central Highlands was hit the evening of the sixth by NVA supported by Soviet light tanks. Supposedly, the attack was repulsed and several of the tanks were knocked out. That was the first use of enemy armor we had heard of since Lang Vei was overrun a year before during Tet of '68.

One of our teams out in the A Shau back in early November had listened to a tracked vehicle moving down the valley at night. It seemed hard to believe that the NVA could hide and maneuver tanks in those jungles without our Ranger and Special Forces teams finding them. If Nixon carried through with the troop withdrawals he had been promising, the bloodbath in Vietnam in the next couple of years would rival the Russian purges. The South Vietnamese military would never be able to stand up to the NVA. They had no heart, and their government and a good part of their military staff were hopelessly corrupt.

First Sergeant Cardin informed Phil Meyers and me that he didn't think we would get our field commissions because neither of us had enough time-in-grade as E-5s. It seemed that the past five years had been nothing more than a frustrating attempt to receive a commission. I knew I could get an appointment to OCS after my DEROS, but I realized that I would never be able to take any harassment from some bare-chested instructor who had never seen any combat outside of Phoenix City. I would end up in the stockade in short order.

Well, I had given it my best. If the army didn't want me, then I would go back to school on the GI bill and get a degree in business management or law.

March 7, 1969

My new platoon sergeant, Staff Sergeant Bowman, ran into my hootch right after we returned from noon chow and asked for volunteers to rappel onto a mountainside somewhere south of Camp Eagle to rescue the crews of a Cobra that had gone down in the jungle and a LOH with three officers aboard which had crashed nearby trying to locate the gunship. There had to be NVA in the vicinity because the Cobra had taken hits while attacking a bunker complex. The LOH had probably crashed because of equipment failure. They had never radioed that they had been fired on.

There had been a heavy fog in the area where the LOH and the Cobra had crashed. No one had spotted any smoke, so there was an excellent chance that the five men had survived. Another LOH went in and located the wreckage of the Cobra but could not find the other bird.

Six of our teams were already out in the field, so the company was short personnel. Two of my people were on R & R and another was away at Recondo School. So I sat there, thinking about all the times that Cobra and LOH pilots had risked their lives to pull my fat out of the fire. Yeah, I had to volunteer. I could never face another chopper pilot if I didn't.

Rich Fadeley volunteered to take in the second team.

Division had decided that it would be safer if twelve of us went in together on the same LZ. Since there were enemy troops in the area, six men would have a difficult time trying to locate a couple of downed choppers and evacuate their crews while maintaining security.

My team would rappel in first. We would secure the LZ while Fadeley's team came in right behind us. We were told to leave our rucks behind. LBE (equipment harness—"load-bearing equipment") and weapons only. They would have us in and out in less than three hours.

I went looking for volunteers to fill out my team. Groff, Kilburn, and I made three. I ran into Larry Saenz as I was leaving the hootch. He had already heard the news and offered to go out as part of the rescue team. I found Biedron and Munoz and asked them if they'd like a chance to earn their pay. Both agreed to go. That would make six. I made sure everyone knew we were going in light, our web gear and weapons being all we would carry. Each of them was to bring an extra bandolier of ammo. I could cope with running out of food or water—although the loss of either could create some problems—but running out of ammo in the middle of a firefight was one of the quickest ways I knew to get your work permit canceled.

Munoz would be the senior RTO, Kilburn the junior. Both Rangers strapped their PR-25 radios directly onto their pack frames. I noticed that Munoz had taken the extra precaution of tying a butt pack under the radio and sticking an extra battery in it. I told Kilburn to do the same and instructed him to add a claymore for balance.

Beidron, Saenz, and I met at the ammo bunker to pick up the extra bandoliers. Biedron and Saenz both grabbed a claymore carrying bag. I removed one of my canteens and jammed four frags into the empty pouch.

We had to hurry; we could already hear the two slicks arriving on the chopper pad. It wouldn't take First Sergeant Cardin and Staff Sergeant Bowman long to rig the rappeling ropes. You could feel the sense of urgency in the air. It would be dark in five hours—we wouldn't have much time. I jammed a couple of survival bars, a compass, and pen-flare gun into my pocket as I made a final trip through my hootch.

I had the uncomfortable feeling that I had forgotten

something important. In the time allotted to gear up and get on the road, it wouldn't have been difficult. I had my leather rappeling gloves, D-ring, and Swiss seat rope. I made sure that everyone else had his. No one had taken the time to apply camouflage paint. Only Biedron and Groff were even wearing jungle cammo uniforms. The rest of us still wore our OD (olive drab) utilities.

We had left our black baseball caps with their white Recondo patches back at our hootches, but only Biedron and Saenz had picked up their boonie caps. The rest of the team tore apart someone's OD undershirt in front of the Ranger lounge and made headbands to cover our hair. I wish that I could say I was nervous, but the mad rush trying to get organized and get airborne caused me to focus only on the matters at hand. I would have to worry about the details afterward.

Fadeley's team arrived at the chopper pad the same time we did. "Contact" Johnson was already there with Bowman, and both NCOs were anxious to get going. They would each be flying belly-man in the slicks. Their job was to make sure that each man hooked up and exited the ship properly. Once the team was out, they had to recover the two ropes quickly so that the rotor wash from the departing Hueys couldn't cause them to entangle in the blades. That would have been disastrous.

As the twelve of us stood around rigging our Swiss seats, they urged us to hurry. Kilburn had some difficulty with his, until Bowman jumped down out of the slick and corrected the problem. We climbed aboard as the two slicks took off immediately toward the south. Bowman screamed in my ear that we would be stopping at FSB (fire support base) Tomahawk to pick up our Cobra escorts and to receive an update on the situation.

I had never worked to the south of Camp Eagle, but I remembered that the same range of mountains that rose to the west of our base camp swung in toward the coast just south of Leech Island. We could see Tomahawk coming up in the distance. It was a typical U.S. firebase. It reminded me of Firebase Jack up near LZ Sally, except Tomahawk sat on a little higher hill than Jack did. Neither of the two firebases was actually in the mountains. They had been established in the foothills to support the troops patrolling the fringe areas.

We set down on a PSP helipad just big enough for the two Hueys. I told the rest of the team to stay aboard until I found out what was going on. Fadeley and I started to walk across the pad to a group of officers clustered on the other side, but stopped when a lieutenant ran up and told us to form up our teams on the edge of the pad.

We turned and signaled our teams to come up just as a LOH popped over the horizon. It circled in to land between two bunkers in the center of the firebase. Two officers got out and started walking toward us. One was Gen. Melvin Zais, the commanding officer of the 101st Airborne Division. The other was a chicken (full) colonel from his staff. It was the third time I had seen the general. He had spent some time talking with me back in November when he had pinned my Silver Star on me. I had talked briefly with him at the division Soldier of the Month review board in December. I was pleased when he looked at me and nodded. He still recognized me.

We drew up in front of him on the edge of the chopper pad. He thanked the twelve of us for volunteering to go in after the two aircrews. I wasn't surprised to discover that all five of the missing men were officers—three warrants, a captain, and a lieutenant colonel. When the general finished speaking, he turned us over to the staff officer at his side. He, too, thanked us for volunteering then got right into the meat of the briefing.

The two downed choppers were within two hundred meters of each other. The Cobra had broken in half on impact and was in double-canopy jungle about two thirds of the way up the side of a steep primary ridgeline that ran through the area. The LOH was two hundred meters west of the Cobra and lower on the mountainside. The Cobra had been shot down assaulting a bunker complex, reportedly by a .51-cal. machine gun. The LOH had gone down twenty minutes later. There had been no commo from the LOH warning of any enemy fire. They had just radioed that they were going into a fog bank to look for the downed Cobra. They never came back out. Another LOH had worked its way back in under the cloud cover and located the Cobra and, after a lengthy search, reported what they thought was the crash site of the other LOH.

There had been a lot of enemy activity in the area over the past few days, even though several infantry companies patrolled it on a regular basis. Intelligence reported two separate NVA battalions in the immediate vicinity. He went on to tell us that no maps were available for the particular area we would be going into, but that all precautions had been taken to place us right on top of the crash sites.

Fadeley pointed out that without maps, we would not be able to plot coordinates and call for artillery support if we made contact with the enemy. The colonel responded that four Cobra gunships would be available for support, as if that should impress us, and then let it go at that. Jesus Christ, two choppers go down in the fog and they want to offer us air support! Well, as long as they can put us on top of the downed birds, how tough could it really be?

Fadeley and I decided that we would go in simultaneously as close together as the two slicks could insert us. Once on the ground, we would link up and move out for the location of the Cobra, figuring that we could get two men out faster than three. Besides, if the Cobra was farther up the side of the mountain, the fog would settle in from the higher altitude much quicker, giving us less time to evacuate the crew of the gunship before we got totally socked in.

Once we had gotten the Cobra crew out, we would move down the mountainside and go after the LOH crew. Hopefully, the fog bank would still be above us by the time we got to them, permitting the Hueys to get back in and bring everyone out before the weather made flying totally impossible.

We hurriedly boarded the two slicks and took off for the mountains to the southwest. The plan had sounded good. We should be able to get in and out in ninety minutes unless we ran into trouble.

Two Cobras joined us a couple of kilometers out from Tomahawk. We flew in formation toward a mountain range not far off in the distance. I had to assume it was a mountain range because the upper half was totally covered by a

dense bank of gray-white clouds that obliterated any sign
of the ridgeline we were looking for.

The information handed down at our briefing had been
based on old data. We didn't have until dark to locate and
evacuate the two aircrews. It was already too late to get
them out. The crash sites were well within those hanging
layers of low clouds. The choppers began orbiting outside
the edge of the fog bank, unsure what to do next. Our
pilot called back to Staff Sergeant Bowman and pointed
out that flight conditions were too bad to continue the mission. He was calling back to base for new instructions.
The message came back that it would be up to us to continue the mission. We all nodded—we'd try it if the pilots
could get us in.

The two Hueys drifted a hundred meters apart and entered the fog bank at an altitude that was designed to put
us a hundred feet over the downed Cobra if we didn't hit
a tree or crash into the side of the mountain first. None of
us dared to breathe as our helicopter eased its way into the
wall of gray.

I was surprised to find that I could see darker shades of
gray just below us as we moved further into the fog bank.
They turned out to be the tops of trees slightly visible
beneath us. At least we knew we weren't flying upside
down. The broken line of jungle provided a reference point
that kept us from feeling totally disoriented. We had lost
visual contact with the other Huey as soon as we had entered the cloud cover. I knew instantly that we were heading into trouble.

After about two minutes worth of feeling his way
through the dense, almost solid layer of air, our pilot signaled that he was over the wreckage of the Cobra. I looked
over the side and could barely make out sixty-to-seventy
foot trees shrouded in the mist. I could not see the downed
Cobra. The jungle seemed to emit some eerie, almost
ethereal vibration that threatened to overpower me. I
sensed sheer, unadulterated terror. I fought back panic as
it tried to root me in place. I couldn't drop down into that
. . . whatever it was. It was like something out of a horror
movie. The only things missing were the tombstones.

Bowman was screaming for us to hook up as he tossed
a rope out each side of the Huey. I watched them as they

uncoiled down into the smoky, hazy maw of the jungle below. I stood and stepped back toward the edge of the cabin floor, willing movement into a body that no longer seemed able to respond. I watched my hands as they looped the rappel rope through the D-ring in my Swiss seat. They performed the task without direction from me. I fought for control; I had to get my shit back together. What was I doing here? The only thought that raced through my mind was the unknown danger that could be waiting for us down there. As team leader, I would be the first one out.

I couldn't remember stepping off the skid into the almost solid haze below. I couldn't even remember the actual rappel. My first recollection was the jolt I felt as my brake hand pressed into the small of my back, just above the canteen pouch full of grenades. I was back in control. I knew I had only seconds to get down to the ground, free myself from the rope, and belay it for the next man. I touched down in the middle of a six-foot-wide high-speed trail. My skin crawled as I hurriedly fed the trailing end of the rope through my D-ring. I wanted to look over my shoulder; something evil was looming there like a giant saber-toothed tiger ready to pounce. My weapon was slung across my back. I needed it in my hands—*now*—*right now*! I reached back and pulled it up over my head, wanting to look at what was behind me. I spun around! A concrete bunker sat nestled back in the vegetation three meters off the trail. I would never have spotted it except for the rotor wash from the Huey whipping down from above.

The other Rangers were dropping down around me. Munoz, Biedron, and Groff all made it safely to the ground. One . . . two . . . three . . . myself, four . . . who's missing? I looked up to see Kilburn, the second man out on my rope, stuck five feet above me. Saenz was in the door, looking back over his shoulder and waiting for Kilburn to finish his rappel. I could see Bowman's face staring over the edge of the cabin floor, trying to figure out what had happened. Finally he signaled for me to get Kilburn off the rope. Instinctively, I reached to my chest and pulled out the K-bar knife I wore taped upside down on my LBE harness. I grabbed the rope dangling below Kilburn and tried to reach up and cut it above where it had fouled with the radio handset cord. I couldn't reach it.

I motioned for Bowman to have the pilot bring the Huey lower. It seemed like it took forever before he responded and dropped a couple of feet lower. I was able to extend my right arm just far enough to slice through the rope above Kilburn's head. Instantly, Saenz was on his way to the ground. The chopper must have drifted back up a few feet, because Saenz ran out of rope six feet above the trail.

Bowman waved and the Huey drifted upward like a hot air balloon and disappeared into the overcast. We could hear it as it moved back out away from the ridgeline and headed for the open country to the northeast. Dead silence fell over us as the noise of the chopper faded in the distance. We moved off the trail into the jungle and set up a hasty perimeter fifteen meters away. I told Munoz to contact Fadeley, find out where he was, and arrange a link-up.

He put the hand-phone to his head and whispered into it for several minutes before turning to tell me that he couldn't reach him on the radio. He tried again on Kilburn's radio but only got static in reply. I couldn't imagine what had happened to the other team. They had been right behind us coming into the fog bank. Even in the overcast, they couldn't have gone in over two hundred meters away from us. We should have been able to establish radio contact with them.

Munoz called the C & C ship and asked them if they were in touch with the other team. They asked us to wait while they tried to establish commo with them. Seconds later, they were back on the air telling us that they had them on the horn but their signal was coming in as weak as ours. The thick cloud cover seemed to be deadening our signals.

The C & C chopper relayed back to us that Fadeley was going to fire a pen-flare so that we could locate each other. They did a countdown and announced the moment it was fired, but we couldn't spot it. I radioed back that we would fire a single shot, no more, and advised them to get a bearing and come to us. We had been the lead chopper, and unless our pilot had really screwed up, we should be in the vicinity of the downed Cobra. We did another countdown and I fired a single shot from my CAR-15 straight up through the trees. I didn't like doing it, but I knew that a single gunshot, unless you were expecting it, was almost impossible to get a bearing on.

In seconds Fadeley relayed that he had heard the shot and was moving in our direction. I asked the relay to find out from what azimuth. He radioed back that Fadeley didn't know. No one on his team had a compass. Great! We had one, but it sure wouldn't help the other team. What a fucking freak show! No map, no food, no poncho liners, no bug juice, no SOI codebook, no artillery, and no air support. Just like they promised. Out in two to three hours! Bullshit, brother! We were going to be in till the clouds lifted. And that could be days.

Fifteen minutes passed. We hid waiting for the sounds of Fadeley's team moving through the jungle. I really didn't know what to expect. Those guys were Rangers, too. They wouldn't be making any noise. Suddenly, I heard someone yell, "Yo, Rangers!" It was Fadeley! I couldn't believe he was yelling out in the middle of the jungle with NVA in the area, but what else could he do? I hollered back, "Rangers! Over here."

From the sound of his voice, he seemed like he was half a klick away, but I realized that in the jungle, especially with the shroud of fog that enveloped us muffling the sound, he was probably less than fifty meters away. I decided to let them work their way to us. There was too good of a chance we would miss each other if both teams were moving in opposite directions. We each had to yell twice more to effect the link-up.

Their point man, Phil Myers, cut the trail just up hill from where I hid, and they followed it down to us. I don't think twelve guys were ever so happy to see each other. Fadeley, a staff sergeant, took overall control of the combined teams. We decided that the slick pilots must have "choked" and dropped us off too far down the mountain from the Cobra's crash site. They had gone in on the proper bearing, but had not been able to judge distance.

We would have to get on line, four or five meters apart, and move up the side of the mountain until we located the wreckage. If we didn't find it by the time we reached the crest, we would move back along the crest fifty meters and make another sweep down the side of the mountain, covering new ground.

We set off up the mountainside, moving slowly and methodically, searching the cover for any sign of wreckage. How could anyone hide a Cobra helicopter? We knew that it would only be a matter of time before we found it. We just hoped that we would find the crewmen alive.

We must have covered a hundred meters before Fadeley located the cockpit and fuselage of the Cobra. He passed the word back down the line that he had found it. When we got to him, he was standing alongside the fuselage, shaking his head. The canopy was open and there was no sign of either of the crewmen. Three Rangers from Fadeley's team stayed with the wreckage while the rest of us got back on line and resumed our sweep of the area.

Twenty minutes later, we located a jungle boot and a flight helmet, but found no signs of the two men or any indication that they had ever been in the area. There was nothing to lead us to believe that the NVA had gotten there ahead of us. The only conclusion we could draw was that the pilot and his gunner had survived the crash and were hiding somewhere in the area or had attempted to E & E on their own. After all, they would have naturally assumed that no rescue would take place until the fog lifted. We could only guess why one of them had removed his boot and left it behind. It had been unlaced just like someone had taken the time to loosen the strings so that it would have been easy to get off. There was no sign of any blood on it to indicate that the owner had been wounded or injured. None of us could explain it.

We called in a sitrep but could only get through to the artillery battery on Firebase Tomahawk. The choppers had returned to the safety of Camp Eagle. The fire control officer manning the battery of 105s on Tomahawk agreed to relay our message back to Camp Eagle for us. We reported that we had located the Cobra but had found no sign of the crew. We also recommended that any attempt to extract us be postponed until the fog lifted the next day.

After about fifteen minutes, the artillerymen radioed back to tell us that they had gotten the message through to our rear. Our "Six" (company commander) had agreed that we should remain in the field overnight and await further instructions in the morning. It wasn't a surprise to any of us, although there was a certain shock in hearing it from an outsider. There was nothing anyone could have done to get us out before morning. We would just have to hope that the fog would lift long enough for them to get a couple of birds in to us the next day.

We moved up the side of the mountain, not wanting to get too far from the crash site, yet not wanting to linger too long in the immediate area. We needed to find a defensible NDP with some heavy concealment, big enough to accommodate twelve men.

Fadeley, Myer, and I discussed the feasibility of splitting up the team into two elements and hiding within a hundred meters of each other until daylight. We were all concerned about our proximity to the well-used high-speed trail down below and the concrete reinforced bunker that I had spotted. There had to be other bunkers in the area, and—well—even the U.S. Army wasn't building bunkers out of concrete.

In the end, we decided to stay together. Twelve men would have a lot better chance of defending themselves than six. We soon located a level area just large enough for twelve men to lay within. It was surrounded by several large, vine-covered mahogany trees. There was a natural berm on the uphill side that offered some protection in case the enemy decided to put small-arms fire into us from above. There wasn't a lot of ground cover to hide us, but in the thick blanket of fog, that by then was swirling around at our feet like billows of smoke, concealment was being provided by Mother Nature.

We weren't spoiling for a fight. We knew that we were without outside support. We couldn't call in a fire mission without a map, and none of us expected any pilots to fly in the kind of soup we were standing in. No one had brought in anywhere close to the usual amount of ammunition and frags we carried on a typical mission. If we were forced into a protracted battle at night with the enemy, we wouldn't last an hour. We just wanted to be left alone until daylight so that we could finish up our mission and get the hell out of there.

Some places just had an evil air about them. We felt as

if the very jungle were after us. We crawled into the protection of the huge trees just as darkness settled in. My team had three claymores with them. We decided to put one on each flank and then to point the third one straight uphill over are E & E route. If we got hit during the night and had to escape and evade, we agreed to rendezvous on the crest of the ridge directly above us. We knew that fog settled in from above, but stayed longest down in the valleys. Our chances of rescue would come sooner at the top of the mountain if the fog lifted in the morning the way it was supposed to.

We kept the claymores in close to the perimeter. The big mahoganies insured that we would receive no backblast from the detonations if we had to blow them. We had no food except for a few ''lifer'' bars and some snacks, which we shared. If one of us had to be hungry, we would all be hungry.

Each man had brought two canteens, so water was not yet a concern. The biggest immediate problem was the lack of poncho liners to protect us from the moist, chill air that had crept in with the fog. I recommended to Fadeley that we set up security shifts with three men on duty while the other nine slept. Each shift should pull a two-hour watch beginning at 2200. But Fadeley preferred to go with twelve one-man shifts covering forty-five minutes each starting at 2100 hours. He was the overall team leader, so we went along with his plan.

I doubted if I would be getting much sleep anyway. I wasn't very tired and was already too chilled to be comfortable. I just prayed that we would make it through the night. The NVA in the area had to have heard us come in earlier, and the gunshot and the shouting could hardly have been missed. The first few hours of night passed quietly. No one moved. A hush had fallen over the jungle, silencing the normal sounds of its creatures and providing a tomblike atmosphere for the sentries to stand watch over. The dense, almost solid fog slowly settled over us like a heavy funeral shroud, suffocating us in its blanket of dead, stale, moist air.

An eerie, soft white light seemed to emanate from above, yet it could have been coming from anywhere around us. It wasn't really a light . . . more of an illumination. It seemed to grow brighter farther off in the distance. The false glow broke up the outlines of the trees around us and gave the effect of shadowy gray, mottled whisps of swamp moss hanging down from overhead. I looked back over the other Rangers lying asleep in no particular formation. I couldn't see where their bodies met the clammy, dank embrace of the jungle floor. They appeared to float suspended, partly above and partly below the mattress of fog that cushioned their sleeping forms. It was like looking out over a battleground where only the specters of the dead remained.

I dared not sleep. Evil seemed to be moving out in the mist. I sensed a deep foreboding of danger. I couldn't understand how the rest of the Rangers had kicked back and gone to sleep. Then, maybe they were only feigning sleep. Wasn't that what I was doing? I stayed alert while the first three men pulled their guard shifts. I was pleased to see that every man woke his relief at the proper time. Good! They weren't sleeping on guard. I wondered if each of them was going through the same personal terror that I was, as they lay there listening for sounds that didn't belong, watching for movement that was out of place. I began to feel drowsy, wanting to give into the escape that sleep would provide, but I fought it. I wanted to be awake if anything happened.

March 8, 1969

A little after midnight I sensed, more than saw, Munoz wake Biedron. It would be my turn next. Dave lay still during his shift, moving only once to remove something that lay beneath him. I was getting sleepy, and knew that I had screwed up. I should have slept earlier. It would soon be my turn to pull guard, and I wasn't sure I could stay awake.

Finally, I felt Dave roll toward me and whisper in my ear, "Linderer, you're on." I whispered back, "Okay." He lay back and immediately fell off to sleep. I could hear his breathing slow down and shallow out as he sought the safe, comfortable security that deep sleep afforded. I envied him. I had never been able to drop off like that on a mission. I had never been able to trust the man on guard enough to give myself over to his care. Then, again, maybe it was myself I didn't trust.

Ten minutes into my shift, my head snapped up, popping my eyes wide open. I had fallen asleep. Fuck! I rolled over and looked at the luminous hands on my watch. It was only 0110. I couldn't have slept for more than a few seconds! I slowly sat up. Maybe I'd stay awake if I didn't lay down! Ten minutes later the strain on my lower back forced me down again. Drowsiness returned with a vengeance. I reached for a sharp stone I had earlier removed from my position. It was right where I had put it. It had gouged me in the hip when I had first tried to sleep, so I had pried it loose and set it to one side. Now I slid it back under my hip, knowing that a little discomfort would drive away the sleep.

It worked for a while, but it wasn't long before I could feel the moisture over my eyes beginning to dry out. Easing my canteen out, I poured a little water into the palm of my right hand, then slammed it into my eyes. I rubbed vigorously, trying to get the lubricating liquid in where it would do some good. I looked at my watch again. It was nearly 0135. Ten more minutes and I could switch places with Kilburn. The cherry hadn't impressed me, getting the cord on his handset tangled in the rappeling rope. What a dumb fucking thing to do! And how about that time he had seen that match flare in the tree line along the Perfume River? Short, stocky little fart! Hell, he's not even built like a Ranger. Then, what's a Ranger supposed to be built like? Me? Maybe there had been a match in that tree line. After all, something had warned me to get out of there. And that screwup on the rappeling rope—remember the time I waited too long to leap out of the Huey on my first mission, and then fell flat on my face while the rest of the team raced for cover. Naw, the kid was okay! He didn't bitch any and at least tried to do his job. It was time to wake him.

I leaned over and shook him gently. He rolled over on his side. Damn, I wish I could sleep that soundly. I shook him again. He sat up and rubbed the sleep from his eyes. I stayed awake until I was sure that he was alert, then lay back. The drowsiness that had plagued me before was gone. God dammit, more of this insomnia bullshit! It must have lasted for ten to fifteen minutes, but I finally felt myself dropping off. I remembered hearing Kilburn lay down again, and wondered if he was going back to sleep. To hell with him! That's his worry. I had pulled my watch, and now I was going to get some sleep.

I didn't know what had happened, but suddenly I was wide awake. My eyes flew open and fought momentarily to focus. It was darker, much darker than when I had finished my guard shift. Something wasn't right, I could feel it. A shadow, yes, a shadow faded out of my vision to the right. I wanted to sit up, but something told me not to move. I slid my left hand over a few inches and felt the comfortable handgrip under the trigger-guard on my CAR-15. It was right where I had left it. I turned my head slowly to the right, eyes straining to find the specter that had passed from my sight. Nothing! Not a goddamned thing. Had I dreamed it? Was my overactive imagination playing tricks on me? My God, was Vietnam doing this to me?

Then I sensed that Kilburn was awake. I rolled over and started to whisper in his ear that I couldn't sleep and would take the rest of his shift for him, when I noticed that he was rigid, shaking violently, like he was freezing to death. He was holding his M-16 at port arms across his chest. Something was very wrong. It was chilly lying there, that I knew, but he was trembling so badly that he seemed to be coming apart.

"What in the hell's the matter?" I whispered as I pressed close to his ear.

He turned his head quickly toward me and whispered back, "Sarge, gooks, gooks, three of them! They walked right into the perimeter. They bent over Saenz and looked at him, then turned around and walked back out again. I couldn't shoot. I couldn't bring my weapon around. Tree in the way.'' He was petrified with fear.

I froze. Damn! Son of a bitch! I knew it. Something had awakened me. I had felt the danger. The pricks had been right in our perimeter. I leaned back over and told Kilburn to start waking everyone up to his right, warning him to do it quietly. I rolled to the left and woke Biedron, telling him to wake everyone to his left. We were going on full alert. The goddamned gooks had found us.

When everyone was awake, I crawled over to Fadeley to confer on a plan of action. We had four more hours of darkness before sunup, and probably another four to six hours before the sun burned the fog off. That was a total of eight to ten hours we had to keep the NVA off of us until help arrived.

I was for E & Eing the hell out of there right then. Fadeley cautioned that he felt we should stay where we were. If we took off in the darkness, we could be playing right into their hands. They had located our position and had probably calculated our strength. If they hadn't attacked already, it was because they either weren't strong enough yet, or they were lying in wait to nail us when we moved out. Either way, we were in big trouble.

Fadeley's advice made sense. At least we had a few claymores out. We were in a defensible position, and had the cover of the trees and the berm in case they hit us. If they caught us outside the perimeter, we would be in the open and at their mercy. Besides, we really didn't have any idea how in the hell we'd get out of there if we did break through. For all we knew, we could be heading toward Laos.

Everyone stayed alert and ready for action the remainder of the night. We expected to be probed again at any second. Personally, I thought that they would crawl up under cover of the fog and then, with whistles blowing and bugles blaring, stand up and overrun our position. They didn't know that we knew that they had discovered us. Surely, they suspected that the element of surprise was in their favor.

Around 0600, I began to wonder if Kilburn had fucked up again. Had he really seen NVA in our perimeter? Maybe it had been monkeys! It wouldn't have been the first time

monkeys had been mistaken for North Vietnamese sol-
ders. No, he had seen something. I had felt it, too. Why
hadn't the cocksuckers come for us? What were they waiting for?

Our commo, which had been worthless during the night,
was restored with the coming of daylight, if you can call
a lightening of the fog daylight. Only the improvement of
our vision indicated that dawn was upon us. It gave no
immediate sign of burning off the blanket of haze that
enveloped us. We contacted the fire control officer on
Tomahawk and told him that we had been compromised
during the night and we were requesting either a reaction
force or an immediate emergency extraction. We asked
him to relay that message to our rear.

Ten minutes later, he came back on the air and told us
that our "Six" said to stay put until he reached the area.
He would advise us then. The artillery officer added that
the entire area was socked in and didn't look like it was
going to burn off in the near future. Well, our only choice
was to sit tight and wait. There had to be a reason why
the NVA hadn't come after us. The only logical explanation was that they couldn't find their way around in the
dense fog any better than we could. Sure, that had to be
the reason. Their scouts had stumbled onto us during the
night but had gotten lost going back for reinforcements.
Or maybe they had come back with their friends but had
been unable to find us again.

We were safe as long as the fog didn't burn off—or until
we couldn't control the hunger that was already starting to
gnaw at our insides. Yeah, we were safe like twelve rats
in a box. We were in some *deep* shit, and we knew it. Our
only hope was for the division to get some help to us
before the NVA did.

Around 1000 hours, we got a call from Captain Cardona
on Tomahawk. He told us that Charlie Company, 2d of
the 501st, was coming in after us. Their call sign was
Alpha Tango. At that time, they were only about a kilometer from our position and moving toward us. They
would approach us from the southeast, coming over the
crest of the primary ridgeline above us.

Apparently they had been patrolling not far from where
the Cobra had gone down, and they had been ordered to

move toward the vicinity of the crash site about the same time we had been notified to ruck up. It would have been nice to know those things! Line doggies meant food and water . . . and company—lots of company. We would feel a hell of a lot safer after we linked up with a hundred paratroopers. Those guys could handle an extended period in the bush without help. No one had told them they would only be out for two to three hours. They probably even had a poncho liner or two.

Now it's not that the twelve of us were afraid, but our secret had been let out—Mr. Charles knew we were in his AO. And when that happens, and there are only a few of you, it's time to get out. It would have been different if we had come equipped, and maybe even had a map or two. Then we would have been able to survive until the weather broke. But the situation we found ourselves in came under the classification of "not having your shit in order." We would be just a token more comfortable when we cast our lot with the boys of Charlie Company.

Two hours passed before we reached the line company on the radio. Surprisingly, their company commander thought they were right above us. He told us to listen up and he would have his point element yell for us. Sure enough, we could hear them up on the ridge. They weren't quite above us yet, but seemed to be within a hundred and fifty meters and closing.

We acknowledged that we could hear them, and the CO radioed back for us to fire a couple of shots so they would know where we were. Fadeley told him that he didn't think that would be advisable. We had NVA in our immediate vicinity, but as long as we knew where Charlie Company was, we would keep them informed of our proximity. The captain radioed back a short time later and told us to start moving straight up the ridge to meet his point element. He said they were following a wide trail that ran up the crest, and the going was pretty easy.

Again, Fadeley rejected the advice, telling him we would rather have him stop and set up a perimeter once he got above us, then send a squad or two down to our NDP. Once we linked up, we would sweep the area and look for the two airmen from the downed Cobra. After all, they were the reason we were all there in the first place.

The infantry commander didn't like the idea, but Fadeley finally convinced him that we weren't coming up that hillside without trying once more to locate the pilot and his gunner. He radioed for us to let him know when they were directly above us, and he would send his recon platoon down to link up with us. They sounded closer by then. We could hear American voices about sixty meters away. Fadeley told us to stay alert, in case the NVA, attracted to the voices above, stumbled into us again.

Just as the American infantry company reached a point directly above us, a long burst of automatic-weapons fire erupted. Fadeley, not knowing what had happened, tried to raise Charlie Company on the radio.

Seconds later, their captain called back, his voice full of anguish. "Lynwood Team One-One, this is Alpha Tango Six. Contact, contact. My point element has been hit. November Victor Alpha between you and my position. Stay put. Stay where you are. Over!"

Fadeley grabbed the handset from his senior RTO and radioed back. "Alpha Tango Six, Lynwood Team One-One. I read you Lima Charlie (loud and clear). We will wait your next transmission. Good luck. Out!"

We could hear the cries of "Medic! Medic up!" from the ridgeline. Their point element had probably walked into a trail watcher. The question was—did he have any friends with him? Fadeley turned and told everyone to get down, we had NVA above us. We were in danger of being caught in the line of fire if the paratroopers opened up and fired downhill toward the enemy.

Suddenly, we heard brush breaking above us. Somebody was running in high gear down the side of the mountain directly at our perimeter. They were making no effort to be quiet, and from the sound of them, there could have been anywhere from one to three of them.

I heard the *snap-click-snap* of selector switches being thumbed to full-automatic. Mine included. The crashing sounds were getting closer. Fadeley was on his knees, peering over the berm, trying to get a glimpse of what or who was coming.

I rose in a squat, weapon ready, trying to see past the team leader. I stepped to the right to get a better view, and there he was . . . fifteen feet away, in a dead sprint.

An NVA soldier was bearing down on us, and closing at a speed too fast to miss our perimeter.

As often happens in combat, everything switched into low gear. The NVA was still coming, but in slow motion. I looked into his eyes, wide with surprise at the sudden recognition of danger. He knew he was about to die. The determined look on his face had changed from excitement, to shock, to fear, and then to resolve, all in the space of a second.

I noticed the olive drab shorts that covered his lower body. He wore a matching short-sleeved shirt on his upper body and had a red bandana around his neck. His head was bare, except for the thick, jet black hair that stood out like it had been electrified. I saw that he was holding his left arm up above his head while he parted brush with his right hand. What caught my eye was the pair of Ho Chi Minh sandals he held aloft in his left hand. I thought, "He's not wearing any shoes!"

A swarm of angry bees whizzed past my head, making me wonder where in the hell they had come from. Then I spotted the AK-47 clenched in the same hand that held the sandals. He was holding his shoes and his weapon clear of the brush so they wouldn't catch on anything as he escaped from the paratroopers on the ridgeline above. He spotted us at the last moment, but still had the presence of mind to level the AK, one-handed, and fire a long burst in our direction. Either he was right handed or just a bad shot. Or maybe Fadeley and I had someone watching over us. I don't know—but the rounds missed us by inches.

I saw Fadeley go down in front of me as I threw myself to the right to escape the burst. Fadeley and I screamed simultaneously, "Blow the claymore . . . blow it . . . blow it!"

Munoz grabbed for the charging handle, squeezing the firing device just as the NVA leaped over the mine. The sudden explosion erupted with the concussion of a two hundred-pound bomb. It had been placed only five feet away, on the reverse side of the low berm. The back-blast from the claymore took the NVA's legs out from under him and slammed him into the ground on the other side of the mound, as dirt and debris showered back over us.

The Vietnamese was down within a hand's reach of our perimeter.

Phil Myers, Fadeley's ATL, jumped to his feet and fired a long burst from his M-16 directly into the wounded NVA soldier, at a distance of less than three feet. The NVA started moaning loudly. I stood up and fired a quick burst at point-blank range, then dropped behind the protection of one of the large mahogany trees. The moaning continued, until Biedron pulled the pin on a fragmentation grenade, released the lever, and then slowly flipped it over the berm.

The second explosion was little more than a *pop* compared to the claymore, but the moaning stopped. No one moved. We didn't know for sure if he was really dead or had just been wounded. The possibility existed that he might not have been alone. Three or four of his pals could be flanking us at that very moment.

I leaned against the tree, praying he had been alone. I was momentarily out of action. My body was shaking so badly that I couldn't hit the magazine release to reload my smoking CAR-15. My heart started pounding as I suddenly realized just how close his burst had been to my head. Jesus Christ, I'd almost gotten it again.

Fadeley picked up the handset and radioed Alpha Tango Six that we had gotten a KIA (killed in action), probably the same NVA who had fired up Charlie Company's point element. Alpha Tango Six quickly called back and reported that he had sustained four WIA (wounded in action), all leg wounds.

When we realized it was over, everyone started to breathe easier. The NVA had been alone—only a trail-watcher. He had accomplished what he had set out to do, taking out four American soldiers. Yes, he had only wounded them, but, in that particular situation, wounding had been better than killing. Instead of four dead soldiers to deal with, Charlie Company had four badly wounded men that it couldn't medevac. And they were hit too badly to carry along with the company. Charlie Company had just gone static. As an offensive unit, they had just been put out of action, single-handedly, by a barefoot peasant boy from north of the DMZ.

Biedron and Myers moved up and checked the body.

He was dead, all right—several times over! The claymore's back-blast had shattered both legs. There were numerous bullet wounds and multiple fragmentation injuries from Biedron's grenade.

He had taken some killing before joining his ancestors. Funny, but I felt no animosity toward him. He had been just another soldier, trying to do his job, when his luck ran out. I even admired him. I imagined the fear he must have felt as the company of American infantrymen approached him. He must have choked back panic as their point element filed past his position. Surely the cocky Americans would discover him before he could bring his weapon into play. But no, they hadn't seen him. Terror must have filled him as he sighted down the barrel of his AK-47 and fired a sustained burst into the close file of paratroopers. Then he had fled the battlefield, not even looking back over his shoulder to see if he was being pursued.

At some point in his flight, he must have thought he would make it. He had wanted to live.

The two Rangers returned with his damaged AK-47, a wallet, and a personal letter. The last two items had been in his pocket. The letter was in Vietnamese—three pages, in the fine hand of a woman. It had probably come from the young Vietnamese girl whose photo we found in the billfold. It struck me that, except for the luck of the draw, it could have just as easily been a North Vietnamese soldier standing there over my dead body, looking at the photo of my girl. The thought tore at my insides. I turned away, unable to look at the mound of perforated flesh that had been, only minutes before, a vigorous, young, healthy individual. He must have had hopes, desires, and ambitions, similar to my own. He had been capable of loving and of being loved.

It was only the second time since arriving in Vietnam that I had been affected in such a way by the death of an enemy. The first time had been back in November, when I had killed three female nurses in an ambush. I had felt instant revulsion and guilt. I had been brought up to protect women, not butcher them. Only the discovery that two of them were carrying U.S. 45-cal. automatics helped me to rationalize what I had done. I told myself that they would have killed me in a second, if I had given them the chance. Yet a stigma of guilt and responsibility had remained with me, long after the deed had been performed. War was such a terrible thing. Why was it such an integral part of mankind?

Alpha Tango Six radioed back that his troops had swept both sides of the ridge, ten to fifteen meters from the crest, and had found no other sign of recent enemy activity. He had formed his company into a perimeter and would not be moving until he got his wounded out. He was overjoyed at the news that we had killed "that NVA cocksucker" who shot his men. I couldn't blame him! There had to be a smug self-satisfaction in seeing revenge so swiftly dealt to someone who had so recently caused you injury. He thanked us for "getting the bastard."

Fadeley told Alpha Tango Six it would be better if we came to his position. He agreed. With four men down, he wasn't in a big hurry to divide his command. Fadeley told us to get ready to move up the hill, with Meyer at point. He told us to talk, laugh, break brush—make all the noise we could. He knew the GIs above us would be sitting with itchy trigger fingers, just waiting for a chance at a little payback. We were cautious. None of us wanted to end up a casualty of friendly fire.

It was a little after 1230 hours when we moved out. We wanted to join the paratroopers as quickly as possible, but knew better than to go off crashing through the brush. We started talking about the C rations that grunts usually carried. They weren't worth a shit, but when you're hungry, they would definitely pass for food. After all, if the body could turn it into a turd, then it had to be chow. Everyone was talking too loud for intrateam conversation.

Thirty meters up the hillside, Myers walked headlong into two Screaming Eagles kneeling over an M-60. They stared at us briefly, then thanked us for killing the gook who shot their buddies. We nodded to them as we walked past their position and moved to the top of the ridge. A large, open trail ran straight up the crest of the ridgeline, just like the captain had said. There wasn't very much cover along the spine. It had obviously been used by several line companies in the past. The NVA didn't clear away the vegetation like that when they used an area.

We dropped the teams off in the center of Charlie Company's perimeter and walked down the hillside in search of their company commander. We needed to give him a report on the wreckage we had found on the hillside and coordinate a search for the missing aircrew before any more time elapsed.

We walked up to a baby-faced captain who, except for the hollow cheeks and the shadows under his eyes, looked all of eighteen years of age. He was talking to two second lieutenants and hadn't seen us approach. When he finally noticed us standing there, he shook our hands and introduced himself as Captain Ross. We returned the courtesy and thanked him for coming to our assistance.

He told us he and his men had been patrolling the area for the past four months. They had lost a lot of people trying to dislodge two stubborn NVA battalions from the AO. He said the terrain was particularly steep and the jungle unusually dense. The NVA were dug in, with tunnels, spider holes, and reinforced bunkers. We told him about the high-speed trail we had found plus the concrete bunker near it. He whistled. His unit hadn't found any concrete bunkers, but he sure didn't doubt they existed.

The captain told us he was trying to get a dust-off in for his wounded, but the prospect didn't look good. The weather report called for at least three more days of fog. The humidity was high, and there was no breeze available to blow the low cloud cover back toward Laos. He asked whether we wanted to get out if he could get the choppers in. We told him we would if we could. We had only been inserted for two to three hours on the ground and had not come in equipped for an extended mission.

He asked us if we had eaten. When we shook our heads, he sent a staff sergeant to get some extra food from his troops, with a "Sergeant Bradley, see to it that these Rangers get everything that they need."

Fadeley asked how he intended to get a medevac in. He said that he was going to have it come in high over his position and circle until he could get a fix on it. Once he had it directly overhead, he was going to talk the pilot in by bringing him straight down onto the crown of a nearby saddle. The clearing there was about sixty by eighty feet and was level enough to handle a chopper. When we nodded, he said, "Once my wounded are evacuated, I'll try to get a couple of slicks in for you and your men."

We thanked him and asked if they had enough water to furnish a canteen or two for our men. He smiled and told us to see the staff sergeant. He was sure our needs would be satisfied. We met the staff sergeant on our way back to our teams. He dropped a case of C rations and four canteens of water on the ground next to us. "Try to make it last, Rangers, we are probably not going to see a resupply for a while."

We nodded in agreement and told our men to break out the chow. We would eat, then try to borrow some additional men from Captain Ross for a second try at the Cobra. We would have to hurry. We still had a LOH to go after, too.

The infantrymen had set up a perimeter in the shape of a long, loose oval. It more or less covered both points of high ground flanking the saddle and the saddle itself. I noticed no one was pulling security. A machine gun emplacement had been set up just off the side of each of the two hilltops. We had passed one of them coming up from below. No other security measures were apparent.

I looked at the other Rangers, and wasn't surprised to see I wasn't the only one who had noticed. When I said something to one of the nearby paratroopers, he merely responded, "Oh, don't worry about it, we're got OPs (observation posts) out on both sides of the ridgeline. There's no way Chuck's going to get to us up here."

We hid our smiles. The fools! In the heavy fog, Chuck could waltz an entire battalion of sappers right past a couple of OPs and they would never know it—until it was too late.

We chowed down, then decided to catch a nap until Captain Ross was ready to go after the downed choppers. We understood his priority decision to get the wounded out first. I would have been disappointed if he had done anything less.

Groff woke me from a sound sleep. I sat up groggily, rubbing the sleep from my eyes. Most of the other Rangers and the majority of the line doggies were still sleeping. Five Rangers were particularly alert, ready to sound the alarm in case the enemy appeared on the scene. Groff said,

"The CO wants to see you and Fadeley over by that trail-watcher's bunker. He says it's important."

I rose stiffly, checking my watch for the time. It was almost 1500 hours. I had been asleep for three hours. I met Fadeley, and the two of us headed over to see what the good captain needed. I was amazed to see that the fog had not thinned a bit. Fadeley commented that it looked like we were going to be in the infantry for a while.

When we got there, the captain said, "Gentlemen, we've got a problem. The dust-offs tried twice to get into us with no luck. The pilot said it was like trying to swim in a pool of cotton. No chance of getting his ship in here without jeopardizing both the chopper and its crew. They almost clipped a treetop on their second try." He kicked angrily at a rusting C rat can near his feet. "It looks like you and your team will have to hump out of here with the rest of us. I hate to abandon the search for those two choppers, but I've got four wounded men that I've got to get to a hospital."

We both nodded in agreement. "Seems like the only thing to do, sir," I responded with a smile on my face. I would have enjoyed taking one good kick at that damned can myself.

Fadeley and I returned to the team and broke the news to them. They weren't nearly as upset as I had suspected. They had pretty well figured on their own that there was a slim chance of getting out ahead of the line doggies. Well, at least we weren't lost, alone, and starving anymore. It was an improvement over the previous night's situation.

As the infantry company started to break camp in preparation for moving back down the spine of the ridge, a pair of Cobra gunships radioed that they were going to try to get into us with a few cases of C rats and some fresh radio batteries. They had monitored the plight of the medevac that had tried to get into us earlier. The pilots of the two Cobras were from the same squadron as the gunship that had been shot down on the side of the mountain below us.

Captain Ross told them to go ahead and try. He would talk them in. Soon we could hear the deep, pulsing sound of the first Cobra as it took up a position over us. It sounded a good thousand feet above us. But with the thick fog muffling the sounds, it was probably much lower. Captain Ross set up his radio in the center of the saddle and put a couple of his men on each of the flanking knolls with flash panels. He was smart enough not to use any smoke grenades, which would only have added to the mist covering the mountaintop.

We watched as he coached the first gunship down through the cloud cover. The engine noise grew louder, until it seemed like it was in the perimeter with us. Suddenly, the Cobra's rotor wash began swirling the thick layer of fog around us until we could see the skids of the chopper break though into the pocket of dense, moisture-laden air around our perimeter. It appeared that our ceiling was in the neighborhood of fifty feet or less. When you're flying around in the fog and there are trees and mountaintops all around, fifty feet isn't a very good neighborhood to be in.

The gunship hung suspended for several seconds as the pilot oriented himself to the ground beneath him. Finally, he spotted the paratrooper on the east side of the saddle flashing a red-orange marker panel at him. He slowly jockeyed the sleek gunship over toward the small clearing on the crest of the knoll and brought it gently down in the very center of the LZ. He cut his engine back to low idle and opened his cockpit as the second Cobra began its descent. It didn't seem like there was room enough on the ridge for two of the powerful gunships. Two minutes later, the bottom of the next "snake" materialized through the low-hanging cloud bank and moved toward the west side of the saddle to make a rather hard landing on a large rock ledge just off the crest on the other side of the saddle.

The gunners of both Cobras were soon handing down cases of C rations, along with four extra radio batteries and two five-gallon jerry cans of water. It seemed like a small amount of booty for the risk those two brave pilots had taken, but it would be greatly appreciated by those of us who were days away from seeing another resupply. The two pilots remained in their cockpits, both ships on low idle. I could tell they were communicating with Captain Ross, who had not left his position in the center of the saddle.

Suddenly, I saw the captain pass the handset to his RTO and take off in a run to where his four wounded paratroopers lay. After conversing with them and the three medics treating their wounds, he motioned for several of his men to help with the wounded.

"What in the hell could they be up to?" I said to Munoz as we stood staring. Eight line doggies picked up their four wounded buddies in cradle-carries and brought them over to where the helicopters waited. Two of the wounded were taken to each ship. I knew there wasn't enough room in the cockpit of a Cobra to carry one extra man—definitely not two. Then I saw the company commander go to the fuselage on one of the Cobras and unfold a small, rectangular piece of metal out of the side of the ship below the cockpit on the right side. It was a seat! No shit, an actual seat! It was just big enough for one person to sit on, if he was strapped in.

Now I understood what they were up to. The two Cobras were going to attempt to medevac the wounded on the little jump seats located on each side of their fuselages. Two of the men seemed to be in great pain from their wounds. The medics ran up and injected each of them with morphine. The other two appeared to be in less pain and seemed anxious to get on with the program.

When they were finally strapped in, the Cobras revved their turbines and slowly lifted into the overhead cloud bank. They turned, in unison, on a heading due south, and moved off through the clouds at a much-reduced airspeed.

I was totally amazed. I had never seen anything like that before. I had never realized the Cobra's capacity for handling emergency extractions. I wondered if the wounded being taken out would change Captain Ross's plans for us to hump out to Tomahawk.

We looked up to see him crossing the perimeter toward us. When he reached us, he told Fadeley we would be staying to look for the crews of the two downed helicopters. That was the promise he had given the two Cobra pilots. The missing crewmen had been friends of theirs.

Fadeley agreed. It wasn't worth risking the lives of two more chopper crews just to try to get us out. The Rangers would stay in until the weather lifted or we all humped out from under it. Captain Ross decided that, with the hour or two we had before night set in, he would send his first platoon down the mountainside to the wreckage of the Cobra to sweep the area one more time.

We offered to go with them, but he refused, saying that he was trying to get the coordinates for the location of the downed LOH scout chopper from brigade. If it was close, he wanted us to take his recon platoon and attempt to find it before dark.

We returned to the Rangers and briefed them on the plans, hoping we could still get the job done before dark. None of us relished the idea of staying under this blanket of clouds any longer than we had to.

An hour passed before Captain Ross came over and told us there had been some question as to the actual crash site of the LOH, and it had just been determined the site was a klick west of where they had first thought it had gone in. Our company commander wanted to rappel two more Ranger teams into the general vicinity early the next day, weather permitting.

At dusk, the first platoon returned to the perimeter. They had found no sign of the Cobra pilot and his gunner. They had found signs that the NVA had been all over the wreckage since we first discovered it. The NVA had removed the radio and the ammunition. The guns and rocket pods were still in place, but they could tell that the enemy had attempted to remove them as well.

The line doggies had placed explosives on the wreckage, set to go off in thirty minutes. A sudden blast a hundred and fifty meters down the mountainside came as a complete surprise, even though we had expected it. I only hoped the enemy had returned for the guns and had been caught in the blast.

The first platoon had also discovered the site of our last NDP. The dead NVA's body had been removed. His friends had come after him sometime during the day. Made sense! He was running downhill after he popped the four paratroopers. Needless to say, he wasn't running just to get away from the American imperialists. No, he had to have been running toward something—like a base camp full of North Vietnamese soldiers. He would have made it

if his path of escape had been ten degrees left or right of
the one he had chosen.

It had been his bad luck to choose the only possible
route that would mean death for him. He had not reached
his destination. But from the direction of his escape path,
we knew his friends had to be in the valley below . . .
somewhere. They knew we were in the area, and if they
were as good as Captain Ross said, they would be down
there waiting for us. My mind kept wandering back to that
concrete bunker. If they were holed up in a bunch of those,
we were going to be in some deep shit.

Darkness brought a new terror for the twelve Rangers
on that ridgeline. We broke up into four elements of three
men each. We were given ponchos and shown how to tie
them to short stakes to provide overhead cover against the
dampness. We were assigned no particular place on the
perimeter, nor were we assigned to post security watches
at our positions. It hadn't made any sense until we discovered the reason why.

The paratroopers of Charlie Company, set out eight or
ten trip-flares, about ten claymores, and, except for one
man who monitored the battalion "push" (radio frequency), all of them rolled over and went to sleep.

Now, you must realize the initial impression this made
on the security-minded Rangers in their midst. We freaked!
What in the holy hell was going on? One hundred and
thirty-seven American soldiers, out in the middle of Indian
country—and I mean *Indian country*—and one hundred
and twenty-four of them drop soundly off to sleep.

It wasn't that the enemy didn't know we were there. We
had spent the past twenty-four hours doing everything but
putting up billboards and running a marching band up and
down the side of the mountain, just to let them know exactly where we were and how many of us there were.
C'mon, you guys! Ray Charles could find those trip-flares
and claymores on his worst night. You ain't foolin' nobody!

God, I had heard about the VC having suicide squads,
but we had found ourselves in the middle of a U.S. infantry company with an overall compulsive death wish.
Maybe the line doggies knew something we didn't, I don't
know. But what I did know was that twelve owl-eyed

Rangers pulled guard during the entire night while a U.S. airborne infantry company slept like babes all around them.

March 9, 1969

The camp began stirring at 0600. No throats had been cut. No one was missing. No one had seen or heard anything. The grunts appeared to be totally refreshed and revitalized by their long night's sleep. The bloodshot eyes of the twelve Rangers gave mute testimony to the type of night we had spent.

The line doggies must have thought we were nothing but a bunch of pussies when we elected to sleep in for a couple of hours more.

We woke around 0900. The line unit was busily engaged in cleaning weapons and trying to dry out gear soaked by the evening mist. The latter task seemed hopeless. The humidity must have been 100 percent, but at least the air wasn't hot. The heavy fog blocked enough of the sun's rays to keep the temperature in the low 80s during the day. The nights were actually chilly. However, the humidity was high enough that we stayed uncomfortable during the daylight hours, as well.

When Charlie Company had finished cleaning its weapons, we borrowed rags, bore brushes, cleaning rods, patches, oil, and a little solvent to give ours a good going over. We never broke our weapons down and cleaned them in the field unless we really got them screwed up or something. It wasn't worth the risk to get caught half steppin' by the NVA while laagered up in an NDP with your weapon torn down and spread across your lap.

We carried small, dry cleaning brushes to remove most of the grit and twigs that invariably collected in the bolt, the chamber, and the magazines. But we seldom touched the bore unless we happened to jam the end of the weapon into the ground. Usually, one or two of the guys on the team would carry a cleaning rod just for that purpose, or in the event a casing would expand in the chamber and fail to eject. Most of us kept a piece of Saran Wrap, a cellophane cigarette pack cover, a balloon, or a rubber over the flash suppressors on our weapons when we were in the bush. We used a rubber band to hold them securely in place. They did an excellent job in keeping the bore clean. The first shot you fired would normally dispose of the cover without any problem. Besides, there was a certain irony to killing an NVA soldier with the business end of a Trojan Deluxe.

Anyway, it was a treat to be able to field strip and clean our weapons in the middle of the boonies. A clean weapon was one less thing to worry about when the shit was about to hit the fan.

The twelve Rangers made a meal out of six C rations, then took a smoke break to keep our minds off our hunger. Smoking, too, was a treat for us. With few exceptions, we never smoked in the field.

The rest of the day was spent lounging about the ridgetop, trying to pass the time. Captain Ross suggested going back down to look for the LOH crew, then sweeping back through the area where the Cobra had gone in. When we were about ready to pull out, the fog thickened to where we couldn't see across the ridgeline, so, at the last minute, the CO canceled the patrol and ordered everyone to stay within the perimeter.

It was risky to go outside the trip flares just to answer nature's call. No one knew what was waiting out there. And a body could get turned around and lost quickly in the dense cloud cover that hung over us.

The twelve Rangers pulled security again that evening as the camp slept. We must have been good at it, because the enemy let another night go by without trying to sweep us off the mountain. I did notice that a few of the infantrymen appeared a little nervous just before dark. I suspected that the situation was getting to some of them, too. Maybe we wouldn't be the only ones with bloodshot eyes in the morning.

March 10, 1969

Captain Ross's runner woke us at 0830 and told us that two other Ranger teams was inserting west of our location, about three klicks away. We listened on the radio, as they rappeled into the jungle in the midst of the same dense fog we had gone into two days earlier. We had no idea why they were going in so far to our west. The missing LOH was supposedly over two klicks from where they were inserting.

Captain Ross told us that, early that morning, another LOH had discovered a small window in the thick cloud cover and had gone back to look for the wreckage of the first scout helicopter. After an hour of hovering just over the treetops, it had gotten lost and stumbled onto the crash site while trying to work its way out. They reported that the downed scout chopper appeared to have flown into the trees. There were indications of an explosion. The site was a good distance west of where they had originally reported it.

Battalion HQ wanted someone to go in to secure the crash site and check for survivors. It didn't appear likely, but an effort had to be made just the same. Naturally, the Rangers got the job.

The Ranger teams came in that morning and rappeled right on top of the downed LOH. As soon as they reached the ground, they reported that the LOH had definitely exploded and burned on impact. There were no survivors.

The teams requested plastic body bags to remove the crew. The corpses had burned in the crash and came apart when any attempt was made to move them. One of the team members had stepped backward and put his foot through the chest of one of the dead crewman. He vomited in his gas mask while extracting his boot.

I didn't envy the Rangers on the heavy team. I only hoped they had all brought gas masks with them.

It was late in the day by the time the body bags were flown in. The teams loaded the corpses and lifted them out one at a time in a wire body basket connected to a steel cable.

As luck would have it, heavy fog settled back in just as they finished, and they couldn't get another chopper in to remove the Rangers. They, too, would have to spend some unscheduled time on the ground before their mission would be accomplished.

We monitored the team's radio traffic and finally figured out that John Sours, Ron "Mother" Rucker, Ricky "New Guy" Lawhon, Frank Anderson, Doc Glasser, Pete Peterson, and Joe "J. B." Bielesch were some of the Rangers on the team. Rucker, Sours, Glasser, Peterson, and Bielesch were seasoned Rangers. The other two were replacements who had only been in the company since December, but they had been two of the best.

Bielesch had been appointed heavy team leader, with Rucker as ATL, even though Sours had more time in grade and more experience running a team. All in all, Bielesch had a good team with him.

For some reason, we could hear them over the frequency, but they couldn't pick up our transmissions. We radioed one of the gunships orbiting outside the fog bank and asked the pilot to relay a message to the Ranger team below them. The message was for them to move up to the top of the ridgeline they were on and then head east. If Captain Ross's map was accurate, they would run into us about 2500 meters down the ridge.

They relayed back that they had taken a few rounds from the surrounding jungle when they had inserted, and they had heard movement up the hillside from the crash site after they had gotten the bodies out. It wouldn't be to their best interest to try to make it up the mountain. The movement and the gunfire had come from that area. They decided to head off in another direction and find some place to hide until they could get out. They were "going to cover." There must have been gooks everywhere.

We spent another uneventful night pulling security for

Charlie Company, and praying that Bielesch's heavy team would make it through till morning without being hit.

March 11, 1969

Another uneventful night. Fadeley and I talked to Captain Ross's and asked permission to drop off the ridgeline for one last sweep of the area. When we finished, we wanted to move down into the valley and then west to link up with the other Ranger team that had gone in after the downed LOH.

He wanted to know why, so we told him the other team was in a worse predicament than we had been in before Charlie Company had arrived on the scene. There was still no way of telling how long it would be before any of us got out of there, and those twelve men were going to have a tough time staying alive without help. We had already requested permission from our Six earlier that morning, and he had given his approval for the link-up.

Captain Ross told us he understood and offered to send his thirteen-man recon platoon with us. We thanked him for the added security and told Charlie Company we wanted to start as soon as possible. He said Charlie Company would remain on top of the ridge until we effected a link-up. If we got into any trouble, they would come arunning.

Around 1100 hours, we slipped off the crest of the ridge, on line, and moved down to the east side of the crash site. Again we found no sign of the missing Cobra crew. It appeared they had been captured or were trying to hump out on their own. Either way, their chances of survival were not good. The NVA hated snake pilots every bit as much as they hated Rangers.

We continued patrolling toward the valley, in file this time, with a two-man recon element walking point. We didn't put out any flankers but zigzagged to avoid am-

bushes. I noticed that the Rangers could teach Charlie
Company's recon people a lot about noise discipline.

We had borrowed a couple of maps of the area from
two of the platoon leaders and had formed a pretty good
idea of where we wanted to go. There was a "blue-line"
at the floor of the valley, indicating water. Everyone was
about out, so we decided to stop at the stream and refill
our canteens. After resupplying, we would turn west and
head up the valley to meet up with J. B.'s team. When the
link-up was accomplished, we would either rejoin the rest
of Charlie Company or, if the fog had finally lifted, move
to an LZ for extraction.

We still couldn't raise Bielesch on the radio. I could not
remember ever having had that type of commo problem
over such a short distance before. Apparently, dense fog
stopped radio waves almost as effectively as high mountains.

We reached the stream around 1530 hours. It wasn't a
large stream, but there was enough water in it to slake the
thirst of twenty-five dry soldiers and fill their canteens to
the brim. We set up a perimeter on both sides of the water
and watched the surrounding jungle intently while everyone took a turn in the stream. I noticed the recon men
were showing a little nervousness for the very first time.
I was anxious to get out of there and on up the valley. We
were in a bad spot if the NVA decided to hit us. They
were around. You could almost feel them watching. I wondered why they had held off as long as they had. Maybe
they had decided to leave us alone as long as we didn't
stumble into whatever it was they had in there. Sometimes
they avoided contact even when the odds were in their
favor.

We stayed in file and moved up the valley, the Rangers
at the head of the column. Myers walked point with
Biedron at slack, directly behind him. The going was
rough, with thick vegetation, laced with vines and
creepers, running to the edge of the stream bank. We
tried to stay on the edge of it, fearing an ambush if we
remained down in the stream where the walking was
easier. I was pleased to see that Myers crossed back and
forth across the stream every fifty to one hundred me-

ters. He knew his stuff. If we were going to run into the enemy, we weren't going to make it easy on him.

Close to dusk, we realized we weren't going to make it to Bielesch's location. We had just established weak, but clear commo with the other team. They told us they were staying put until we got closer, then they would try to move out and link up. They sensed enemy troops all around them.

Fadeley radioed Bielesch that we were going to set up a perimeter for the night. As near as we could tell, we were still 1200 meters apart—too much ground to cover at night. He gave Bielesch a compass heading to our location and told him to rendezvous on us if they had to E & E during the night. The password would be J. B.'s first name. The countersign would be Fadeley's first name.

Bielesch called back in a few minutes and told us they were moving out to a better location, and that they would see us in the morning.

We moved onto a high mound nestled in the upper loop of an S-shaped curve in the streambed. We had good cover all around, and if the NVA hit us there, we would be able to make one hell of a fight of it.

We set out eight claymores, covering every approach to our perimeter. Fadeley organized four-man watches, one and a half hours each, beginning at 2130. The recon men didn't mind taking their share of the duty. I was on the watch running from 0030 to 0200. I baby-sat the radio, breaking squelch three times every hour, on the hour, to let Bielesch know that we were all right. He answered by breaking twice. Neither team had commo with Tomahawk, but we were still in touch with Charlie Company on the ridgeline to our southeast.

Funny how much more noise goes on at night. We had several false alarms. Creatures—some large, some small—prowled the brush on both sides of the stream. Once Biedron woke me to say he had heard something big coming upstream. I listened for a few minutes but never heard anything.

March 12, 1969

We were glad to see daylight come, even though the cloud cover hadn't improved. The heavy fog seemed to have settled permanently in the mountains around us. A pretty determined breeze was needed to clear it out. We were beginning our sixth day under its dominion and we were getting a little skeptical about ever getting out again. We were losing our tans!

The recon men shared the rest of their chow with us. There hadn't nearly enough to satisfy the gnawing hunger each of us felt. We knew we were reaching the end of our endurance, unless we could find a way out of these mountains or get resupplied in the next twenty-four hours. And the constant moisture was causing emersion-foot problems among both the recon people and the Rangers.

We continued up the valley, which seemed to narrow as we headed west. Myers was still at point, but Saenz had moved up to the slack position. Biedron was suffering from a fungus that turned his feet raw.

About noon, we passed a large secondary ridge that dropped off the main ridgeline above us and swung down to parallel the blue-line, until it finally petered out about fifty meters upstream. The ridge showed up on the map, so we were able to get an exact fix on our position. We were less than three hundred meters from Bielesch's last NDP.

We got them on the radio and told them we were getting close to their location, and advised them to move out from their NDP and come downstream to link. They agreed, but asked us to remain in radio communication with them so we wouldn't walk into each other unexpectedly. There would be no signal shots or yelling this time. If Charlie didn't know where we were, we weren't about to lead him to us.

It took us another hour to cover the final three hundred meters. We were on the north side of the stream when our point man spotted Sours and Rucker standing in some brush next to a large, dead tree, twenty-five meters on the opposite bank. Thank God for Sours's red hair! There was no doubt it was him. We crossed over and joined them on their side. Relief swept over both groups as we shook hands all around.

Bielesch told us they had cut across a fresh trail crossing the stream less than a hundred meters behind them. The enemy was sending out patrols either to find us or to keep tabs on us.

Quickly, we turned the column and headed back downstream, with Sours and Rucker at point. It bothered me to see them following the same trail we had made coming up. But as soon as they reached the secondary ridge we had passed earlier, they recrossed the stream and broke through the underbrush on the other side.

They continued down the valley, staying fifty meters away from the blue-line. The thick underbrush gave way to thinner, double-canopy jungle. The going was much easier than it had been coming up the valley.

We called Charlie Company to inform Captain Ross of our link-up, and advised him we were on our way back. He told us one of his platoons had located the Cobra pilot three hundred meters east of the wreckage while on a routine patrol. He told them that his gunner, who had been wounded when they had been hit, had gotten separated during the first night on the ground. They had been forced to hide from an NVA patrol. The pilot had remained in hiding until the American patrol had almost stumbled over him. He had not seen his gunner again.

Captain Ross advised us to return to the top of the ridge as quickly as possible. The pilot was in bad shape, and the paratroopers were low on food and water. The captain was planning a forced march east to Highway 1.

We had our own problems. Biedron, Kilburn, and two men on the recon squad had developed severe emersion-foot. Kilburn took off his boots and socks during a break, and discovered that the bottom layer of skin on both feet had remained in his socks. The areas between his toes were raw and bleeding. A couple of the recon people had a little foot powder left, and willingly offered it, but his condition was already beyond field-expedient medical treatment. A check of everyone else turned up the additional three cases, and indicated that ten to twelve more would crop up in the next twenty-four hours. We would never be able to climb back up the mountain to link up with Charlie Company and then hump the six klicks back to Highway 1.

We got Captain Ross back on the horn to apprise him of our situation. He recommended we laager up for the night, then continue down the valley the next day. There was a small village about three klicks to the east of our position. The inhabitants were reputedly VC sympathizers, but we would be able to get some food there, and possibly be picked up by an ARVN armored column. There was a platoon of "tracks" operating at the mouth of the valley, near Highway 1.

He also reported he had received word from battalion that the weather was due to improve the following day. If it did, the division could get choppers in to extract everyone.

It was already after 1600 hours, so we set up another NDP in the same location we had stayed the night before. Again, we were acting contrary to our training, but the site was the closest thing to a defensible position we had come across. Besides, thirty-seven men would have a difficult time trying to find a place to hide unnoticed. At this stage of the game, cover was more important than concealment.

We posted five six-man and one seven-man guard shifts, each for an hour and a half duration. Everyone was getting tired. I wondered if it was from all the humping or from mental stress.

The night was quiet—almost too quiet. Around 0130 hours, the insects and animals went suddenly silent. There was no decrease of volume. It was like someone had thrown a master switch. I wasn't on guard, but I happened to be awake when it happened. I could sense the nervousness among the sentries. I held my breath for what seemed like minutes, listening for sounds of the enemy maneuvering into position. Nothing. Not a leaf stirred . . . not a twig snapped. Nothing! I was beginning to think I had lost my hearing, when the ordinary sounds of the night began to return—softly at first, then increasingly louder.

Whatever had been out there had gone. Nature's alarm system warned us that we were not alone.

March 13, 1969

Dawn came on the seventh day of the mission. We had spent a bad night, sleeping fitfully and trying to stay warm against a sudden drizzle that started around 0330. All of us were weak with hunger, having eaten no more than one full meal per day for the past week. The rain only added to our misery, but at least it indicated that the weather was changing.

We stayed in our NDP long enough to send a recon element to sweep the perimeter. We didn't want to walk into a trap when we left cover. It returned in fifteen minutes, having found nothing out of place in the jungle around us.

Our four emersion-foot casualties worsened. They were joined by another from the recon squad. The staff sergeant in charge of the grunts told Fadeley he didn't think his men could cover three hundred meters, let alone three klicks. Fadeley agreed. Biedron and Kilburn were in too much pain to walk out.

The decision was made to cross the stream and find a flat area to cut an emergency LZ. We had to evacuate our injured or the rest of us were going to be trapped, too.

We moved out around 1100 hours and crossed to the south side of the stream. The jungle seemed to have moved back away from the water. As the fog began to thin a little, we could tell the valley was actually widening out. The going was easier. There was still a lot of underbrush, but the normal creepers, wait-a-minute vines, and ankle-length shrubs were missing. I figured the stream must have flooded periodically, sweeping the ground cover away. It was a blessing to us.

Two hundred meters south of our NDP, we came upon an area where most of the trees had been knocked down. It might have once been a garden plot or a village site. But, as far as we were concerned, it was the perfect spot for a one-ship landing zone.

Fadeley and the recon squad leader put half the men on security around the forty-meter perimeter while the rest of us set about with machetes and K-bar combat knives to clear the smaller underbrush. Fadeley contacted Charlie Company to tell them we were cutting an LZ and gave them the coordinates. They would relay our message to Tomahawk and request a couple of medevacs for our five emersion-foot victims. We set the time for 1300.

It took us an hour to clear an area big enough to handle a single Huey. We still had to knock down six ten-to-twenty-foot-high trees that grew out from the LZ. It would have taken hours to hack them down with the four machetes the recon people had among them. A claymore strapped to each of them would do the job much faster. We had used claymores before for just that very purpose. They were quite effective on trees with a diameter of up to twelve inches.

We set the six mines in place, pointing each of the claymores toward the south. We fed the electrical wires back toward the stream and connected them to their firing devices. We decided to blow them ten minutes before the choppers arrived on the scene.

We were set up in a horseshoe-shaped perimeter waiting for the moment to blow the mines when we noticed that the fog was starting to burn off. We contacted Charlie Company and were informed that battalion had reported a breeze had kicked up in the past half hour. It was pushing the fog back toward the west. Charlie Company had been told to break off its march and to wait where it was for extraction. Captain Ross told us to try to contact our Six, who was flying C & C over Tomahawk.

Munoz picked him up quickly, but the signal was weak. We found out the fog was burning off very quickly. Captain Cardona had six slicks and a pair of Cobras at Tomahawk waiting to come in and get us. He had canceled our two dust offs. We nearly cheered when Munoz passed the word that we would soon be getting out.

We could see blue sky above our perimeter when Fadeley called the C & C ship and reported it was clear enough over him to bring the choppers in. Captain Cardona informed us the flight of eight ships would be coming in from the direction of Highway 1. The fog had cleared out of the valley to our east, but was still socked in between us and Tomahawk.

We blew the claymores at 1315. The choppers were three klicks away and heading in our direction. After the smoke from the explosions had cleared, we discovered that a twelve-inch-thick hardwood was still upright in the center of the LZ. Two Rangers ran over to it and started rocking it back and forth until it fell over with a crash.

The CO radioed that the slicks would have to come in one at a time to extract us. The valley narrowed just to our west, and the area over and behind us was still partially covered with fog. He called for us to pop a smoke.

Fadeley tossed a purple smoke out in the center of the LZ. We watched silently as the canister hissed, then popped, as a dense plume of grape-colored smoke billowed out, drifting up toward the retreating clouds.

The first Huey came thundering up the valley three hundred feet above us. It banked sharply and came around in a tight turn. I ran out into the LZ, and holding my weapon in both hands above my head, proceeded to guide the ship into the small LZ. What we had figured as enough space for a single Huey had turned out to be a tight fit, at best. I held the CAR-15 straight out to my front to signal the pilot to hover while he drifted clear of a single eight-foot stump just off his tail rotor. Finally, I was able to lower my weapon onto the ground as he cleared the obstacle and settled in for a touch down in the center of the clearing.

Seven of the recon men were up, running for the Huey as the pilot prepared for a quick lift-off. When all were on board, I signaled for the pilot to take off. He lifted slowly, having trouble with the weight of seven grunts and a crew of four in the heavy, humid air. It took him several seconds to clear the surrounding trees and gain enough altitude to complete his turn and head back down the valley.

The next chopper was already over the LZ as the first

one nosed down and pulled away. I watched the pilot through his Plexiglas shield as he frantically looked left and right as he brought the chopper straight down. He came in too fast and hit hard as he dropped his ship into the LZ. He broke one of the curved support struts that attached the skids to the Huey's undercarriage. The pilot must have realized that he had suffered structural damage. He held the chopper in a ground-kissing hover as the remaining six men of the recon squad dashed across the clearing to the safety of the Huey's cabin. The pilot climbed out as quickly as he had come in. Must have been a cherry.

The third chopper was a hundred meters out and already on a final approach. This pilot was coming on in without the benefit of my signals. I could see the two door-gunners hanging out each side of the ship, directing the pilot's approach. Only the umbilical cord of their safety ropes kept them from pitching headlong onto the LZ. I yelled for Fadeley to get Biedron and Kilburn out on that flight. He didn't want to go on that ship, but I was out on the LZ playing Mr. Pathfinder and he didn't have a choice. I looked around at our shrinking perimeter as the first Ranger team loaded on board. There were only eighteen of us left. Our team integrity had been destroyed when Fadeley had taken two of my men out and had left two of his on the ground. Bielesch yelled and pointed to six Rangers who were to go out on the next ship.

Finally, there were only twelve of us remaining around the LZ. The fifth Huey approached the LZ, and I looked over at J.B. He pointed at me and then motioned skyward. The remainder of my team and two of Fadeley's men were going out on this bird.

I signaled the approaching chopper that he was right on the money, as he came in fast, but flared up at the last minute to set his ship softly down on the LZ. I took off in a running crouch for the left side of the bird, doing a reverse half gainer to land on the edge of the cabin floor with my feet dangling down toward the skids. The other five Rangers piled in from the other side. I felt the ship lift, slowly at first, then gain momentum as it nosed over and sped down the valley. I heard someone yell, ''Gooks— they got gooks on the perimeter.'' I looked down, but it was too late. We were already fifty meters from the LZ, and the tail boom was blocking my view. I could tell by the way the pilot was climbing that something was wrong. He was trying to get out of the area as quickly as possible.

Munoz was monitoring the extraction of Bielesch's team on his radio as we flew down the valley. He screamed that Rucker had spotted an enemy soldier standing up across the perimeter as our bird had lifted out. The NVA had been right behind where I had been directing the landings. Rucker and Sours had killed him. Our pilot had then reported movement in the cover to the south and east of the LZ. He and the port-side door gunner had spotted NVA soldiers moving up through the trees as we were lifting out. It had happened too fast for the gunners to respond.

The last Huey was on final approach when the word came over the airway that there were gooks on the LZ. To their credit, they attempted to go in anyway. But Bielesch got on the radio and told them to abort the extraction. The enemy was already on top of them. Bielesch quickly tossed another smoke out into the center of the LZ and called for the Cobras to blast everything on the east, south, and west sides of the LZ.

The two gunships came in with automatic cannon fire and chopped up everything in the area of the LZ except for the side of the perimeter where the last six Rangers lay hiding in the brush. Each ship made two passes. Bielesch directed them to come in again, while the extraction ship tried to slip back in under the cover of their miniguns. Rucker had killed another NVA across the LZ with a frag. The enemy soldiers seemed confused, not understanding who was there or where they were. The pickup worked perfectly. The two Cobras came in hot, miniguns droning as they shredded the jungle around the LZ. The slick pilot brought his ship in low and fast to hover just over the clearing, as the Cobras circled around for another pass. Bielesch, Sours, Rucker, Peterson, Anderson, and Glasser sprinted for the chopper, expecting at any moment to see the surrounding jungle erupt with the green tracers of enemy automatic-weapons fire. Rucker turned just as he reached the cabin door and fired a burst at another NVA who had just stood up in the bushes to the front of the ship.

Farther down the valley, one of the door gunners pointed back toward the direction we had come from, and then

flashed a thumbs up as he nodded his head and grinned. I
knew that Bielesch's team had gotten out.

Munoz handed me a cigarette. I wondered how in the
hell he had gotten it lit in the wind tunnel of the Huey's
cabin. But that wasn't really important. I cupped it in both
hands to keep the rush of air roaring past me from tearing
it away and drew the smoke deeply into my lungs. The
tobacco tasted delicious. I passed the half-smoked butt
over my shoulder to Groff and leaned back against him,
as our chopper broke out of the valley and swung back to
the north. Our two-to-three hour mission had lasted seven
days, but somehow, we had all survived!

The chopper turned west again and flew to Firebase
Tomahawk. We still had to drop off the recon squad. When
we set down on the chopper pad at the firebase, we were
surprised to find General Zais waiting. We dismounted the
choppers, moved across the pad, and formed up in teams.
By the way he was beaming, we knew what was coming,
but we hoped it wouldn't take long. All we wanted was a
good meal and a hot shower. The general didn't keep us
in suspense. He was a soldier's soldier, and he knew our
priorities. He thanked us for the sacrifices we had made
in accomplishing our mission, and told us that he would
always have a warm spot in his heart for the Rangers. We
were carrying on a rich tradition established by our pre-
decessors, the 1st Brigade LRRPs and F Company, 58th
Infantry (LRP). Then he dismissed us, saying he had seen
to it that we had a big feast waiting for us back at the Cav
mess hall, and he wasn't about to stand between a good
meal and four starving Ranger teams.

We quickly reboarded the choppers for the ten-minute
flight back to Camp Eagle. We had been gone so long that
I couldn't remember what it looked like. The entire company was at the pad to welcome us. The warmth and appreciation we got from our fellow Rangers was more
gratifying than any five-minute speech from a general officer.

They huddled around us, offering to carry our weapons
and web gear to our hootches. Several of them expressed
concern about our haggard appearance and general physical condition. Once they had assured themselves we were
okay the jokes and jibes began—good naturedly, of course.

Schwartz asked if I had a good time on my R & R. Miller wanted to know if I had brought him anything back from Bangkok. Chambers told me that I had been gone so long he had naturally assumed I wasn't coming back, so he had written Barb and offered to take my place at our wedding in June. He added that she would undoubtedly be getting a better deal. You had to know Chambers!

The chow was everything we had hoped it would be, and more. Honest to God steaks, with real meat on them, baked potatoes, green beans, homemade rolls, and fresh salads. We were told to take all we wanted. I ate so much that I ended up giving my pie to Rucker. After a long soak in a warm shower, I put on some clean fatigues and waddled down to the Ranger lounge to drink myself into oblivion. I had a lot of celebrating to do. I was still alive, and, after filling in the seven days on my short-timer's calendar, I had just discovered that I was down to eighty-three days and a wake-up.

Zo came in and told us that, while we were out in the jungle playing "house" with the infantry, Mr. Poley had been killed up north of Camp Evans. He had flown his Huey into a fog-covered mountaintop, returning after picking up a chopper load of wounded Marines. He had volunteered when no one else would take the mission. Zo had rappeled in to get the bodies two days later. He and Mr. Poley had really been close. Our drinking took on a much more somber tone after that.

March 14, 1969

Sometime in the early morning hours, a 122mm rocket had gone through the tin roof of my hootch and exploded in the back of my skull. It was the only reasonable explanation for the tremendous headache that greeted me when I awoke that afternoon. I was lucky to have survived the impact of the rocket, and even luckier to have not suffocated when the herd of wild elephants shit in my mouth. I was suffering from the granddaddy of all hangovers. The wonderful meal I had consumed the evening before, soured by copious amounts of beer, lay splattered over the newspapers strewn across the floor of our four-hole crapper. I had been unable to lift my head high enough to "greet the seat." I felt like a total ass until Schwartz told me that I hadn't been the first, or the last, to "shed his bread in the head."

A couple of hours later, I had recovered enough to walk around without feeling like I had just stepped off the tilt-a-whirl at the local carnival. Chambers popped through the front door of my hootch and asked if I had heard what Mother Rucker had done the night before. Shaking my head brought new jolts of pain and made me aware that there was still something loose in the upper quadrant of my skull. He ignored my expression of agony and continued with his story. It seemed that Mom had also been feeling his oats, and had gotten his bowels in an uproar over something that happened when his team inserted on the last mission. They had just arrived over their LZ and were hooking onto their rappeling ropes. First Sergeant Cardin—not-so-affectionately known as "Cubby" to the Rangers—was flying belly-man on Rucker's insertion ship. Now normally, it was the belly-man's job to see that everyone got hooked up and into their rappel as quickly as possible, and then to recover the ropes as the chopper pulled away from the area. But in that particular situation, Cubby had acted a little overzealously and shoved Mom out the open door before he had a chance to grab the trailing end of the rope with his brake hand. Mother had been forced to grab the rope above him with both hands, slowing himself enough to prevent injury on landing, but burning his palms in the process.

The evening after the mission, when we were all down at the Ranger lounge pickling our brains, Rucker had suddenly announced he was really pissed about what Cardin had done to him. It was wrong, anyway you looked at it, and he didn't have to put up with that shit, even if the man was a "goddamned lifer pig." He stated that he was going to go up to the TOC (tactical operations center) and have a little chat with that son of a bitch who had tossed him out of the chopper.

Everyone thought he was just blowing smoke, so no one made an effort to stop him. Mother staggered up to the orderly room and barged in to find the first sergeant seated behind his desk with the lights off. Rucker, showing very little respect for the NCO's rank or position, called him a couple of choice names and asked him what in the hell he thought he was doing tossing him out the chopper like he had. Cubby's reply was not what good old Mom had wanted to hear. And the .45-caliber automatic the first sergeant shoved in his face was not what good old Mom had wanted to see, either.

Rucker vaulted over the desk, catching a blow across his forehead from Top's pistol, before he disarmed him and tossed it across the floor. He was in the process of pounding some wisdom into the ex–Special Forces soldier, when a couple of Rangers barged in and broke up the affair. But Mother had gotten in some damaging blows in the meantime. After the two Rangers had separated them, Rucker was just sober enough to realize he was in some big trouble—somewhere between life in Leavenworth and death by firing squad. Of course, he was also just drunk enough that he really didn't give a rat's ass.

Captain Cardona and Lieutenant Williams arrived on the scene seconds later. After finding out what had happened, they dismissed Rucker and stayed to talk to First Sergeant Cardin. The officers made the decision to ignore the incident and got Cardin to agree not to press for a court-martial. They should have let Mom kill him.

I couldn't believe all of that had happened without my having been aware of it. But then, I had slept right through that 122mm rocket that had hit my hootch, too.

March 15, 1969

Captain Cardona, in an unusual display of warmth, told us at morning formation that all four of the Ranger teams that had participated in the search and rescue mission were being given the remainder of the day to rest and relax at Coco Beach. He also included two other teams that had been out in the field, west of Camp Eagle, during the same period.

We hurriedly gathered up swim suits, cut-off fatigue pants, or, in some cases, those OD (olive drab) undershorts that no one ever wore, and made a mad dash for the deuce-and-a-half parked below the orderly room.

Someone had already iced up several cases of Schlitz and had loaded them on board. A few air mattresses that had survived dry rot and perforation were brought along and jealously guarded by their lucky owners. My own had long since succumbed to the perils of hootch life, and I had not been issued another after my return from the convalescent center.

Rucker had a knot on his head as big as a baseball grenade when he climbed into the truck beside me. He told me what had transpired the evening before. I had to sympathize with him. I pointed out that Cubby had obviously never heard the story of Captain Shepherd, the commander of the old LRP company, who had stomped on a toe-popper mine entering his tent one night. He, too, had shown contempt and a general lack of respect for the men he commanded. It seemed that some people took to learning, real hard.

The beach was great. We stopped at a little village outside Hue and picked up some fresh giant prawns and a large basket of green saltwater crabs. We had stopped there before. They were delicious, steamed over a pit of seaweed and red-hot coals. The saltwater performed its miracle cure on the ringworm, emersion foot, bacterial fungi, and the open sores we had picked up on the last mission. A long soak in the briny sea, followed by a couple of hours of sunbathing, renewed the body and the spirit. Some of the Rangers passed around pipes full of pot, while others attacked the barrels of ice-cold beer. Both vices served to mellow the stressed-out Rangers.

By 1600, we were ready to return to the company area. Rucker had finally calmed down, no longer out to hang the skin of Cubby from the flagpole above the Ranger lounge. All was forgiven, but not forgotten. Rucker had shoved it back into the hidden recesses of his mind, where all the hurt, pain, and bad memories were stored. Each of us kept such a place. It was a personal place, that no one else was allowed to enter. It was the place where the bogeyman dwelled, were the bad things could fester and rot, out of sight and out of mind. We were young. There would be a time in the future when we would dig back into that attic of nightmares and bad memories, to pull out all the bitterness, hatred, and guilt we had hidden there in our youth. But not yet! No, we weren't ready for that type of trauma. We were still of the mind-set to live for today. "Fuck it, don't mean nothin'." "Shit happens, man!" "Don't get behind me when your bullet comes, Bro'."

March 16, 1969

The fun and games were over. I received a warning order for a new mission. Rucker and I were to take a team out behind Nui Ke Mountain. Same old shit—find the rockets that were plastering Camp Eagle! This time we were to take out a team full of new guys. I didn't feel right in calling them cherries anymore. They had all had their cherries broken over the past two months. Groff, Lawhon, Kilburn, and Greg Krahl made up the rest of the team.

We were to insert at first light on the seventeenth in the valley behind Bald Mountain. I had been in this area so many times it felt like home.

March 17, 1969

We went in on a small, brush-clogged clearing half-way up the reverse slope of the mountain. We stumbled through the wait-a-minute vines for 10 to 15 meters before hitting the relative safety of the jungle. It felt good to be back in the field again.

We laid dog for fifteen minutes while Rucker got commo with the TOC. I was surprised the reception was so clear with Old Baldy between us and Camp Eagle. You could never figure out commo: it was good when you thought it wouldn't be, bad when it should have been as clear as a bell.

I shot azimuths to the top of Nui Ke and back to the peak of Bald Mountain, just to make sure we were where we were supposed to be. I had been inserted in the wrong LZ one time too many to trust anyone else's judgment. It paid off in spades to double-check one's location at the beginning of a mission.

We moved cautiously through the double-canopy down toward the valley to our west. I remembered the little stream that meandered through the steep-sided valley floor at the base of the mountain. The water was cold and clear. There were several trails in our AO. Some were old and overgrown, while others were unusually well-maintained. It seemed we always had teams reconning in and around the general vicinity. More often than not, our teams found the enemy either moving through the area or set up in platoon to company-size base camps. It was our own private hunting preserve.

We heard the running water before we saw it. I was at point and held the team a few meters back while we listened for sounds that would indicate the presence of the enemy.

I was pleased with the way the new men performed. They had maintained proper interval coming down into the valley, and their noise discipline belied their inexperience. It was unusual to see such a performance in Rangers with less than six missions under their belts.

Once we had determined we were alone, I moved the team down through the heavy underbrush along the stream to the very edge of the water. It was almost cool among the rocks that littered both sides of the stream. Leeches clung to the leaves of the bushes at the edge of the water, blindly reaching for us as their sensing devices zeroed in on our body heat. I watched, fascinated, as the sluglike little bastards rose up on their tails and swayed back and forth as I moved my hand across their fronts. What uncomplicated lives they led, lying lazily along a jungle stream until the next meal happened along. They had become masters of the ambush, while their airborne neighbors, the mosquitoes, had perfected the art of aerial attack.

I intended to move north, about a hundred meters up the stream, to where the valley widened and the triple-canopy began. That was usually the area where we ran into Mr. Charles. He liked the triple-canopy. It hid his trails from above and provided shade from the heat. The ground cover thinned out in triple-canopy. Giant ferns and huge, green, elephant-eared broadleafs broke up the park-like terrain beneath the 150-foot-high teak and mahogany trees.

The overhead cover was so dense that sunlight often failed to penetrate, leaving us wandering in a world of perpetual dusk, to darkness, to dusk again. Night brought blackness. Not the kind of blackness you would associate with the night—this blackness was a total absence of light. Like being born blind, where not even the memory of light slips through the mantle of darkness that shrouds the mind. It settles in around you with a suffocating closeness that muffles outside sounds, yet amplifies the pounding of your heart. Here and there, patches of phosphorous glow eerily on the jungle floor. They throw off no real illumination, but their presence restores some sense of depth perception and keeps you from feeling like you've been entombed.

Only the realization that the enemy was as sightless as we were enabled us to sit out the night and wait patiently for the coming of dawn. Rangers had to learn to conquer their fear of the triple-canopy jungle. It often inspired such terror in new men that they became a security risk. They would spend more time watching the trees than the terrain around them.

Once we had learned to deal with it, we discovered that our talents of stealth and concealment were at their best under the protective blanket of the towering trees. We could hide totally undetected and let enemy troops pass within a few feet of us. Besides the lush vegetation that hid us so well, the deep, dark shadows of the jungle made our discovery by the enemy virtually impossible.

An eternal symphony of moisture droplets fell from the uppermost branches, working their way slowly, in leapfrog fashion, to *plink-plunk* their way to the ground. It didn't seem to make a difference whether rain was pouring down at the time or it hadn't rained in days. The rhythm of pellets of water bouncing from leaf to leaf was a constant reminder of where we were. The heavy dampness soaked into the ground, growing layers of moss that felt like plush carpeting under our feet.

The only perils we faced patrolling the heavily forested triple-canopy jungles were the risk of getting lost and the difficulty of extraction. We usually discovered rather quickly that, in triple-canopy, our topo maps indicated only major terrain features, totally overlooking such things as secondary ridges, hog-backs, ravines, saddles, and degree of slope. Combine that with the inability to get a fix on known terrain features, and it is understandable that we had a slight tendency to nervousness while under the high growth. We often had to call in artillery, in the blind, to get a fix on our position.

If we were unfortunate enough to be compromised beneath triple-canopy jungle, we had to E & E to the nearest clearing, bomb crater, or streambed to be safely extracted. In some cases, that could take hours. With the enemy hot on our trail, it could quickly become a test of endurance. If our luck was good, a McGuire rig or jungle penetrator would be dropped down through the trees to pluck us from harm's way, but that was the exception, not the rule.

It was early afternoon, when we reached the shelter of the triple-canopy. I noticed the nervousness in a couple of the new men. Patrolling in these conditions would take some getting used to. We discovered a well-used trail fifty meters up the opposite ridge. It blended perfectly with the surrounding terrain. We hadn't spotted it until we were right on top of it. It wasn't standard procedure to walk trails, but I decided to risk it. It would be a waste of time to parallel the trail five to ten meters back in the jungle, as we had been trained. It meandered back and forth, and we would never be able to keep it in sight. Besides, trying to maintain our footing while traversing the steep, moisture-slick sides of the mountain would be next to impossible, without sounding like an assaulting infantry regiment.

We followed the trail up over the crest of the mountain. The roots of the huge trees lining it snaked back and forth across the path, forming spaced and well-defined steps and made climbing much easier.

I moved slowly, stopping often to listen. I was pleased that no sounds came from behind me. I had to look back over my shoulder on more than one occasion to make sure I hadn't walked off and left the rest of the team. The triple-canopy turned to double-canopy as we approached the crest of the mountain. Sunlight penetrated the overhead vegetation. I stopped as we reached the crest. Huge vines hung down from the treetops. In the distance we could hear monkeys moving away through the highest branches. We had spooked them. Their panicked flight would alert every NVA in the vicinity of the mountaintop.

I moved off the trail to the right and dropped down the side of the mountain, maintaining a gradual, lateral descent. We needed to get into some heavy cover within the hour and set up an NDP for the evening. I was surprised to find that the north slope of the mountain was covered with double-canopy, unlike the east slope we had ascended. Movement was a little more difficult, but the sight of the sky above us made us feel a little more secure.

I located a level spot along a downed tree and signaled that we would NDP at that location. Rucker called in a sitrep while I oriented the map to find our exact coordinates.

I was sitting back against my rucksack, my folded map laid across my drawn-up knees, when I spotted the biggest centipede I had ever seen. The damn thing came out from under the log on my left and dashed right under my legs. I was too amazed to move. It must have been ten or twelve inches long, with a jet black body and bright orange legs. I just couldn't help but wonder about all the unknown creatures that had crawled over, under, and around me during the many nights I had lain in ambush along jungle trails, or had laagered up in heavy cover in more NDPs than I could remember. They had caused their share of nightmares, as my mind had conjured up all types of imaginary denizens. Seeing them during the daylight didn't lessen my imagination any. In Vietnam, nightmares were reality.

We set out four claymores, two aimed uphill and one on each flank. The hillside below us was open enough that I felt we could cover it with frags, in case the enemy came at us from that direction.

In the morning we would move on down the north slope, then swing back around to the east side of our AO. If my calculations were correct, we would come up on the north side of Bald Mountain sometime before the next evening. We would spend one more night out in the bush before being extracted on the morning of the nineteenth.

The entire northeast corner of the AO was composed of low ground cover and bamboo thickets. Finding an LZ would be easy.

March 18, 1969

The second night passed quietly. Once, around 0200, we heard a heavy volume of automatic-weapons fire erupt a few klicks northeast of our position, in the direction of Firebase Birmingham. Probably some line company having a mad-minute. It wasn't sustained fire, so we didn't figure it was a perimeter probe or a firefight. It could have been an ambush, but we couldn't detect the blasts of claymores that usually signaled the initiation of an American ambush.

Rucker flipped his radio all around the current frequencies, but never picked up any traffic on the net indicating the cause of the gunfire.

At daybreak, I had the Rangers chow down in groups of two. I had decided to go first class on this particular mission and had brought along a small bottle of Tabasco sauce. A few drops of the tangy liquid, sprinkled in my beef-'n'-rice LRRP ration, added a little zest to a normally boring meal.

When we had finished eating, I moved to the edge of the perimeter and dropped down on my knees to relieve myself. Rangers had long ago learned to urinate in the kneeling position, because the sound of piss spraying against ground cover carried fifteen to twenty meters in the jungle. The trick was to avoid the splashback. When I was done, I reached down and pulled a pile of dampened leaves over the target area to mask the strong, telltale ammonia smell that Americans were known for. It was a dead giveaway in the jungle. The Vietnamese left an even stronger odor when they voided. It smelled more like cat piss. Even their crap smelled different from ours, giving off a distinctive odor of rotten fish. On more than one occasion, it had alerted our teams to their presence long before we had spotted them.

We really had to be extra careful roaming around the jungle. Our senses of sight, hearing, and smell had developed to such a degree that we had become little more than walking sensors. Our eyes, ears, and noses continually collected data from our surroundings. It was quickly transmitted to our brains for processing, identification, and storage. What bothered me was that there was no reason to doubt that our enemies had not developed the same capabilities.

We pulled in our claymores, then moved out in team formation to the east. We soon reached the valley floor, but the final twenty meters coming off the ridge had been disastrous. The forty-five-degree slope had changed abruptly to a steeper sixty-degree gradient, and we had been forced to slip and slide down the muddy embankment until we reached the valley below. We clutched at each vine, small tree, and shrub we passed in an unsuccessful effort to control our descent, but had only succeeded in leaving a noticeable mud slide behind us. There was no way to go back and cover it up.

I moved the team quickly across the wooded valley to the gentle slope of the opposite ridge, stopping only to refill our canteens as we crossed the stream. Once on the other side, we paralleled the base of the ridge in a north-easterly direction until we figured we had put several hundred meters between us and our beaver slide.

We climbed up the side of the ridge for about thirty meters or so, and set up an NDP in a small, shallow washout overlooking the valley below. Thick clusters of twenty-foot-tall trees formed a fencelike hedge behind us, protecting us from being spotted by anyone farther up the side of the ridge.

It was early in the afternoon, but I decided to stay there, under cover, until the next day's extraction. We were in a good position to watch the valley below, and we could hear anyone coming down the trail on the opposite ridge-line. Besides, if someone had picked up our trail and had decided to track us, I wanted to be above them when they closed in on us.

We spent another quiet night, listening for sounds that

weren't supposed to be there. It was good to be away from the leeches, but their winged comrades, the mosquitoes, found us right after the sun went down. We buttoned our sleeves tightly to keep them away from our skin, and pulled our boonie towels over our heads so that only our faces showed. The continuous buzzing drowned out all other sound. I had to squint to keep them out of my eyes. Unfortunately, my nose was incapable of squinting. I inhaled three or four of them before I broke down and rubbed a little insect repellent over my face. I didn't like to use it in the bush, but in the calm of the evening, I didn't think the smell would carry far.

March 19, 1969

The sun rose over the mountain behind us, keeping us in shadow until after 0900. Our extraction had been moved up to 1030 hours to permit two other teams to be inserted southwest of us, near Firebase Normandy.

We were sitting quietly, waiting for the call from Captain Cardona to move to our PZ, when we heard voices above us on the other side of the tree line. They weren't speaking English. That meant only one thing out in the jungle. We had several Vietnamese, forty to sixty meters away, engaged in a heated dialogue that could have very easily been about us. We dropped into prone defensive positions, facing outward, while Rucker called in the information.

Suddenly, one . . . two . . . three . . . four 122mm rockets took off with a *whoosh* from a position a hundred meters up the hill from us. We hugged the ground instinctively, as our RTO reported the multiple launches.

Captain Cardona radioed that he was ten minutes out and told us to move to our LZ a hundred meters to our north. He asked for the coordinates of the rocket launch site, saying he would put a fire mission on it as soon as we got to our PZ. We informed him that the coordinates were only an estimate, since the launches had occurred just over the crest of the ridgeline from us. We had not been able to pinpoint the exact location. I doubted if the fire mission would hit anything, anyway. The NVA were usually long gone within seconds of the launches.

We radioed back, giving the coordinates of the trail on the opposite mountainside and recommending they put WPs up and down the area in about fifteen minutes. With a little luck, they would catch them returning to their base camp. The white phosphorus rounds might nail a few of them. It would at least trap some smoke under all that foliage. H & E would only explode in the treetops, causing more fright than damage.

The way to the PZ was relatively open. We were on a natural shelf that ran along the side of the ridge and opened onto a small hill that flanked the major ridge above us. It was a good spot for an extraction. I could see the back side of Bald Mountain just over the crest of the ridgeline. It looked pretty imposing at such close range. It was amazing how much cover was on the reverse slope. The side facing Camp Eagle looked like someone kept it freshly mowed.

We stopped just off the top of the little hill to our front. We could cover the twenty meters in seconds when the chopper came in. The sound of the Huey grew louder as it followed the contour of Bald Mountain around to our location. Suddenly we saw it, two hundred meters out and a hundred feet up. I tossed a green smoke grenade out into the center of the hilltop, as Rucker talked the slick into our PZ. I ran out to the edge of the clearing and guided the pilot in, as the rest of the team fanned out behind me to secure our back-trail. The pilot put the chopper down ten meters to my front, as the team broke from cover and sprinted for the beckoning safety of the open cabin. Looking back over my shoulder, I quickly followed them up, jumping for the empty space they had saved for me.

As much as Rangers looked forward to being extracted after a long, stressful mission, they still dreaded that final dash to the waiting chopper. There was no other time on a mission that we felt so vulnerable. That quick dash from cover, across an open area to the helicopter, always brought an overpowering surge of adrenaline. It would send your heart pounding as you sprinted for safety, neck jammed deep into your shoulders in an unconscious effort to make yourself smaller. The expectation of a bullet tearing through your back was always there.

Some guys said insertions had the same effect on them, but I disagreed. On an insertion, you were running to cover, not away from it. You were at least able to see where the bullet was coming from, even if you couldn't hear it. On an extraction, you couldn't hear or see it. Your eyes were on the chopper. If the bullet came, it was always in the back. It made a difference.

The flight back was short, almost as short as I was getting. I was down to seventy-seven days and a wake-up. If I got any shorter, I would have to stand on a footlocker to shake hands with Miller

March 20, 1969

Phil Myers and I received word that our commissions to second lieutenant were being processed. Division had sent word down through the channels that it would take another six weeks to complete the paperwork and cut the orders. First Sergeant Cardin told us we would both be transferred to the Americal Division for commissioning. It was against SOP, or tradition, or something, to be commissioned in the same outfit you had been serving as an enlisted man. It didn't make a lot of sense, but at the time, I was too excited to argue. My life-long ambition was finally being realized, and I really didn't care what price I had to pay to achieve it. Not even if I had to give up my R & R, which was very possible.

I had also just received word that I was scheduled to

leave April 29 for Honolulu. The only thing that bothered
the two of us was that we were going to be leaving the
best company, in the finest division in Vietnam, to go to
one of the worst-led and poorest-motivated units in Southeast Asia—on either side.

March 21, 1969

We got a return trip from the Donut Dollies. The Red
Cross sent two different girls this time. Same games and
refreshments. Maybe the REMFs enjoyed this shit, but we
would have gotten more out of a beer bust and some music.

Now if the Red Cross had its act together, it would have
shipped the girls around in groups of about fifty with a
beer trailer and a stereo. Most of us had forgotten how to
dance and have a good time. It would have been a good
primer for returning home to the States.

My fiancée had written me about the latest dance fads
they were doing back in the World. There had been several
new ones since I had arrived in-country. I would have to
spend more time watching than rug-cutting when I returned.

We got rocketed again. Three of them, early in the afternoon. Two hit outside the perimeter, while the last one
exploded harmlessly among the revetments sheltering the
Cobras in the Cav compound. We were fortunate the 122s
weren't more accurate. The poor bastards lug those damn
things all the way down from the north, and then have a
hell of a time landing them in a military base as large as
Camp Eagle. I'll bet there was more than one enemy
rocket specialist running around in the jungle with some
officer's Ho Chi Minh sandal sticking out of his backside.
Maybe if they'd moved the launchers just a little bit
closer . . .

March 23, 1969

God what I nightmare I had! I awoke in a cold sweat around three in the morning, gripping the sides of my cot. Normally, I don't remember my dreams, but this one I could have made drawings of. It was not really a dream, but something more vivid—like an ominous premonition. I was on a mission in the A Shau. Chambers, Sours, Closson, and Rucker were the only other Rangers on the team. We were way up on a hilltop overlooking a multiple trail system. Gooks were coming and going like it was downtown Hanoi. We kept calling in that there were thousands of NVA soldiers around us, but no one would believe us. Someone radioed back and told us to capture a few of them, and then they would come in and pull us out. We were all too damn short to be taking those kinds of chances so we decided to just lay dog until they finally extracted us.

Suddenly, there were dinks everywhere, coming up the hillside all around us. We kept killing them, but more would take their place. We ran out of ammunition and started throwing grenades. We slaughtered so many that they had to climb over the dead to get at us. Then a tremendous explosion ripped through our position. When the smoke cleared, I could see myself lying there dead, next to the mangled bodies of Sours and Closson. Chambers was next to us with his legs blown off. Rucker lay a few feet away with his arms gone. I hadn't had those kinds of dreams since I was a kid. I pulled my poncho liner up over my head and tried to go back to sleep, but I was too wide awake to do anything but think about the nightmare.

It was totally ridiculous! We hadn't been pulling any missions near the A Shau in months. We seldom operated in five-man teams, and besides, I had never been out on a mission with Chambers. Too many contrary facts to justify a premonition, yet I couldn't get it out of my mind. It had been too goddamned real to just forget it.

I kept thinking about it after I got up. When I went to breakfast at the mess tent with Schwartz and Rucker, I decided to share my dream with them, figuring they would make a joke out of it and relieve me of some of the anxiety I was suffering. Schwartz told me I was screwy. He said a dream like that had to be nothing but a farce. None of us were good enough shots to kill that many gooks. Then, just to make light of the whole thing, he asked me if he could have my Penn double-E camera—just in case the prophesy came true.

Rucker took my dream a little more seriously. After all, he was one of the key characters. He told Jim he had heard a lot of stories about soldiers who had dreams that had forecast their being killed in action. In some instances the prediction had come to pass. He seemed lost in thought momentarily, then finally grinned and warned me that if I really wanted to start this prophesying crap, he wasn't going to go out with me anymore. That would guarantee that the prediction would never come true.

Later in the day, Sours and Chambers came over to my hootch and asked me if I knew what day we were supposed to get our shit blown away. They both wanted to schedule their R & Rs so that they wouldn't be there when it happened.

Finally, Closson came by and wanted to know when I had started shooting heroin. Good old Schwartsy—before he was finished, it would be all over the company area. Well, I decided I would be better off if I just let it blow over and made a joke of it. I was getting too damn short to get killed now.

March 25, 1969

After two more days of Ranger-style embellishment, my dream had indeed taken on the trappings of a major prophesy. A couple of the guys wanted to know if I was any relation to Nostradamus. One Ranger from the first platoon volunteered to go along—he said he'd never seen that many gooks die. I tried to handle the ridicule and teasing good-naturedly, but by the end of the day, I had just about had enough.

March 26, 1969

A warning order came down in the morning for a mission outside Firebase Jack. There had been an increasing amount of enemy activity in the immediate vicinity of the firebase over the past two weeks, and division G-2 (Intelligence) was worried. They passed the information on to G-3 (Operations), who requested a full-scale reconnaissance of the area. The Rangers got the job.

I was back on Closson's team as ATL. Rucker was assigned to the same team but not as an RTO. He told me that Closson told him he could walk point. Marcy and Fadeley were taking another team out with Marcy as TL. The third team would be lead by Zo with Schwartz as ATL.

We would all be flown out to Jack late in the afternoon,

then walk off the firebase in three different directions to move into our RZs. We would be out three days. Our primary mission was to monitor enemy traffic through the area and, if possible, get a prisoner or two. Our secondary mission, kill a few of them. We would be close enough to Jack to get all the support we needed, so the division gave us the okay to start whatever kind of trouble we wanted.

The best thing about the mission was nobody razzed me about my premonition. I was relieved. I was beginning to feel like the company comedian.

The team leaders returned from an overflight of the area just before dark. In our premission briefing, Closson told us that our RZ was to the southwest of Jack. There was a small stream meandering through a large area of high elephant grass. Line patrols from the infantry company on Firebase Jack had recently been running across fresh trails parallel to the stream on both sides. Our mission was to monitor enemy movement on those trails and to try for a snatch.

Marcy's team was going due west of Jack to the base of the mountains to sit on a major trail junction near the intersection of two rivers. Sensors back in the mountains had picked up heavy enemy movement along both trails.

Zo was going to the northwest of Firebase Jack. Scout choppers had spotted several enemy soldiers, on two separate occasions, hanging around the overgrown earthen berm of an old French fortress. The chopper had fired on them both times, but the NVA had disappeared into the tall elephant grass.

Closson pointed out that we would be staging out of Camp Evans. Firebase Jack was one of the support bases for the brigade base camp northwest of Hue and north of LZ Sally.

March 27, 1969

We drew our equipment after morning mess. I loaded up on grenades, both frags and willie petes. If we were going to be working in elephant grass, they would be more useful than bullets. Closson had Lawhon and Hillman pack extra claymores. That would give us eight on the mission.

Lawhon and Kilburn would be humping the two radios, while Rucker got a break for a change and would walk point. I wanted to walk his slack, but Closson wanted to be up front where he could monitor our movement. Since I was the only Ranger left with much experience, I put myself at rear security. The three newer men would be strung out between us. On the way back to our hootch Rucker and I stopped by supply and picked up a couple of strobe lights and some extra pen-flares. Rangers didn't get to work the open terrain very often. It required different equipment and a different strategy—we would be moving only at night.

Closson told us that Firebase Jack was a small fire-support base located in the open, rolling foothills about four and a half klicks west-southwest of Camp Evans. It sat on a little knoll, about forty feet higher than the surrounding terrain. A battery of 155s, with an infantry company providing perimeter security, was stationed there. A six-man Ranger X-ray (radio relay) team would be assigned to the firebase to provide us with commo to our rear.

Jack was only three klicks east of the mountains that Charlie called home, so anything could happen out there. The enemy could be just gathering information, or possibly planning to hit Jack or Evans with a ground assault. Closson told us that it wouldn't take much to deal Jack a mortal blow. The firebase didn't look very defensible, and the elephant grass had only been cut back from the perimeter wire about fifty meters.

We looked at a map of the area. The contour lines were definitely few and far between. I noticed the villages of Ap Lai Thanh and Ap Thanh Tan were both within a few klicks of Jack and Evans. Each was lightly defended by small contingents of PFs (Popular Force troops). It was conceivable that one or both of the towns was the focal point of the recent enemy activity. Our three Ranger teams would have a lot of ground to cover in such a short period of time.

Closson told everyone to shit, shower, and shave, and to be on the chopper pad at 1530. It would be a good half-hour flight to Camp Evans. We would be there less than ten minutes before we were flown out to Firebase Jack. Our slicks and Cobras would be on call at the Camp Evans helipad. In addition, an infantry company would be on standby alert as a ready reaction force, if and when we required one.

At 1520 hours, an eighteen-man Ranger team and a six-man commo team were geared up and ready to go. Excitement was in the air. Most of us had the impression we were going to get to kick some ass on this one.

We climbed aboard our choppers and flew north, in the direction of Camp Evans. It wasn't long until we spotted the city of Hue to our right as we crossed over the Perfume River. A few minutes later, LZ Sally appeared just below us on our left. I was surprised at the size of it. It was big, almost the size of a battalion base camp with room for supporting units. I couldn't understand why they referred to it as an LZ!

We finally approached Evans. It was a rather large installation, not as big as Camp Eagle, but not far off. It squatted among the low, rolling foothills just east of the rugged mountains separating the coastal plains from the North end of the A Shau Valley. Evans had originally been the home of the 1st Air Cav Division until they had moved south in the summer of '68. The 101st had sent one of its brigades in to take over the TAOR previously patrolled by the Cav. It was quite a responsibility to fill in for an entire division with one third the manpower. But the 2d Brigade of the Screaming Eagles had been doing a remarkable job of keeping the NVA in the mountains where they belonged.

We landed on a narrow stretch of tarmac long enough to accommodate ten to twelve choppers at one time. Captain Cardona stepped down from his C & C ship and walked over to each ship, telling the Rangers to rest in place until he returned. Then he shuffled across the flight line to a heavily sandbagged operations bunker forty meters away.

He returned, several minutes later, and signaled for us to reboard the choppers. We lifted off and headed west for the short hop to Firebase Jack.

I couldn't say I was impressed by my first view of Jack. Closson had been right. There wasn't much to it. The first thing I noticed, as we circled to approach from the west, was the six 155mm artillery pieces sitting in circular firing pits. A three-foot-high ring of sandbags protected each gun from shrapnel and direct small-arms fire. A few HE rounds lay stacked nearby. Sandbagged trenches ran from each gun to separate fortified ammo bunkers.

The perimeter was small, maybe seventy-five meters across. There was an above-ground mess hall off to one side of a commo shack and a large command bunker. Several other large bunkers were scattered around the area, obviously there to house the infantry company that guarded the redlegs (artillerymen).

Machine-gun emplacements in well-fortified bunkers were spaced every thirty meters around the perimeter. Reinforced trenches ran between them. I looked down at the back gate where the road from Ap Lai Thanh and Ap Thanh Tan ran up to the perimeter. I was appalled by the single elevated bunker guarding the metal-framed, barbed-wire–covered gate—an obvious weak spot in the perimeter defenses. After a single RPG round took out the bunker, a squad of old ladies from a quilting bee could pull the gate open and walk through. I imagined that the front gate guarding the road to Camp Evans was not in any better shape.

The pilots dropped us off at the road outside the back gate. We had to land one ship at a time, because the dust blown up by the rotor wash blinded everything and everybody within a hundred meters. Once on the ground, we walked up the slight rise to the gate and passed through under the disinterested eyes of the bunker guards., I hoped they paid more attention after dark!

An E-7 from the line company's headquarters platoon met us just inside the wire and told us he was there to brief us on what to expect. John Looney, in charge of the radio relay team, asked the NCO where his commo people could set up their radios. They were directed to a bunker just up the perimeter from the back gate. We huddled around the operations NCO as he gave us a rundown on their latest intelligence. Over the past two weeks, four of their fire teams had blown successful ambushes within a thousand meters of the wire. They had never gotten kills larger than three NVA at a time. The dead enemy soldiers were healthy, well-armed, and lightly equipped. They had found no documents on any of them, but had turned up a map laying out all the gun emplacements, bunkers, and weak spots in the wire. They even had the locations of all the claymores pinpointed. The infantry company's commander was a little concerned. I could understand why. Somebody was getting ready to blow their shit away. I think I would have been more than just a little concerned. I would have been trying to move my R & R up a week or two.

The NCO told us that for the last three nights they had been putting LPs (listening posts) out in the elephant grass surrounding the firebase. On four different occasions, the LPs had heard movement in the grass around them, but had not made contact. Jack was being scouted.

When he finished briefing us, the E-7 asked how we intended to recon the area outside the wire. The team leaders pointed out that it seemed that the bulk of the movement had been detected to the west of the firebase. Since the enemy was obviously observing everything that went on at Jack, we would walk off the firebase after dark through the east, or front, gate. Once we were outside the perimeter, we would swing back around to the west and move out in echelon formation by teams. Closson's team would be on the left. Zoschak's team would be out front in the center of the echelon. And Marcy's team would secure the right flank. We would stay in formation until we reached a point 1500 meters outside the wire, where we would split off and move to our respective recon zones.

Our team would swing to the right and set up an OP

along a small stream that ran to the south of the firebase. One of the firebase's patrols had reported a narrow, well-used trail running along the north side of the stream. We would set up a six-claymore ambush back in the grass and see what came by.

Zoschak's team would head due west three klicks, until it came to the intersection of two small rivers that came out of the mountains. Three main trails came together near the intersection. They were to set up an OP on some nearby high ground and monitor any enemy traffic coming down the trails or using the rivers.

Marcy's team would swing to the northwest and set up an OP ambush along a new high-speed trail just west of an old, abandoned French fortress about two klicks from Jack.

Once the three teams were in place, we would stay out for three days or longer, until we were able to find out what Mr. Charles had up his sleeve.

When the briefing was over, we dropped our rucks and went over to view the big 155s up close. It was as near as most of us had ever gotten to the big guns that had bailed us out on so many occasions. The artillerymen were as impressed with us as we were with their field pieces. They told us the one thing they hated about their jobs was that they never got to see the results of their work. They enjoyed firing for us because we normally could see our targets when we called for a fire mission, and usually radioed back to inform them of the results.

The line companies often requested artillery support on suspected or dug-in enemy positions. By the time the grunts checked out the impact area, Charlie, if he had ever been there in the first place, had long since *di di mau*ed out of the neighborhood. So they seldom reported successful fire missions. The compliments from the cannon-cockers made us appreciate them even more. We let them know that most of us wouldn't be here today if it hadn't been for their fast response and deadly aim. We were astute enough never to pass up a chance to improve relations with the arty people or the chopper pilots. Mutual respect was a major factor in the speed and dedication of their response to our calls for help.

About a half hour from dusk, we reassembled by teams and went through a final equipment check. The senior

RTOs set up a squelch-break code to implement basic communication between the teams while we moved to our RZs. We would stay on identical compass headings to maintain the thirty-meter intervals between the teams, but we would have to stay in touch with each other to maintain a similar pace.

We waited until total darkness was upon us before moving out through the gate. The infantry company manning Jack had pulled in all its ambush patrols and OPs. No one wanted to risk friendly casualties by bumping into one another out there in the dark. We passed through the gate in single file, having decided to form up in an echelon once we had reached the west side of the firebase. We would wait until we were a couple hundred meters outside the wire before executing the tricky procedure.

All went well as we moved into the six-to-eight foot-high grass and swung around the firebase. Marcy's team was in the lead, with Zo's team next, and then us. The going must have been tough on the first few men in the column who had to break trail for the rest of us. The elephant grass cut like a razor when it slid across exposed flesh. Thank God most of us had brought the leather gloves we used for rappeling!

We finally reached a point we estimated was due west of the firebase. Zo climbed atop the shoulders of a team member and shot an azimuth back toward Jack. We were right on the money! The team leader set a compass heading of 270 degrees and signaled the three teams to form up in the three-pronged echelon that would take us out through the tall grass to our jump-off points.

Rucker was walking point for our team, with Closson right behind him at slack. Lawhon was senior RTO, then Hillman, and Kilburn with the Prick-25 for the arty net, and finally myself at rear security. I didn't like walking drag, but it had its advantages in the deep elephant grass. The men ahead of me left a trail that made walking drag almost a pleasure.

There was little I could do to cover our back-trail. The elephant grass didn't want to come back up after six men had passed over it. I tried to pull the grass back into place behind me, but soon realized my efforts were futile. I could only hope that the stiff blades of grass would recover on their own by morning.

We had probably gone only seven or eight hundred meters when the man to my front, Kilburn, suddenly came to a dead stop. I turned to cover our back-trail and waited for the end of what I had assumed was a short break. A couple of minutes passed before I felt Kilburn's hand on my shoulder. He whispered in my ear that Closson wanted me up front. I told him to watch the rear and slid around him in the grass to move up to the point.

It was very dark in the grass. Only the illumination provided by a sky full of bright, shining stars enabled us to see a distance of three to four meters. When I reached Closson, he was kneeling next to Rucker, who seemed to be watching intently to the front. Closson was studying something at his feet. I knelt next to him so he could whisper to me without standing up. I heard him mutter, "Rucker stumbled across something in the grass. Looks like commo wire, running from Jack back toward the direction we're heading." I leaned over, and there it was, a strand of the pale blue commo wire the NVA used with their land lines. I had seen it before out in the A Shau. An effort had been made to hide it, but Rucker's sharp eyes had detected the horizontal line that was out of place among a sea of vertical grass.

I asked Closson if he had signaled the other two teams that we had halted. He nodded in the affirmative, then asked what I thought we should do. I told him that the wire appeared to be heading the same way we were, and if we continued moving in that direction, we were bound to run into the people on the other end of the line. I didn't think that was a very wise move under the circumstances. They would hear us long before we heard them. I had never been on the kill-zone end of an ambush and really didn't fancy it now. I was just too damn short for that kind of crap. He agreed.

He moved back to Lawhon, secured the handset, breaking squelch three times to signal the other two teams that the message was coming from him. He next broke squelch four more times, the signal to assemble on the team sending the message. When they answered by breaking squelch once and twice respectively, Closson passed the word back through the team that the other two teams were linking up with us. He told them not to fire on anyone coming through the grass on our right flank.

It took ten minutes for the other two teams to come in. Zo had waited for Marcy's team to link up with his before moving over to us. We set up in a circular perimeter while the three team leaders discussed our options. Zo wanted to put one team on the wire with the other two teams ahead on each flank, then follow the wire back to its point of origin. He thought we could flush the spying little bastards into one of the flank teams and put an end to their snooping. Marcy wanted to go after the receiver on the other end of the wire. He felt we would nab some bigger game on that end of the line than on the transmitting end. He liked Zo's inverted echelon formation. He felt it would be the least risky.

Closson wisely pointed out that to go after either commo team in the dark was foolish. There was little chance of their moving out of the area. They had a good thing going out there in the tall elephant grass. They would stay put and continue sending info back to their intelligence people as long as they didn't become too suspicious. He thought we would be wiser to move off to one side or the other and set up an NDP. In the morning we could try to move around behind them and establish a cordon on their backtrail. Once we were in place, we'd have the grunts sweep out from the firebase and flush them right into us. They wouldn't know we were there until it was too late.

The other two team leaders agreed with his plan. It was not as risky as trying to take on an enemy force of unknown size in the middle of the night. They would be coming to us, with the element of surprise in our favor, not theirs.

Marcy recommended we move to the north and set up our NDP in the old French fortress. We would have some cover within its walls and be able to monitor any activity on the trail that passed a few meters to the west of it.

The team leaders decided to move off to the northwest, in single file, until we reached the site of the fort. It was dangerous walking strung out in the elephant grass, but there was no other way to get there without leaving multiple trails through the thick cover. At least the single trail would not betray our numbers to any enemy soldier who stumbled across it in the darkness.

We moved out with Marcy's team at point. I remained at drag and tried to cover up our back-trail as much as I could. It wasn't easy. Eighteen heavily loaded Rangers moving across a dense field of elephant grass at night couldn't help but leave a lasting impression on the environment. The best I could do was to make the trail look like it was a couple of days old, but I knew it wouldn't fool anybody in the daylight.

I was surprised when the team came to a complete stop out in the grass, just a hundred and fifty meters from where we had started. Word was soon passed back down the column that the point element had discovered the old fort. It was overgrown and abandoned. It appeared to have been deserted for a number of years. Trees, twelve to fifteen feet high, grew from the inside of the berm, and waist-high grass covered the entire inner courtyard. Nothing remained of the old bunkers and fighting positions except weed-clogged depressions in the grass.

Marcy's team slipped in to check out the old enclosure, while the other two teams doubled up on each other to form a defensive perimeter. The team returned a short time later to report that the fort was empty. No one seemed to have used it for ages.

We got back to our feet and moved quickly through the last twenty meters of tall grass and into the shelter of the abandoned French position. We set up in a triangular perimeter across the southwest corner of the old fortress. The six-foot-high berm offered protection from attack on two sides. The open side of the triangle faced the interior of the fort.

Each team leader established a guard post on his side of the perimeter. Our team put a sentry on top of the south wall, while Marcy's team took the west wall. Zo's team covered the inside of the fort. We had no idea what the dimensions of the old fortress were, but assumed it had held at least a company of legionnaires. If their permanent camps were constructed on the order of ours, it must have been somewhere in the neighborhood of a hundred meters square.

It was 2230 hours before we got settled for the night. We snacked on a few lifer bars and C rat chocolates while Zo called in a sitrep to our X-ray team back on Firebase

Jack. He relayed our plan for the next day to Looney and told him to get the word back to Captain Cardona for final approval. He would have to arrange for the use of the infantry company as the hammer for our anvil.

Looney radioed back a half hour later to tell us to put the plan on hold until morning. The CO wanted to conduct a low-level aerial survey of the AO before we pulled off our operation. Great! There goes the surprise party.

Every twenty or thirty minutes flares from Firebase Jack popped over their perimeter. I assumed our discovery had made them nervous. It would be hard to get a good night's sleep knowing there were gooks outside the wire gathering information on your strengths and weaknesses. They obviously were not employed by the census bureau. Something was coming down the pipe. You cold feel it in the air.

March 28, 1969

At sunrise, Zo shot a compass heading back toward Jack and discovered that that big-assed, orange ball of solar energy appeared to be coming up directly from the center of the firebase. A few of us crawled up on top of the berm to see if we could spot the low hill where Jack sat guarding the southwestern approach to Camp Evans. Even though we were only a thousand meters away, we couldn't make out the firebase against the skyline. Their range of vision must have just as limited as ours. It wasn't really hot yet, but the humidity and lack of breeze threatened unbearable heat by midmorning.

We weren't in our environment out in the grasslands. Most of our missions had been deep in the mountains to our west or along the Perfume or Song Bo rivers. The shade of the double- and triple-canopy jungles and the dense stands of bamboo along the rivers had usually sheltered us from the worst of the Vietnam heat. We had heard the sun could be a killer down in the lowlands, east of our mountain recon zones. We had little idea just how bad it would be.

By 1000, it was pushing 100 degrees Fahrenheit. No protective shade or cooling waters to bring the temperature down a few degrees. No word had filtered back from the CO, okaying our plan. We sat under the bushes and small trees growing from the inside of the berm, trying to lessen the effect of the sun's rays.

At noon, the X-ray team radioed back and told us to stay put until "higher-higher" made a decision what to do. So that was it! Now division was in on our plans. Bullshit!

Minutes later, Rucker came running over to were I was sitting beneath my poncho liner. I had draped it over some low-hanging shrubs to create a little shade. He squatted and whispered that he had been up on the south berm of the fortress, glassing the tree line on the other side of the field of elephant grass with a pair of binoculars. He thought he had spotted something out of the ordinary and wanted my opinion on what it was.

I was reluctant to leave my meager spot of shade, but the heat was already turning it into a pizza oven. I got up and followed Mother to an open spot between two thick bushes sprouting from the top of the berm. We bellied up to the opening and looked out over the top of the tall elephant grass to a narrow tree line two hundred meters away. The tree line ran from east to west, bisecting the wide expanse of grassland.

He pointed toward the eastern end of the tree line due south of where we lay hidden in the brush, then handed me the binoculars, saying, "Look just to the right of that tall tree just in from the end there. See anything that doesn't belong?"

I put the glasses to my eyes, adjusting the focus with my right index finger. Finally, a clear picture of the tree line swam into view. Much of the trees were hidden by the tall grass. I scanned an area of thirty to forty meters, looking for someone or something man-made. I didn't see anything. The lower six to eight feet of the tree line had to be below the top of the elephant grass, so I would not be able to spot anything on the ground anyway.

I shifted my attention to the treetops. Had he spotted an observer or something up there in a tree stand? It wouldn't have been the first time Mr. Charles had played monkey to spot American soldiers before they got in range. No, nothing. What was I looking for? Then I saw it! A long, straight shaft—too thin to be another tree. It was narrow in diameter and didn't seem to have a natural taper. I couldn't spot any limbs growing from it, but at such a distance I didn't really expect to. I followed it as it rose through the branches of the tallest tree, stopping abruptly just beneath the uppermost branches of its host. Was it a radio antenna? What else could it be? There was no shine or reflection. How in the hell had Mom spotted it? I answered the question myself when I suddenly realized that I had only recognized the long, rigid antenna because it had seemed totally out of place amid the forked, angular limbs of the trees. No item in nature was that mathematically exact in form, that perfectly sculpted by creation, to stand the test of zero-degree variance in the horizontal or the vertical plane. Only man had achieved the ability to design and manufacture the "unbroken line" and to formulate the concept of the "shortest distance between two points." It had to be an antenna of some sort.

I handed the glasses back to Rucker and told him to keep his eyes on it. I was going back for Closson and the other team leaders. Rucker and I both knew what we thought we had seen, but the acid test was the team leaders—they would have to make the decision and act upon the information.

I ran over to where Closson, Marcy, Fadeley, and Zo were sitting around a large plastic-covered map of the AO. They were attempting to figure the logical terminus of the commo wire based on terrain and cover. I squatted next to them and said to no one in particular, "You guys need to come over here and see what Rucker found."

Zo asked, "What is it?"

I waited for a second before answering, not wanting to plant any ideas in their heads. "You'll have to see for-yourselves. We're just not sure, but it sure is suspicious looking!"

The five of us crossed the fifteen meters of open terrain to where Rucker lay with his back to us among the bushes. Closson slid in next to him. Taking the glasses from Rucker and sighting along his outstretched arm and pointing finger, Closson studied the distant tree line.

Several minutes passed before he looked back over his shoulder and said, "Looks like a radio antenna to me."

Zo, Fadeley, and Marcy each took their turn at spotting and identifying the object of our curiosity. Each Ranger agreed that it was indeed a radio antenna, and where you found a radio antenna, you could pretty damn well bet you'd find a transmitter/receiver. Pay dirt! We had just discovered the terminus of the commo wire.

The team leaders hurried back to their radios to call in the sighting to the X-ray team. We had several options. We could call in an air strike or a fire mission and knock out the site. We could carry through with our original hammer and anvil operation. Or we could take it out ourselves. Now that we knew where the receiver was located, we could move through the grass after dark and get into position to hit them at first light the next day, before they knew what was happening.

We decided that the third option could yield a prisoner or two and would be the most likely to nail the radio and its entire commo team. It would be tough trying to get in position without being detected, but we had the whole night to accomplish it. The commo team would probably be asleep during the wee hours of the morning, and they would never expect American soldiers to move up on them in the darkness. The noisy U.S. infantryman never moved at night. Well, that didn't hold true for Rangers. The night belonged to us.

We decided to move out in single file sometime after 2300 hours, taking a full five hours to get into position. We would get as close as we could, sighting in on the tall tree as a reference. When we reached a point within twenty meters of the tree line, we would swing on line—the point man being the pivot—until we came up eighteen Rangers abreast facing the tree line. We'd hit them on signal at first light.

At 2315, we moved out as planned. Schwartz was at point, with Zo close behind at slack. Zo had shot an azi-

muth to the tall tree just before sunset and was keeping
Schwartz on a compass heading of 190 degrees. Zo's RTO
was counting paces to keep track of the distance we were
covering.

We must have been in the grass close to forty-five minutes, and had probably covered half the two hundred meters to the tree line, when the static on Lawhon's radio
went crazy. Someone was breaking squelch rapidly, trying
to signal danger. Everyone froze in place. No one moved
a muscle. Something was wrong somewhere in the column, but none of us knew where.

Ten minutes went by before I saw Lawhon reach forward and give Closson the handset. I could barely make
him out in the faint illumination of the starlight, nodding
his head as he spoke to someone on the other end. Finally
he turned to Lawhon and whispered something ever so
slowly in his ear. When he finished, he looked past his
RTO at the rest of the team and held one finger to his lips,
then made the sign for ''men walking'' and pointed to the
front of the column. Zo's team had movement to its front!

A few minutes later, Closson turned and whispered
again to his RTO, who in turn passed it back to the man
behind him. When the message finally reached me, I listened intently as Kilburn said, ''A lot of gooks just passed
Schwartz and Zo. More than fifty. Heading for Jack. Zo's
team will fall back on us. Marcy's team is moving up. Set
up tight, wagon-wheel perimeter on our location.''

Jesus H. Christ! Sappers on their way to hit Jack and
we damn near walked into them. Suddenly, Phil Myers,
Marcy's point man, moved up behind me and told me that
their drag was reporting movement behind us. Had to be
another group of sappers. Son of a bitch, what if they
cut the trail we just made? They could follow it right up
our ass.

About that time the other two teams moved in on us
from both sides and hurriedly set up a perimeter. Zo motioned for everyone to freeze, while we listened for any
signs of the enemy maneuvering around us.

Everything was quiet for the next ten minutes. Not a
sound came from the alert Rangers hidden in the tall grass.
Then Zo was in the middle of us, placing each man in a
defensive position facing outward. Only he seemed aware

of the total picture. Rucker was on my left, Kilburn on my right. I could barely make out Myers on the other side of our junior RTO. There was a noise behind me. I turned to see Zo and Marcy, along with Zo's senior RTO and Marcy's junior RTO, setting up a command position in the center of our perimeter. They were slowly bending the elephant grass to the ground. I assumed they were trying to clear the inside of the perimeter to enable them to observe the Rangers on the outside of the defensive position. We had plenty of concealment, but no cover. I had no idea how far a bullet could plunge through elephant grass without losing it's punch.

The word moved around the perimeter, "No rifle fire, only grenades." I quickly unhooked four frags and placed them next to my knees. Man this was no place for a firefight! They would be on top of us before we spotted them. I'd be better off using a grenade in my fist, like a rock, and clubbing the bastards up-side their heads with it.

Rucker whispered to me, "Every other man, starting with you, move out about five meters and set up a claymore to your front. Slight angle to deflect the back-blast away from us." I quickly dropped my ruck, pulling the antipersonnel mine from its position under the flap. I laid the clacker next to my grenades. I passed the message on to Kilburn as I began uncoiling five meters of electrical cord, then slithered out away from the perimeter to set up the mine. When I reached the point where the slack wire drew taut, I raised up in a squatting position, holding the claymore up in front of me. I unfolded the bipod legs and jammed them down into the earth at my feet. I fed the blasting cap at the end of the electrical wire down through one of the guides, next to the sighting device on the top edge of the mine. When I finished, I screwed the guide down tightly, securing the cap in place, and looked back over my shoulder to line up the claymore with the direction of the wire. I made sure it sat at a forty-five-degree angle to the perimeter. The back-blast could be deadly at five meters.

I flip-flopped position and crawled back along the wire, using it to guide me back to my place on the perimeter. Myers was just returning from putting out his claymore. I attached the reverse end of the wire to the firing mechanism at my feet and made sure the safety was on before setting it back down.

I heard Zo behind me warning the X-ray team that they had at least two enemy forces, approximate size fifty or more, heading for their location. He advised them to prepare for an immediate ground attack. He then called the fire control officer at Firebase Jack and gave him our location and the coordinates for four pre-plots, each 150 meters outside our perimeter. If we got hit during the night, we would need artillery quick and close.

The voice on the other end of the radio advised that our location was too close to his tubes to fire support for us. He advised us to contact Firebase Rakkassan for support. Man, Rakkassan was twelve klicks to our south and back in the mountains!

I looked at my watch. It was 0020! We still had six more hours until daylight. A hell of a lot could happen in six hours.

The waiting began. At 0100, Zo called in a sitrep—negative. The X-ray team whispered back that all was quiet on their end, too.

At 0200 hours, Zo radioed in another negative sitrep. Something was coming. We could all feel it. It was too damn quiet. Looney called back and said that the crickets had stopped chirping outside the wire. The 155s had been set to fire fleshette rounds in defilade. The firebase was on 100 percent alert. They would be ready when the attack came.

At 0220, the ground attack on Firebase Jack began. The deafening roar of a claymore initiated the battle. With only a second's pause, M-16s and M-60s joined in. We listened for the deeper *bap . . . bap . . . bap* sounds of the AK-47s and the steady hammering bursts of the RPD. For the first sixty seconds, it sounded as if the battle was all one-sided, with Screaming Eagles doing all the fighting. Soon, the *krumppp . . . krumppp . . . krumppp* or mortars impacting joined in. We couldn't tell whose they were, but whoever was using them was putting out rounds at a frantic pace.

Wham . . . wham—more claymores, or maybe it was satchel charges! I remembered the lightly guarded rear gate at Jack. Surely it had been breached by the NVA early in the fight. Our X-ray team was in the bunker next to the security position guarding that rear gate.

The battle was still raging fifteen minutes later. Two Cobra gunships from Camp Evans had arrived on station and were taking turns making minigun runs along the west side of the beleaguered firebase. We could hear the steady high-speed burping sound of the rapid-firing guns as their red tracers chewed up the charging NVA soldiers. Thousands of bright-red tracers ricocheted obtusely off into the night. Jesus, what a firefight. Jack must have been getting a real pasting.

Suddenly the elephant grass was full of sounds; sounds that we couldn't at first identify. It was almost like a brushing noise. It seemed off in the distance when we initially heard it. But the volume increased steadily, until it was on both sides of us, then all around us. My God, it was the sound of elephant grass brushing on the clothing of rapidly moving men—a lot of rapidly moving men.

It had to be the main assault. The original attack on Firebase Jack had been a diversion. The real one was just now coming—and it was coming right through us. It sounded like hundreds of men were passing around us. They were in a hurry to get to where they were going. Once in a while they would stop, and dead silence would replace the sounds of the scurrying NVA soldiers. A few seconds would pass while they got their bearings, then it would start all over again.

This lasted for half an hour. I don't know how many of them passed through us, but the knowledge of the numbers would have terrified the men on Firebase Jack.

The movement started to peter out about a half hour after it began. Zo had already reported the current intel to the X-ray team. They had somehow survived the initial assault, but had been forced into fighting within the perimeter defense after a number of sappers had breached the wire and penetrated past the bunker line. The new information about the main attack that was about to hit them left them audibly shaken.

They called back in a few minutes and told us that the firebase commander had called for a Spooky gunship. The C-47 with its Gatling guns was expected at any moment. I had never seen one of the slow-flying fixed-wing gun platforms work out before, but I had been told it was devastating in a static defense role. It would have its hands full tonight! There were one hell of a lot of hostile people between us and Firebase Jack.

Then we heard the real attack begin. It started as a crackling sound, like a heavy volume of large-caliber automatic-weapons fire. None of us recognized it at first. I heard Zo mutter, "Fuck, those are RPGs!" I turned to look back at him. Man, no way! Nobody had that many RPGs in one place. The rocket-propelled grenade launchers were normally used to support an infantry attack by knocking out the hard positions and the machine-gun emplacements. If the sounds we were hearing were RPGs, then the entire attacking force must have been assaulting with them.

I had seen what a single RPG could do. The firebase was catching them by the hundreds. Those poor bastards on Jack were going through hell.

More enemy troops began moving past us again—closer this time. Jack would never survive an assault by so many NVA. They were obviously intent on wiping out the firebase. The Spooky was Jack's only salvation.

Suddenly a claymore exploded on the north side of our perimeter. Marcy's team! Someone on Marcy's team had engaged. We were in it now!

Selector switches clicked from SAFE to AUTOMATIC as each Ranger prepared to sell his life for maximum value. The NVA would have to pay dearly to take us out.

Zo's harsh whisper broke the silence. "No weapons . . . no weapons! Only grenades and claymores. Make sure you know where they are before you blast 'em."

I held on to the CAR-15 with my right hand and reached down to pick up the claymore's clacker with my left. I would blow it first, then use my grenades.

Ten minutes passed. Nothing happened! The movement around us had increased again a few minutes after the claymore had gone off. But then it seemed to have quickly moved off away from us toward the firebase. What were the bastards up to? Were we not big enough game for them? Maybe they weren't sure what they had hit when our claymore had detonated. They could have written it off as a booby trap. But more likely they were under orders to annihilate Jack at all costs. They would be back for us later.

Just when we were beginning to think we had been granted a reprieve, we heard them again. This time they were on two sides of us—north and east. They were moving quickly, in a big hurry to get someplace.

I put the claymore's firing device down and picked up a frag. It would be better to save the claymore for when they actually assaulted our position. The grenades would do a better job as long as they were only trying to locate our position.

We could hear them out in the grass, moving around and talking in brief, muffled conversation. Two grenades exploded twenty meters to my front. I wasn't sure who had thrown them, but I suspected that it was Myers and Garrison from Marcy's team. The movement had been closest to their position. Other Rangers began pitching frags out into the grass around them.

I thumbed the pin out of the grenade I was holding, letting the lever fly. I counted, "One thousand one . . . one thousand two . . ." and flipped it about fifteen meters out in front of my position.

After the explosion, I quickly retrieved my other frag and lobbed it out a little farther from where the first one had landed.

Shrapnel was flying everywhere as our grenades detonated out in the tall grass. The Rangers were trying to confuse the enemy as to our location and to prevent them from mounting an organized attack on our perimeter. It was critical that we keep them off balance until we got some help.

The ground assault against Firebase Jack was still going on. The heavy volume of fire would quickly build up to a frightening crescendo, then suddenly peter away to a few desultory shots—never quite dying out altogether. Then the RPGs' B-40 rockets would start up again, only to be met by another heavy volume of U.S. small-arms fire.

The Cobras had used up their ordnance and returned to Evans to rearm. In their absence, the NVA launched a massive ground assault on the north and west sides of Jack's perimeter. We could hear the hollow pounding of the 155s as they fired into the ranks of the charging NVA at point-blank range.

Minutes later, Closson whispered that the beehive rounds from the big guns had broken the back of the NVA attack. They were pulling back from the perimeter of the firebase. Looney had radioed that the infantry troops were mopping up sappers inside the wire. Spooky had just arrived on station and was circling overhead in case the enemy decided to try another assault. He cautioned us to prepare for an attack on our position and warned us that the NVA still had a lot of people out there. They had failed to take the firebase and would be looking to vent their frustrations on anyone unlucky enough to get in their way. If they retreated west back toward the mountains they had come from, we would be right in their path.

Soon we heard the NVA survivors coming. They were making no effort to conceal their movements. They were coming fast and seemed to be scattered through the grass. It would only be a matter of time before one or more of them stumbled into us.

Zo got on the horn and asked for the circling Spooky. The attack on Jack was apparently over. The ultimate risk had now shifted to us. If we got hit by the full force of the retreating NVA, we would be overrun in a matter of minutes.

The Spooky pilot came up on our net and asked for a heading from Firebase Jack to our perimeter. Zo told him that we were about a thousand meters out on a heading of 265 degrees. Then the team leader turned and whispered loudly, "Who's got a strobe?" Rucker, myself, and three other Rangers where carrying strobe lights. In the glare of a descending parachute flare, I saw Zo motion for Rucker to take up position in the center of the perimeter and turn on his strobe when he gave the signal.

In seconds, the blacked-out C-47 was above us, going into a circular orbit high overhead. Zo pulled the handset away from his ear and said, "Mom, hit the strobe—*now*."

Instantaneously, the pulsing light from Rucker's strobe began blinking crazily. Stupidly, I looked directly at it, destroying my night vision. I turned my head away, squinting to shut out as much of the illumination as possible. The strobe light would act as a beacon, marking our position for the Spooky gunship circling overhead. Unfortunately, it would also expose our position to every NVA soldier within a half mile of our perimeter.

I heard a noise high above me that sounded a lot like someone tearing a large piece of canvas in two. It would have had to have been one hell of a large sheet of canvas, because the ripping sound didn't fade away. I looked up to see a red hose of tracers snaking down toward our perimeter. Man, it was coming right for us. Someone had screwed up and called the miniguns in on our strobe. I dove to the ground, subconsciously flinching as I waited for the rounds to chop us apart. The sound of the bullets impacting twenty-five meters outside our perimeter caused me to curl into a tight ball in an attempt to make myself as small a target as possible.

Finally, I realized that the Spooky was not firing on us. The deadly miniguns were laying down a solid wall of lead around our perimeter, stitching the ground in a deadly circle twenty-five meters out. I was amazed at the accuracy of the twin-engined gunship circling fifteen hundred feet above us. I had seen Spookies work out before, but it had always been at great distance. Sitting on the bull's-eye while one chewed up everything around you was an experience that one would not soon forget. I had no doubt that as long as our friend stayed overhead, no enemy soldier would come any closer than twenty-five meters from our position.

We tightened up our perimeter and hugged the ground as the gunship continued its deadly workout. Only Rucker exposed himself, as he knelt in the center of the perimeter holding the strobe light above his head. I wondered what the chance was of the gunship drifting a little too much to one side or the other and shredding our position with a brief burst of minigun fire. I didn't believe that anything could be that accurate for any extended period of time, especially at night. I was wrong!

An explosion erupted behind me. It was too dull to have been a claymore or a frag. I heard someone whisper that Marvel McCann had been hit by a ChiCom grenade. The Indian from California had been nicked in the back of the neck by a piece of shrapnel. It wasn't serious enough to require a medevac, but it alerted us to the fact that our position was now known to the enemy.

The Spooky remained on station until 0345. It radioed that it was running low on fuel and ammunition and would have to return to Da Nang. A replacement would be over us in about ten minutes, but we would be on our own until then. He gave us the call sign for the next Spooky and wished us good luck before signing off.

As the C-47 left its orbit and headed south, a Cobra gunship came over us and requested that we switch our strobe back on. He was going to attempt a couple of passes around our perimeter in an effort to keep the enemy off of us until the next Spooky arrived. Rucker hit the strobe again as the Snake began its first run along the north edge of our perimeter. Aerial rockets *whoosh*ed down and exploded in the tall grass in front of our position. One of them hit close enough to us to shower us with dirt and debris. Marcy yelled that Fadeley had been hit. Zo grabbed the radio and screamed into the handset, ''Break off! Break off! You're hitting us.''

The Cobra flashed past in the night, swinging wide to the north as it pulled off its attack. The pilot radioed back that he wouldn't make another pass. His voice sounded broken.

Rucker turned off the strobe light and dropped back into the grass next to me. He whispered in my face, ''Man, this looks bad, doesn't it?'' I nodded in agreement, not knowing if he could see me.

Lawhon reported that Fadeley had been hit in the head, but it had only been a nick. He was conscious and ready to get back into action. So far, we had been very lucky!

A couple of minutes passed before the second Spooky came on station. Zo crawled over and told Rucker to hold up his strobe light again. I knew Mother's arm had to be in pretty bad shape. He had knelt for nearly two hours with the beacon flashing above his head. I told him to switch places with me. He nodded his appreciation and moved over to where I had been crouched in the grass. I handed him the firing device to my claymore and indicated the direction it was facing. He offered his strobe light to me, but I held mine up to show him that he had not been the only one with enough foresight to bring one along. We slid past each other, exchanging positions in the dark.

Dragging my rucksack behind me, I moved into the center of our little perimeter. Someone had mashed all the grass back toward the outer positions. Zo sat next to his RTO as he carried on a three-way conversation with the Spooky and the X-ray team on the firebase.

I laid the rucksack in the grass, frame side down, using it for a makeshift seat. Then I held the strobe high overhead and switched it on. The bright, flashing light pulsated in my hand.

I nearly dropped the strobe when the second Spooky zeroed in on our perimeter and cut loose with a barrage of red death. The rounds hit outside our perimeter and splashed back up into the sky, reminding me of molten lava washing over a cliff. I couldn't control an unconscious shudder when I saw the tracers bouncing all over the place. I hoped the gunners were as good as the ones in the first Spooky.

It would be daylight in another hour and a half. If we could hold out until then, the gooks would be gone. They wouldn't stand a chance in the open when the sun came up. The Cobras would be swarming at first light, and we had already been told an infantry company would be combat-assaulted into us in the morning.

It was after 0500, and my arm was beginning to cramp. I had been holding the strobe above my head for more than an hour, and it had gained at least fifty pounds. It would be daylight soon. I had to hold on.

The Rangers had stopped throwing frags into the grass, and the sounds of movement had dropped off in the last thirty minutes. What were the gooks up to? Were they out there ready to attack the moment we let down our guard, or had they hurried back into the mountains to avoid getting caught in the open when the sun rose behind Firebase Jack?

March 29, 1969

The sky was beginning to lighten to the east. My arm had gone numb. I had slid down alongside my ruck so I could use it to support my elbow. It was the only way I could keep the strobe upright. Zo crawled next to me and told me to shut it off. The second Spooky had run low on fuel and had just returned to base. Four Cobras were coming out to baby-sit us until the reaction force reached into us.

My arm dropped across the top of my rucksack. I had nothing left to offer. I couldn't have whipped a salute if General Westmoreland himself had materialized before me. Matter of fact, I doubted I could even have offered a handshake.

We had survived being surrounded by a large NVA force as it assaulted Firebase Jack. We had only two WIAs, and they both had light wounds. We had been unbelievably lucky once again. It almost made me believe the rumor that Jesus Christ had been a Ranger before he decided to save mankind. I shoved the strobe deep into a thigh pocket and slumped against my rucksack. No more! No more! I needed a break before I could be productive again.

The sun was now a big orange ball in the east. We could see Firebase Jack at its base, still smoking from the battle of the evening before. I wondered how hard they had been hit. They had stopped the infantry in the wire, but several of the sappers had penetrated the perimeter before the real attack started. They had gotten through the wire even though the firebase had been alerted and the grunts had been ready for them. My God, what would have happened if we had not been out in the grass?

Looney told us that a line company was being pulled out of the field and would be CAing into us around 0800. We were to remain in place until they arrived. He told us the commander of the firebase wanted to personally thank us for the early warning. He didn't think they would have been able to beat off the NVA without it. I felt very proud when Zo stood in the middle of the perimeter and relayed the captain's words to us. We had done a good job. There were a lot of grunts and redlegs on Firebase Jack who were alive today because of us.

The team leaders had every other man chow down while the rest of us pulled security. With all the excitement, I hadn't realized how hungry and thirsty I had become. My stomach felt like an apartment complex for a hundred nervous leeches, and my mouth was an alum douche. I took a long, hard swig from one of my canteens. The warm, stale water tasted delicious going down. I flipped the canteen to Rucker, who grimaced when he reached to catch it. I had forgotten. His arms had to be as sore as mine. He nodded his thanks, took a long swig, and spilled it down the front of his blouse, just as shots rang out directly across the perimeter.

"It's a gook over by the tree line!" shouted Marvel McCann. He had stood to stretch, and was rubbing the dressing on his neck wound when he spotted the NVA soldier standing in the chest-high grass, fifty meters to the south. The gook was just off the end of the tree line where Rucker had spotted the radio antenna the morning before. Marvel wasn't sure if he had killed the gook, but he had dropped in the grass like he had been hit. He wanted to take a couple of Rangers out to check the area, but Marcy told him to wait for the reaction force. If the gook was dead, he wouldn't be going anywhere. And if he wasn't, it would be better to let him bleed for a while. Just like going after a crippled deer. You chase too soon and they just run off. You can't push 'em. Better off just to let them stiffen up and bleed to death. Besides, running over there too soon could get somebody killed. And for what—a body count? We would wait for the reaction force.

It was 1030 before the line company CAed into the elephant grass. The temperature had climbed to over 100 degrees, and we were drenched in our own sweat. We weren't used to the lowland heat. There was no shade, and the sun made us pay for each minute spent in the open. I missed the mountains. It could get hot there, too, but nothing like the frying pan we were in.

Once the line company was on the ground, they spent another half hour trying to get on line and move over to link up with us. Their Six kept radioing back that they were already finding numerous blood trails in the grass to their front.

Finally their point element ran into our right flank, as we stood strung out in the elephant grass. When we had joined forces, we moved out slowly through the dense cover, looking for the enemy dead we knew had to be there.

It took us more than an hour and a half to cover two hundred meters. Everyone was hitting blood trails and finding abandoned NVA equipment. No one found any bodies.

Two Huey slicks circled above us the entire time. Brass! Fucking rear-echelon, chair-borne officers, out looking for a body count. Assholes! We kill 'em and they want to hang the heads over their fireplaces. Let them get down here in the trenches with us and walk through this goddamn awful suffocating grass. If they didn't get us out of this ass-kickin' roasting oven soon, they'd be looking for our bodies.

We kept moving toward the tree line. Seemed like a waste of time now. The gooks would be gone. The NVA commo people had called for the attack on Firebase Jack. It was over now. They wouldn't have waited around to count coup.

The sun drew higher in the sky, beating down directly on us. There was no cover anywhere. Just the damn searing, ungodly hot rays focusing on the Rangers and para-troopers moving through the elephant grass. Closson's team was on the right flank as the hundred plus U.S. soldiers swept toward the tree line. I was on the very end. I looked at Rucker and Lawhon. Both were beet red and puffing as we pushed ahead. The sun was getting to me, too; I was already soaked. Maybe the tree line would be cooler. There were trees and a stream in the tree line. Yeah, water and shade. It had to be better there.

Another fifty meters. Lawhon was looking bad—heat exhaustion. I had seen it before. I whistled to get Closson's attention. He wouldn't respond. The team leader just kept plowing ahead, concentrating on the tree line, like the rest of us.

It was only twenty-five meters away. We could cool off when we reached it. Just a few more steps. Lawhon was staggering, head swaying side to side. I told Rucker to watch him and moved in his direction. He wasn't going to make it to the trees. Fuckin' heat!

Then we were there. Lawhon collapsed in a heap next to the brush at the base of the trees. I moved toward him, intent on giving him aid, but discovered that my legs were no longer functioning properly. They felt like they each weighed a hundred pounds. My eyes weren't focusing. The trees didn't look right . . . swaying . . .

I don't know how long I was out. When I came to, Zo and Marcy were kneeling over me, draping a wet, smelly towel across my face. I felt clammy, but my skin seemed almost dry. Two other Rangers were working on Lawhon—no, it was Closson. Damn, he was down, too. Lawhon lay on the other side of Closson. Fadeley and Garrison were trying to bring him around. The young Ranger looked bad, his face appeared flushed and swollen.

I tried to sit up—nothing. My body wouldn't respond to the messages my brain was feeding it. Zo was saying, "Stay down, dammit. We got dust offs comin' in. You guys are goin' to the hospital."

They poured precious water from their canteens over us, trying to cool down the sky-rocketing temperatures raging through our bodies. The heat exhaustion had snuck up on us, catching us before we had known it was happening.

I told myself that I just needed to rest for a while, maybe catch a few Z's. Then I'd be ready to move out again.

I awoke to the sounds of helicopters. Two of them were sitting out in the shoulder-high elephant grass, the rotor wash fanning the razor-sharp grass against the ground. In my dazed state, they looked like two oversize dragonflies sitting on nests. I could see the huge red crosses painted on their noses. What was wrong? Had somebody gotten hit? Then they were picking me up, carrying me toward one of the waiting choppers.

"What the fuck's going on?" I croaked to anyone who

would listen. "Put me down. I'm okay." I looked up to see Zo's face above me. He seemed to be smiling, but either his face or his smile were upside down.

They slid me in across the floor of the cabin. The crew chief hurriedly shoved me against the back wall. I could see Lawhon and Closson being loaded aboard the other chopper.

Then I saw Zo turn away from me and yell, "Mother, get your ass on board. You look like shit, too."

Then the chopper was taking off, turning as it climbed away from the LZ. I got one quick glimpse of the U.S. soldiers strung out through the tall grass, then I could only see the sky outside the open door of the medevac. Rucker lay next to me. Zo was right! He did look like shit.

I relaxed, willing to let the cool wind flowing through the open cabin blow over me. It didn't seem to cool me at all. I felt like I was on fire. Some shade, maybe some cool water, and I'd be ready to go again.

The medevac set down on a PSP pad with a huge red cross painted inside a white circle. It hadn't seemed as if we'd been airborne very long. Must be Camp Evans!

Bunch of guys in utility pants and OD T-shirts pulling us out of the Hueys and putting us on stretchers. Grunt, you assholes! It ain't no Vietnamese you're carryin'.

Inside now. Cool! Everything's so clean and cool. They seem to be in a big hurry. Sliding me onto a bed. Man, I'm filthy. Let me get cleaned up first. Well, piss on you then. I don't have to wash these sheets. Jesus H. Christ! Is that ice they're pouring all over me? Break out the JB! Can't be wastin' this shit! Man, I ought to be freezin' my ass off. Feels good, like somebody's ticklin' me all over.

An orderly showed up with a couple of tall bottles of ice-cold, frosty Coke with long white straws protruding from the top of each. "Here," he said, "drink these. You need to get as much cold liquid into you as you can. I'll be back with some more as soon as you down these." Fuckin' unbelievable! Ice-cold Coke! Ten minutes ago I was sweating my ass off out in the boonies trying to flush out a bunch of NVA. Now I'm lying in ice cubes up to my chin sippin' soda. What a way to fight a war!

After my fourth cold Coke, I started to feel like my old self again. Things seemed to make sense again. I could feel the ice, or what was left of it. The shit was definitely cold. I tried to climb out of the bed, but discovered that I was physically drained—like somebody had just pulled me out from under a squad of Marines with a hard-on for U.S. Army Rangers.

My vision had cleared. I could see Lawhon, Closson, and Rucker across the aisle from me, also packed in ice and sipping Cokes through straws. They held up their bottles and toasted me. They each had dumb grins plastered across their faces. My own grin, beneath all the dirt, beard, and washed-out camouflage paint, must have looked just as goofy to them.

An orderly with a chart draped across his left arm stopped at the foot of my bed and asked me my name. I said, "Hell, I don't know. But don't worry, my insurance will cover everything—well maybe not the Cokes."

Rucker busted out laughing. "Hey, I got the Cokes. Closson, you get the ice. Ricky New Guy can pick up the tip."

That cracked everybody up. Everybody, that is, except the orderly. "Okay, you guys. Cut the crap, now. I need to get this information so we can discharge you goldbricks. At least we know you haven't suffered any brain damage."

Closson grinned and said, "Shit, man, we're Rangers. We ain't got no brains."

When the laughter subsided, we gave the frustrated REMF the information he needed, and he charged out through a pair of swinging doors at the end of the ward. Some guys just don't have as well-developed sense of humor as we Rangers have!

None of us could believe how fast we had recovered from heat exhaustion. We must have really been overheated. All of that wonderful ice had turned into puddles of cool water around us.

The medic returned with a doctor who briefly looked us over, then pronounced that we were fit to return to our unit. He seemed flushed with pride over the miraculous recoveries he had wrought. I must admit, we were all pretty impressed ourselves. He told us that he was sending us back to Camp Eagle, but recommended that we wait a couple of days before going back out in the field again.

That was fine by me. I only had sixty-seven days and a wake-up to go.

We climbed out of the beds, dripping water over the tiled floors of the dispensary. I noticed that the sheets were plastic. Must have been a special ward reserved just for sunstroke cases. The orderly handed each of us a written release and told us that a copy would be filed with our medical records at division. We were to give the release to someone at our unit dispensary.

We walked down to the end of the ward and retrieved our weapons and gear. Another orderly looked up from his Superman comic long enough to tell us to wait out on the chopper pad. A slick would be along by-and-by to give us a lift back to Camp Eagle.

It was still hot outside, but nothing like the stifling, man-killing heat that had made casualties out of us in the elephant grass west of Firebase Jack. We wondered how the rest of the guys had made out after they had medevaced us out of the bush. None of them had shown up at the hospital. Fadeley and McCann had been hit during the fight. Were they still out in the field with the rest of the teams, or had they all been extracted? I sure hoped that they had been brought in. If they were still out there while we were winging our way back to the rear, we would all be branded as a bunch of pussies when they returned from the mission.

We sat on the horizontal, wooden electrical poles ringing the chopper pad and waited around for an hour before a slick from the 101st Aviation Battalion landed to drop off some medical supplies. Closson walked over to the pilot's side of the ship and asked him if he was going back to Eagle. When he nodded in the affirmative, the team leader asked him if we could catch a ride back with him. He nodded his head and hooked his left thumb back over his shoulder.

We tossed our gear into the cabin and climbed in. The sun had already dried our soaked jungle fatigues. The portside door gunner tossed a pack of Winstons to us, and we quickly passed them around before the chopper got airborne.

The ride back was a treat. The cool air blowing through the cabin soon erased the remnants of the heat exhaustion we had suffered earlier in the day. The twenty-minute flight was over too soon. The pilot set us down on the Ranger acid pad and took off again before we had a chance to properly thank him for the lift.

Dan Croker, George Thomas, Miller, and Sours came out of the Ranger lounge to welcome us back. Their comments were expected, but still rankled us as we walked off the pad lugging our gear. "You profilin' motherfuckers! Couldn't take the heat, huh? You poor little goldbricks get too much sun today? Hope you girls had a good time visiting the wounded soldiers at the hospital." I shot them a look that was meant to kill, not cripple, and they all ran laughing back into the lounge. Fuckin' dickheads!

March 30, 1969

The rest of the teams had been pulled out right after we had been medevaced. I guess it took at least four heat-stroke casualties to convince the lifers at brigade to extract us. The rest of the Rangers and the line company had found no enemy bodies during their sweep of the elephant grass. But the fifty-six separate blood trails they found told the true story. Jack had accounted for another hundred and twelve NVA bodies inside and outside their perimeter wire, including an NVA sapper found hiding in the back of the mess hall the morning after the fight. The mess sergeant who discovered him shot him to death with a .45 pistol. Too merciful a death! He should have just fed him.

Only six GIs had been killed on Jack. Another fifteen had been wounded. Our X-ray team had escaped unscathed after some horrendous fighting.

The beehive rounds fired by the 155s had broken the attack. No one could have stood up to the thousands of steel darts fired at point-blank range. We had been given credit for saving the firebase from being overrun. Our early

warning had put the infantry and artillerymen on Jack on
full alert and had enabled them to catch the sappers infil-
trating the wire. It was a nice gesture. No one had ever
formally expressed their appreciation of our services before.

Chambers had missed a good mission. The pussy had
been away enjoying himself at MACV Recondo School
down in Nha Trang while we were out dealing with the
enemy. I guess we were lucky that he had been away. He
would have never given us any slack if he had been around
when the chopper brought us back from the hospital.

March 31, 1969

Closson, Lawhon, Rucker, and I checked in at sick call
in the morning. We were okay, so the medic who checked
us had the resident doctor release us for full duty. Closson
told me on the way back to the Ranger compound that he
hadn't really been worried about dying when we were out
at Jack. He smiled and told me that he was saving up all
his worrying for that mission into the A Shau I had fore-
casted. Another goddamned clown! That was all I needed.

April 1, 1969

April Fool's Day! It was the same day that Chambers
was scheduled to graduate from Recondo School. How
appropriate! We couldn't wait for the big clown to return.

His everpresent sense of humor and his harassing satire served to keep us on our toes. You had to be prepared when he was around; shit-burning detail was better duty than being on the receiving end of one of his humorous bash sessions. None of us would ever let on that we really appreciated his wit. He found the funny side to every situation.

Myers and I received word that we were going to be transferred to the Americal Division at Chu Lai at the end of April or the first part of May. We would receive our commissions to second lieutenant when we arrived at our new units. I was scheduled to leave for R & R on the twenty-ninth of April. Well, if it came down to choosing one over the other, I would skip the vacation. I had tried too hard and too long for the commission. I would only have thirty-five days or so left in-country after commissioning, and I really couldn't think of a better way to spend it.

April 2, 1969

I went over to division HQ to sign some papers for the commissioning. I had to wait an hour to get to see someone, and when I was finally called in, it wasn't to sign any papers. The division sergeant major sat me down and told me that he wanted to make sure I understood what the commission entailed. He said that I would be going to Fort Benning after I DEROSed and finished my leave. I had to complete an abbreviated OCS course to make sure that I knew how to conduct myself as an officer and a gentleman. Then, it would be nine months to a year somewhere as a training or range officer—to sharpen my ability to lead men. If I was lucky, I would get another thirty-day leave before the army shipped me back over to Nam as an infantry platoon leader.

Damn, it had never even occurred to me that they would send me back over so soon. I couldn't say anything for a few minutes. I thought about the promise I had made to myself. If I survived this tour, I would never put my girl (soon to be my wife) through this shit again. This tour had been tough enough on her, yet she had handled it like a trooper. Another tour, just a year after our marriage, would kill her.

I asked the sergeant major when I had to sign the paperwork. He told me that I had a week to make up my mind. I thanked him for his information and left his office for the long walk back to the Ranger compound. Damn, damn, damn! What a decision! I had my lifelong dream within my grasp, and I had to chose between its fulfillment and a life with the woman I loved. Well, I had seven days to make up my mind.

April 3, 1969

Chambers returned from Recondo School. The asshole had come back as the hero of his class. We shouldn't have been surprised. The lucky fart had a way of falling into a barrel of shit and come out smelling like a rose. It had been Chambers who was next to the ammo bunker when it blew up several months back. He came away with a slight ringing in his ears.

Each member of every Recondo School class had to go out on a training mission at the end of the three-week course. Each team was usually composed of six students and one course instructor. Each man was required to serve in every team position during the mission—from junior scout to team leader.

The remaining students in Larry's class were sent out in six operational ten-man heavy teams. They were flown to an area about twenty klicks southwest of Da Nang for their training missions. A reinforced company of two hundred CIDGs provided support.

The teams inserted at first light on March 20. The first day proved uneventful. There were trails in the AO, but there didn't seem to be any fresh sign. It looked like it would be little more than a training mission.

On the second day, Chambers was selected to walk point. He moved the team out, putting the dog and pony show on for his training instructor, SfC. Cliff Roberts from 5th Special Forces Group. Roberts was the type of Special Forces soldier who would make John Wayne look like a fake. Roberts, along only as an observer, walked slack position a few meters behind Chambers. As an experienced Ranger, Larry enjoyed the opportunity to show his stuff.

About midday, Chambers led the team in a circle to ambush their back-trail. After setting up briefly, just to show the instructor he knew what he was doing, Chambers led them down a nearby high-speed trail that was to be their monitoring zone for an ambush the next morning.

He stopped the team frequently, listening for a few minutes before moving out again. Chambers was on cloud nine. He enjoyed walking point. That's where all the action was. Good point men enjoyed the respect of everyone on the team. Most guys wouldn't do it. It was the one position where, if you weren't any good, you couldn't disguise it. If you believed in your abilities, there was no place else in patrol formation you would ever want to be. Everyone's life depended on your skill, your judgment, and your performance. You weren't comfortable with anyone else up there.

Chambers was enjoying himself immensely. He was in his element, performing under the eyes of Sergeant First Class Roberts. If he did well, he could come away with the dagger awarded to the honor graduate of each class.

The team members were spaced about five meters apart and were headed up the face of a muddy hill. A deep valley was on their right. The fourth man back was carrying the M-79 and pushing through some heavy wait-a-minute vines when one caught on his trigger and fired off the grenade launcher. Pop! *Ka-wham!* The round exploded about two hundred meters down the hill from where the team crouched frozen in the trail. Roberts turned on the

hapless student and threatened to ram the butt of the grenade launcher down his throat.

While the hapless spec four was paying his dues for his
carelessness, Chambers heard movement to their front. He
snapped his fingers, signaling for the team to freeze where
they were. They listened for ten minutes—nothing! He was
sure something had moved ahead of them.

Chambers moved over the crest of the hill and continued down the trail on the other side. He knew if there
were any gooks around, they would have heard the round
detonate in the valley below. But he doubted they would
know exactly where the round had come from or what had
happened. They would be aware, however, that someone
else was in the area. Chambers moved the team forward
for another two hours until they came to a large clearing
on the side of the hill. It was the kind of clearing where
one usually spotted deer feeding early in the morning.
They waited for ten more minutes, then Chambers moved
them another ten meters down the trail.

He stopped to move brush with his left hand. When he
pulled his hand back, it was wet with thick, yellow mucus—human mucus. Without looking back at his instructor, Chambers held up his hand, palm to the rear, to show
the big NCO what he had discovered. Roberts smiled as
Chambers moved the team forward again.

Chambers's heart was pounding. He could feel the ten-
sion in the air. They were close, real close. He could almost smell them up ahead. He only hoped he would spot
them before they saw him.

They moved on for another hour, through a dense curtain of vines, leaves, and bamboo shoots. It was becoming
increasingly difficult to see for any distance. Chambers
stopped the team to listen again. He was watching the trail
ahead when he saw an NVA soldier sit up in some low
vegetation thirty meters away. It was eerie. One minute
the trail was empty—the next, an NVA soldier was sitting
there trying to see what Chambers was doing. He appeared to be on his knees, talking to someone behind him.
The gook was having a difficult time identifying the strange
soldier on the trail ahead.

Chambers slowly, but deliberately, raised his CAR-15,
silently thumbing the selector switch to FIRE, and placed

three well-aimed shots into the head of the surprised enemy soldier. He was looking at Chambers as the shots tore his head apart, then he fell heavily to the right of the trail and lay still.

Chambers heard more movement coming from down the trail behind the dead NVA. He flipped the selector switch over to AUTOMATIC and emptied the rest of the magazine into the jungle behind the slain enemy.

He turned to run back to the end of the patrol. Rangers were taught to fire, then leapfrog back to the end of the patrol when contact was made. The next man would empty his weapon and likewise fall back to the rear. In this manner, the enemy was kept constantly under fire as the team withdrew. They could cover a lot of ground without breaking contact.

However, Chambers quickly found that only Roberts and a sergeant named Duty, from L Company, had held their positions to cover the men to the front. The remainder of the team was busy hauling ass for the rear. Their heroics left Chambers, Roberts, and Duty without any cover. When Chambers saw what was unfolding ahead of him, he stopped and jammed another magazine into his weapon and turned to face the enemy. Roberts almost bowled Duty over, charging up to the front with the M-79 to support Chambers.

The first round from the grenade launcher exploded fifteen feet in front of Chambers, sending shrapnel whizzing back over their heads. Chambers ignored it, emptying his weapon into the trees where he had killed the first NVA.

Duty moved up to their support, his CAR-15 blazing. Roberts was busy walking high explosive rounds into the mass of vegetation down the trail.

Finally Roberts signaled for the other two to follow him back up the trail to where the rest of the team lay huddled in a hasty defense perimeter. When the three of them reached the band of reluctant heroes, they could smell the sickening aroma of shit in the air.

Roberts got them on their feet and pulled the entire team back another five hundred meters. He radioed in the contact and requested willie pete (white phosphorus) air burst over the area where Chambers had killed the NVA.

With the artillery rounds impacting behind them, Roberts moved the team farther from the area. It was 2030 hours and growing darker by the minute. It was too late for an extraction, and they wouldn't be able to get a re-action force in before morning.

The team crawled into a thicket and stayed hidden until daybreak. They would get little sleep during the night. Enemy troops came looking for them, periodically sweep-ing through the area until daylight.

At 0400 hours, Roberts crawled to where Chambers lay in heavy cover. He wanted to discuss what they would do if they got hit during the night. He needed to make sure Chambers could get the rest of the team out in case some-thing happened to him or they got separated in the dark-ness. He was real pissed at the rest of the patrol for running off when they made contact. Chambers appreciated the attention and recognition Roberts was showing him.

The Special Forces NCO woke Chambers at 0530 and told him he had decided to take the team back up the same trail to see what they could find. He felt the NVA had probably pulled back before the sun came up. He wanted Chambers at point again, telling him he didn't trust any-one else to do it. Roberts promised him he would cover his ass if he walked into something.

Chambers wasn't sure the promise was enough. He knew the odds were good that they would make contact if they went back down the trail.

It took him two hours to reach the spot again. He sig-naled Roberts that they were there, then motioned for the team to wait in place while he moved ahead, alone. After scouting another fifty meters down the trail, Chambers found ten NVA rucksacks and many blood trails going off in several directions. They had hit the jackpot!

Chambers knew better than to touch the equipment. The gooks had had plenty of time to booby trap everything and set up an ambush. Now it was time for Roberts to call in his strike force.

An hour later, Roberts was on the radio directing the link-up with his reaction force. Chambers decided to do a little point recon fifty meters farther down the trail. After he had covered the distance, he stopped to listen and was surprised when an NVA officer stepped out from behind a tree into the middle of the trail.

Chambers whipped his weapon up, thumbing for the selector switch. The NVA panicked and fled. Chambers took off after him and caught the gook with a flying tackle before he had covered ten meters.

The enemy officer began screaming. Chambers tried to keep him quiet, but only succeeded in making him yell louder. The undaunted Ranger grabbed his CAR-15 and shoved it down the throat of the terrified officer. He clammed up immediately.

Roberts arrived moments later, quickly took in the situation, and started to laugh. There was Chambers, astride the officer, struggling to remove the officer's brass belt buckle. The shiny buckle with the bold red star in the center was one of the choicest souvenirs an American soldier could get. In the course of the wrestling match, the CAR-15, still in the NVA's mouth, had slid around to where it was pointing at Larry's crotch. Roberts, still laughing, said, "Don't shoot him, Chambers, you'll blow off your own nuts."

By then, the young NVA officer was nearly in shock. Chambers later found out the gook had never seen an American before and had actually thought Chambers was a Korean when he first spotted him. The Vietnamese were scared to death of ROK soldiers.

Suddenly they could hear choppers coming in with the CIDG troops. Within the hour, a hundred soldiers of the strike force had linked up with the team and were sending out patrols looking for trouble.

An interrogator questioned the enemy POW for several minutes before reporting that he was the platoon leader of an NVA medical unit. They had just arrived that day from North Vietnam, after traveling the Ho Chi Minh Trail for over a month.

Only Chambers could pull off a stunt like that without getting himself killed. He tried hard to play the role of a humble hero, but his head had swollen to the point where he could wear a steel pot without the liner. Ah, what the hell! He deserved every bit of the recognition the guys in the company gave him.

April 5, 1969

We got a warning order for a mission on the seventh. I would be going out again as Closson's ATL. The amazing part of the order was that we would be going into the exact AO along the Song Bo River where we had pulled two previous missions. I told Larry we ought to just skip the overflight since we had the damn place memorized. I wouldn't exactly call it a hot AO, but we had always found a few enemy soldiers in the vicinity.

Our mission was to monitor river traffic again. I already figured we would end up back out on that point where Closson had gotten his heel blown off by our own artillery. We weren't real crazy about going back there, but the site of our previous OP along the river would be hard to improve upon.

Closson told us during the premission briefing to bring extra claymores. He wanted to ring the OP with two layers of the deadly mines, just in case the NVA happened to be running spot checks on our old OP.

We selected an LZ on the first pass, not wanting to spend any more time than necessary flying over the AO. The NVA would get suspicious real fast if a Huey started buzzing the area. We decided to insert about four hundred meters north of the river on the same ridgeline where our OP was situated. It was not the best idea in the world, but the only other choices were on the top of the bald primary ridge where we had made the mistake of inserting during our first mission in the AO or down on one of the gravel bars along the river. The bad news there was that every gook in the area would hear us come in. It would be just too damned obvious that we had landed on the north side of the river, since the south bank was nearly all bluff, right down to the waterline. Once they knew which bank we

were on, they would only have to sweep along the shore
until they flushed us.

I wasn't really worried about the mission being a bad
one, but when you were down to sixty days and a wake-
up, they were all bad. I borrowed Dan Roberts's tape deck
and recorded another tape for Barb. For some reason, a
letter just didn't seem appropriate that evening. I was
looking forward to my DEROS, June 5, but I still had a
nagging concern about that stupid dream I had had a few
weeks earlier. It wasn't like me to be overly cautious. I
felt a yellow streak running down my back that I was anything but proud of.

April 7, 1969

We went in a half hour before dark. I hated last-light
insertions. They were unforgiving. Everything had to go
just right. The LZ had to be cold. You had to go to cover
quickly without getting a good feel for your surroundings.
You could be setting up your NDP in the middle of an
NVA regimental base camp and never know it.

We moved quickly off the LZ, going north to set a false
trail for anyone trying to track us. Two hundred meters
away, we circled around and set up an NDP twenty meters
off our back trail. At least we would hear them following
us through the dried brush.

We only put out three claymores, trying to make as little
noise as possible. No one ate. No one talked. We were
too far from the river to try to reach it in the dark, so we
decided to just spend the first night laying dog. We would
take our time the next day moving into position along the
Song Bo.

April 8, 1969

I was on point as we moved out at 0700. The night had been quiet—almost too quiet. We moved slowly through the dense single-canopy jungle. We had six hundred meters to cover, and I planned to take the entire day getting there. We didn't want to move into position during the daylight hours, so we planned a zigzag course between the ridge we were on and the next one across the valley to our west. I had to time it so we reached the OP position a half hour before dark. We would move past it, making sure it hadn't been tampered with, then swing back around to move into it after nightfall. It made a big difference being familiar with the terrain.

I dropped off the side of the ridge and angled down toward the valley below. I moved away from the river, still trying to lay a misleading trail in case we were followed.

The valley was level and narrow, little more than fifty meters at its widest spot. The vegetation was dense scrub brush and scattered trees with thick clusters of reeds and bamboo along the shallow stream running toward the Song Bo.

I stopped often to listen and wait, never covering more than fifteen to twenty meters at a time. I didn't like the valley any more than I liked the AO. We had hit gooks in there twice before, but I did not believe that we had caused any mass migration from the area. No, they were still around.

I crossed the valley and moved thirty meters up the opposite ridge, still angling away from the river. The cover opened up a bit, so I swung back to the right, circling around downhill and recrossing our back-trail.

Rucker made sure that our crossing was sterile. The gooks would have a difficult time figuring out what we had done, or that we were now moving back in the opposite direction toward the Song Bo.

I stayed on that ridge for another two hours. I was tempted to see what was on the other side, but we weren't being paid to be nosy on this particular mission. Not even when we cut a fresh trail coming up the valley from the river and running up over the crest of the ridge we were on.

The trail was a good reason to recross the valley and move to the general vicinity of our OP. It was already early afternoon. We had three hundred meters to cover in three hours. No hurry!

Closson signaled for me to stop the team at the base of the low ridge across the valley. He wanted to wait awhile longer before we made the final move to reach the OP at dusk. We were only a hundred meters northwest of the point where it overlooked the river.

Fifteen minutes later, we were up and moving diagonally up the ridge. It was a short climb, less than fifty feet up. When we reached the crest, I was glad to see that the bamboo thickets we had hid in before were less than twenty meters away. There was no sign of the enemy on this side of the valley we had just crossed.

I squatted in the shoulder-high brush for fifteen more minutes, listening for sounds that were out of the ordinary. Dusk was approaching. I could hear the birds whistling and calling as they hopped from limb to limb looking for a final morsel of food before they went to roost. The nocturnal insects were beginning to stir, adding their buzzing, clicking, and chirping to the calls of the birds.

The natural sounds around our hidden team told me what I wanted to know. We were alone! The enemy was not ahead, waiting for us.

I waved the team up and moved across the crest of the ridge in a crouch, not wanting to show my head above the brush. Just over the top, I swung back around to the right and entered the bamboo from the east. The natural depression was just as we had left it on the last mission. I was pleased to see that there was no indication that six Rangers had spent several nights there less than five weeks ago. The damage to the bamboo above the site of our OP was still there, though. Shrapnel from the artillery we had brought in had torn great gashes through the tightly packed stalks. The severed branches and narrow leaves had turned yellow in death and littered the ground around the shallow depression.

Closson moved the team into the low spot and motioned for Rucker to move down to the river to check for sign. I circled out in the brush to our north to make sure we hadn't been followed. We both returned ten minutes later, shaking our heads: we had found nothing. Closson looked relieved. He was feeling the pressure, too.

We set eight claymores around our position and moved back inside the perimeter just as darkness settled over us. A full moon was already coming up downstream, reflecting its illumination up the river. It wouldn't be hard to see anything moving on the water tonight!

Closson set six two-hour security watches and assigned one to each member of the team. I drew the 0200–0400 shift. I couldn't understand why the beefy team leader was going with two-hour shifts. He knew the danger of men going to sleep on those long, lonely vigils, especially when they were tired. Well, it was his team, and it wasn't my place to criticize.

I stayed awake until around 2300. Closson had moved up to the hole in the bamboo where he could monitor the river right after he had eaten his evening meal. He was still there when I dropped off to sleep.

April 9, 1969

Rucker woke me at 0200. I sat up, rubbing the sleep from my eyes and looked over to the observation point. Closson was still there, watching the river. I grabbed the 9mm Sten gun I was carrying and crawled up next to him. He looked bushed! I told him to get some sack, I would take his place. He nodded and slid back into the NDP.

The ground was still warm where he had lain. I couldn't understand why he had pulled an eight-hour guard shift, since his normal spot in the security rotation was 0400–0600, right after mine. I decided to pull a double shift and let him sleep—unless I found it impossible to remain awake.

The moon had traversed a 180-degree path during the night and was just sinking behind the mountains to the west. I could no longer see the river out in front of me. Now it was time for my ears to replace my eyes. I cupped a hand behind each ear, amplifying the sounds around me. It was a trick I had learned hunting deer back in Missouri. It tripled sound amplitude and eliminated any distractions from the rear.

I would turn to the north every so often, to listen in that direction—just to make sure that our friends from the last mission along the Song Bo didn't come calling again.

The night passed quietly. I surprised myself, pulling the team leader's shift without getting groggy. He didn't say anything when I woke everyone at 0600. There would be time during the day to catch a few Zs, since we were to remain in the OP for another night.

We chowed down on our first meal of the day. The spaghetti LRRP was good for a change. We had taken advantage of the light fog around us and heated water for our LRRP rations and coffee. We used marble-size balls of C-4 to bring the water in our canteen cups to a fast boil. The C-4 gave off no odor or smoke when it was lit, and burned with more intensity than heat tabs.

I downed my antimalarial pill with the last of my coffee and immediately wished for a second cup. I took a couple swigs of the tepid, plastic-tasting water instead and promised myself another cup of coffee at midday.

Rucker dug a small pit and everyone buried his empty ration pouches. I licked my plastic spoon clean and stuck it back in my left chest pocket with my cigarettes. One would have really tasted good right then, but the smoke would have been visible for several hundred meters. I would save them for after the extraction.

A few clouds moved in from the west early in the afternoon. They looked harmless, but within minutes were busy soaking us to the bone with a heavy rain shower.

There was no protection from the big, cold drops that pounded us like they were trying to settle an old grudge. We could only sit and wait it out.

The clouds moved on as suddenly as they had come up. We were sopping wet, but the sun soon came back out, with the promise of drying us out in short order. We took out our poncho liners and spread them over the tops of the small shrubs around our perimeter. They would dry quickly. We didn't like hanging our laundry out for everyone to see, but none of us wanted to spend another chilly night along the river wrapped in a wet blanket. At least they were camouflaged!

Just before dark, we ate our second meal of the day. We downed it cold. The mountains to our west had us in shadow long before it was time to eat, so the bright light from burning balls of C-4 would be visible in the semi-darkness.

About 2330, we heard movement down in the valley, just over the side of the ridge from our OP. It was close to the water, maybe thirty meters or less. We only heard it once, but there was no mistaking it. We weren't sure what it was, but it had sounded like someone falling over a log or a rock—a sliding sound followed immediately by a dull thump.

We awoke the team and waited anxiously for perhaps a half an hour. Nothing! Whoever or whatever it had been was either still sitting there wishing he was more graceful, or he had snuck away in the night with the dexterity of a panther.

Just to be safe, Closson doubled up the guard shifts for the rest of the night. It was not a time to throw caution to the wind. We knew the gooks were active in the area; it was just a matter of time before they stumbled into us.

April 10, 1969

Closson had reported the movement at the next sitrep. At 0630, Captain Cardona reported that the 2/17th Cav wanted to send a LOH scout ship out to overfly our AO and look for signs of the enemy.

Closson didn't like the idea at all. The scout ship would only draw attention to our presence. The gooks—if they had indeed been gooks—had probably long since departed the area.

Around 0830, we heard the tenor hum of the LOH as it buzzed up the river past our position. I was up in the observation spot when it darted by. It seemed close enough to reach out and grab. It moved another hundred meters up the river before swinging right and disappearing behind the ridgeline across the valley from us.

We didn't see him or hear him again for the next fifteen minutes. I had begun to wonder if something had happened to him, when he popped up over the long ridgeline and shot across our AO, heading down the river.

Ten minutes later, our X-ray team on Firebase Rakkassan called to say that the scout chopper had spotted fresh sandal tracks leading up a small, sandy stream on the back side of the ridge to our west. They were so fresh that the pilot could see the marks on a rock where the man had come out of the water. It was right at a spot where the entrance to a cave faced the stream.

Captain Cardona was ecstatic. He was flying in two more Ranger teams, armed with C-4 explosives. He wanted us to go in and capture the NVA cave dweller, then turn his little rock palace into a gravel bar.

Zo's and Gregory's teams were rucking up to come in at that very moment. The CO wanted us to move upriver about two hundred meters and secure an LZ for them on a gravel bar where the little stream ran into the Song Bo. The two teams would be on the ground in less than an hour from then, so we had to pull in our claymores and get humping.

We were soon picking our way up the riverbank. The going was easy except for a couple of spots where we had to move inland because the river had eroded the shore away, leaving a ten-foot-high washout to maneuver around.

We reached the gravel bar just before 1000 hours and moved out into the brush on the north side to set up security. I looked over at the high mountains just across the river to our south. A couple of NVA sharpshooters or a .51-cal. machine gun could have a field day when the two Ranger teams inserted onto the barren gravel bar. We were already in the only concealment around, and we were visible to anyone on the high ground across the river. It would have been much better if the two teams had come in next to our OP. We would have been in control of the high ground and probably just as close to our objective by a short hump cross country.

It was just amazing how much knowledge and foresight manifested itself from the relative safety of a base camp. If only we stupid grunts out in the field could make such enlightened decisions from our personal observations! Captain Eklund had been the only officer I had seen during my ten months in-country who had thought first to seek the advice of his team leaders before making snap decisions that might affect their survival. This new officer was too busy playing "Yahweh on the Mount" to realize that the information he was getting second hand, we were looking at face-to-face.

A full half hour passed before our X-ray team announced that the two teams were enroute to our location. That meant another twenty-minute wait until they arrived. If we had been spotted moving into position, Mr. Charles had had all the time that he needed to prepare a welcoming party.

The radio crackled to life! It was the LOH pilot. He was three minutes out and coming up the river. He told us that he was going back up to mark the location of the cave and give us a bearing. Closson told him that it would be better if he waited out of sight and sound until the other two teams arrived with the explosives. Too much activity in the area would spook any NVA around the location of the cave.

The scout ship pilot reported that he would cover the area until we got to the site. No one could leave without being spotted. The man didn't know how sneaky Luke the Gook could be!

Captain Cardona broke in to say that the two slicks were five minutes out. We stayed in the cover as the LOH passed our position and swung in over the little stream. We heard him move about two hundred meters to the north, then circle back. The cave entrance couldn't be very far away.

The C & C chopper radioed for us to pop a smoke on the LZ. Rucker turned and pitched a yellow smoke grenade out in the center of the gravel bar.

Seconds later, the first Huey came in low and flared up over the flat section of open shoreline. Zo's team was out and running before the chopper had a chance to touch down. I stood up in the grass and waved him our way as the next slick came in behind him. I waited for the .51 caliber on the ridge across the river to open up. It didn't.

Gregory's team waited until the skids came to rest before unassing the Huey and following Zo's team into the brush. We circled up, waiting for the slicks to depart before attempting to communicate.

When the noise of the departing choppers had faded in the distance, the three team leaders met in the center of the perimeter to discuss the game plan. They decided to move up the streambed, with Zo's team on the west bank and the other two teams on the east. If any of the teams got hit, the Rangers on the opposite shore would maneuver around and flank the enemy positions.

Zo's team was carrying forty pounds of C-4, fifty feet of det cord, and a couple dozen blasting caps with a crimper. It seemed like enough explosives to do the job, but I couldn't think of anyone on any of the teams who had been trained in demolitions. But surely the CO wouldn't have sent us to blow a cave without making sure someone knew what he was doing!

We moved out in two columns, with Zo's team crossing the stream to move up the opposite bank. It was going to be tough going. The thick brush ran all the way down to the edge of the stream. Almost immediately, we were forced to move away from the water ten to fifteen meters just to keep up with the team on the opposite shore. We were out of sight of each other and were forced to keep in touch by radio.

A hundred meters upstream, Zo's RTO reported that a bluff had forced them to move out into the wide, shallow stream. It was either that, or a climb up to the top of the ridge to bypass it from above. He called the LOH and asked the pilot to scout the bank ahead for an ambush. This was beginning to look like Custer's approach to the Little Bighorn.

The LOH pilot made a quick run down one side of the stream and back up the other. He reported that it looked clear to him. The cave was less than a hundred meters away.

Zo's team reached it ten minutes later and radioed that they were at the site. He was setting up security on the ridge above it, while we moved into position.

It didn't take us long to move through the thinning single-canopy and reach the stream. We could see four of the Rangers on Team 23 fanned out across the high ground above the narrow entrance to the cave. It didn't look like much! Just a slit in the limestone bluff. It really didn't appear large enough to permit a normal-size American soldier to enter it. Where was Miller when you needed him?

Our two teams stepped out into the stream and spread out ten to fifteen meters apart, setting up security positions and completing the perimeter around the cave entrance.

Zo and Schwartz moved up to the opening in the bluff and tossed a CS grenade back into the recesses of the cavern. The dull pop could barely be heard from where I squatted thirty meters away. A lot of the gas billowed back out of the cave and drifted straight up the face of the limestone bluff above it. The Rangers pulling security up on top had to move to the flanks to escape the fumes.

Zo tossed a concussion grenade into the slit. The blast threw a cloud of fine dust and debris out into the stream. I guess he figured it was now safe to move back up to the cave, because I saw him drop his rucksack right at the mouth as he peered back in through the narrow opening.

He soon backed out and squatted next to his pack. I watched as he extracted several sticks of C-4 and set them to the side. Gregory moved across the stream to help him rig the charges as Schwartz covered the entrance with his CAR-15.

He waited patiently as the two team leaders discussed the best place to lay the shaped charges to get maximum effect. I watched them finally decide to attach the four one-pound sticks of plastique along the roof of the cave. It appeared that they could go back no farther than five feet before running out of room. They uncoiled about a ten-foot length of det cord and crimped a blasting cap on one end. Gregory fed it back to where Zo waited to attach it to the charges. The two of them backed out of the cave and ignited the lead end of the fuse. Gregory took off running down the bank, while Zo calmly walked out to midstream and waited for the explosion.

When it came, it was loud enough, but it seemed to do little more than to knock a few rocks out of the entrance of the cave.

All of us looked at each other as if to say, "Well, obviously that wasn't a big enough charge!"

Zo waded back over to the opening and stood looking at it, feet apart, hands on his hips. Then he turned and pulled ten more narrow blocks of explosives from his ruck.

He repeated his previous steps, but this time he set a ten-pound charge against the roof of the cave. When he was finished, he backed out and lit the fuse. Gregory ran a little farther downstream than last time. Zo turned and walked back out to midstream and climbed up on a large boulder sitting there like a speaker's platform.

The explosion was much more powerful. Several good-size pieces of rock preceded the huge ball of dust that rolled out of the cave's entrance. A few small stones rained down to pepper the surface of the stream forty feet away. But the damned cave was still intact. There was no visible damage to the structure anywhere. This was beginning to get a little embarrassing, besides creating a dangerous situation for the teams. The NVA in the hills around us had to have heard the blasting. Surely they would come and check it out, at least for curiosity's sake.

Zo waded back for the final time. He dumped the re-

maining twenty-six pounds of C-4 at his feet and stood
looking at the pile of white sticks as he scratched the back
of his head. He motioned for Gregory to help him as they
carried the rest of the explosives back into the cave. They
were going to use them all this time. If that didn't do the
job, there were always the B-52s. All of this for a little
crack in a limestone bluff.

It took them fifteen minutes to set the charges in place
and run the det cord back to the mouth of the cave. Zo
ignited the fuse and waded back out to his perch in midstream. Gregory ran about one hundred feet downstream
and turned to watch the explosion.

I looked at the four Rangers strung out on the bluff
above and the other eleven scattered in a fifty-meter circle
around the near side of the stream. They were all hoping
that this time would do the job.

Now I have never witnessed a volcanic eruption before,
and if I ever do, I hope that I'm farther away than fifty
meters. The blast knocked me off my feet and left me
sitting up to my armpits in the stream. The four Rangers
on the bluff above the cave were tossed to the side like rag
dolls. Even the Rangers posted across the stream to the
north and those to the south appeared to be numbed by
the force of the blast. I could see them yelling to each
other to find out if anyone had been hurt, but I couldn't
hear anything but the ringing that was going on inside my
head. I got slowly to my feet and looked over to where Zo
had been sitting on the huge boulder. He wasn't there anymore! I couldn't see him anywhere. It was as if the blast
had vaporized him.

All at once, rocks, gravel, and other debris began raining down on us from above. I covered my head and dove
back under the protection of the trees along the shore.
Rocks the size of softballs began landing in the stream to
my front.

It was over as quickly as it had begun. I stood up, looking across the stream at the location of the cave. What had
just a short time ago been a narrow passageway back into
a solid bluff was now a deep gorge, running twenty meters
back into the ridge. Unbelievable!

And there was Zo, standing waist deep in the water,
thirty feet back from the boulder he had been sitting on

when the blast had occurred. I almost split my gut laughing when he turned to me and said, "I think that last one did it!"

The Rangers slowly moved in to look at the results of Zo's handiwork. Everyone seemed to have forgotten where we were for the time being. Our security had gone to hell and no one was attempting to reestablish it.

Finally, Closson said, "Hey, party's over. Let's get the fuck out of here." It took a few minutes to gather our thoughts and organize ourselves for our return to the LZ. Zo didn't seem to be quite himself yet, and I was worried that he might have been injured in the blast. He saw my look of concern and flashed me one of those big, stupid grins he was famous for.

We formed up in file and moved down the far side of the stream. The water was only knee deep, so the going was easy. The only problem was that we were strung out in the open for over sixty meters by the time we got lined out.

We moved quickly downstream, as Gregory got on the horn and called for our extraction ships. It would be a half hour or longer before they would reach us. Great! We could have half the NVA from the A Shau Valley on us before they arrived.

Rucker, up on point with Schwartz, suddenly threw up his hand and pointed up to the ridgetop to our west. He held up two fingers and then gave the sign for danger. He had spotted a couple of gooks up there, and they were pacing us.

Zo had regained some of his senses and motioned for everyone to pick up the pace. We had to get back to the LZ. If we had to make a stand, that would be the best place. He called for gunships. They, too, would take thirty minutes to get there.

We saw the Song Bo up ahead. The entire column moved quickly but cautiously. The gravel bar was our LZ, but it could just as likely be our killing field. We didn't know if the NVA had gotten ahead of us or not.

Schwartz waded through the deepening water and moved over to the east bank just north of the gravel bar. He scouted out in a quick cloverleaf pattern to check the cover alongside the LZ. He returned the signal that it was clear.

The three teams ran the last twenty meters along the bank and scattered out in the brush along the riverbank.

Zo was on the radio reporting the NVA sightings when the first shot rang out from somewhere up on the ridge to our west. That was where Rucker had spotted the two gooks.

Everyone dove to the ground, not sure where the shot had hit. *Bam . . . zinggggg!* A second one went high over us. It sounded like it had been fired from over two hundred meters away. They were still up on the ridge, trying to pin us down.

Several of us stood up in the brush and returned fire, not expecting to hit anything but just trying to let the bastards know that they had better not get too damn gutsy.

Gregory yelled for Penchansky to start lobbing a few M-79 rounds up on the ridge. Ski fired about six HE rounds along the crest about ten meters apart. That would discourage them from trying to move in any closer. He opened the 79 and dropped a canister round back into the chamber, then jerked the stock up to close the breach. The grenade launcher went off. I was only ten feet away when it fired, but I remember thinking about the explosion that I knew would come. Nothing happened!

Ski stood there in shock looking at the weapon that had misfired in his hands. There had been no explosion. Thank God it had been a canister round. Then I saw Reneer, Gregory's RTO. He was holding his right thigh and grimacing in pain. He had been sitting on the ground beneath Ski when the M-79 went off, and had caught part of the charge in his leg.

Zo was on the other radio calling for a dust off, as one of the medics tied a tourniquet around Reneer's upper thigh. The wound didn't seem to be bleeding a lot, but the double-O buckshot had caused some serious tissue damage.

Zo yelled that a medevac was on its way from Camp Evans. There were a couple of more quick, inaccurate shots from the ridgeline to our left. Several of us opened up on the suspected portions of the enemy snipers. Zo warned the dust off pilot that the LZ was "hot."

We heard the single Huey coming up the river. It was two hundred meters downstream when we saw it. The bright red cross painted on its nose stood out even at that distance. Gregory ran out into the middle of the gravel bar and guided the Huey into our LZ. The pilot jammed the chopper down so hard, he broke one of his skid braces when he hit.

Two of the Rangers carried Reneer in a basket carry over to the crewmen on the dust off and helped him onto the litter lying across the cabin floor.

The chopper's AC pulled pitch, lifting the ship clear of the gravel bar, then nosed down as he executed a sharp turning bank to the left and shot back down the river less than fifty feet off the deck. That pilot was good!

We stayed down in the bushes along the edge of the LZ. Another shot rang out from above us. What in the hell were they up to? They weren't even coming close. They were trying to keep us there, for some reason. The only logical explanation was that they had help coming.

Zo said that if the extraction ships didn't show up in the next ten minutes, we were going to E & E downstream to the east. If we got caught, at least we would be closer to the rear and in a better defensive position than this flat-assed gravel bar.

Seconds later we heard it—the deep throbbing pulse of Huey turbines reverberating off the water. They were coming upstream, just like the medevac had done. Zo told Gregory to take his team out first, since he was short a man.

The first slick popped up over the ridge behind us and swung in over the top of us, executing a near stall as the pilot turned the chopper into a tight spiral. Somebody tossed a smoke grenade out on the gravel bar just as the ship settled in.

Gregory's team was up and running through the rotor-swept red smoke. I saw them disappear into the open cabin as the chopper lifted off and swung downstream.

The next Huey came in from the north and dropped in like a decoying mallard. Zo screamed for Closson to get out. We ran for the chopper, hurtling inside as it began lifting off to make room for the final ship.

I looked out the port side of the Huey and saw Zo's bird coming in just as the gravel bar passed from view.

We flew down the Song Bo, little more than a hundred

feet above the water. The pilot was more concerned with
gaining airspeed than altitude. I felt the door gunner's hand
on my shoulder and looked up to see him pointing back
upstream and then flashing a thumbs up. Zo's team had
gotten out okay.

I reached into my breast pocket and pulled out the pack
of Winstons I had been saving. They were soaked. The
blast at the cave that had knocked me into the stream must
have done it. It had happened less than ninety minutes
before, and I had already forgotten it. Vietnam was getting
to me. I was way too short for that kind of stuff anymore.
Only fifty-five days and a wake-up and I would be on a
freedom bird bound for the world. Jesus, what could happen in fifty-five days?

April 11, 1969

The day after my return from the Song Bo, I told Myers that I had made up my mind to turn down the direct
commission I had been offered. I told him I didn't think I
could put up with a couple of months of Mickey Mouse
shit back at Benning, and the idea of coming back over to
the Nam as a platoon leader twelve months later wasn't
turning me on, either. I wanted to tell him the bush had
been getting to me for the last three or four weeks, and I
was beginning to doubt my ability to perform in the field,
but decided to keep those reasons to myself. It didn't pay
to advertise that you were losing your nerve.

I was totally unprepared for his response. He told me
that he, too, had decided to refuse the commission, basically for the same reasons I had given.

We marched down to the orderly room and reported our
decision to First Sergeant Cardin. He told us that he understood, but that they wouldn't be too happy about it up
at division. Battlefield commissions in Vietnam were not

as commonplace as they had been during World War II. Division had planned on playing it up big time for the public relations impact. He asked us to come back around 1600 and sign the paperwork, and he would take care of the rest.

All the way back to the hootch, I had second thoughts about my decision. The commission had been what I had wanted since I was a kid, and now I was throwing away my chance as if it had never really mattered. I guessed that it had only been a kid's silly dream in the first place. The honor and glory of a career in the military as an officer and a gentleman seemed to have disappeared from my list of priorities. During the past ten months, the combat I had participated in had somehow dispelled all of that honor-and-glory stuff. I had grown up a lot, and my ideals had changed. I was tired. It must have been the result of the adrenaline high I had been on since I had arrived incountry. The withdrawal was just beginning to hit me, and I wasn't ready for it. My mind was trying to prepare me for my DEROS and marriage, yet my body was still in Nam. The dichotomy of it all was tearing me apart. I needed out, and out soon.

A couple of hours later, Zo stopped by and told me that Barry Golden had been killed in action down near Bien Hoa. He had bought it flying door gunner on a Huey slick with some aviation unit out of Ben Cat. He had transferred out of the company a couple of months back, right after extending for an early out. I had heard that he had been pressured to file the 1049 (transfer request form) by the CO. His drug use had been getting out of hand, and he was becoming a disciplinary problem. Golden had been top drawer in the field, but toward the end had used the hard stuff to keep himself in a constant fog between missions. Tragic! He was a double tragedy of the Vietnam conflict.

April 12, 1969

I received a money order for three hundred dollars from Barb. She had taken it out of our joint account and mailed it to me for my R & R. I felt like an ass, spending a tenth of what we had saved during my tour. That money could have done a lot for us after we were married. Her accompanying letter pleaded with me to relax and enjoy myself. She only wished that I would relent and let her fly over to Honolulu so that we could be married there. I had refused. We had agreed to have a big church wedding. All of the arrangements had been made and the invitations were addressed and ready to be mailed out. As much as I wanted her with me, I couldn't see ruining our wedding plans. The noble fool strikes again!

At least the R & R would get me out of the field for seven to ten days. And if I was smart, I could stretch my time away from the outfit to a couple of weeks. Maybe one or two more missions before R & R. By the time I returned to the unit I would be under three weeks, and nobody had to go out with less than three weeks left in-country. Yeah, I'd do the R & R scene. Why not? I owed it to myself. Others had manipulated their R & Rs to get them out of the field early. Why not me? The idea made all the sense in the world and sounded more than convincing to me, yet I had this overwhelming feeling that I was fucking my buddies.

April 13, 1969

We got a warning order for a mission at first light on the fourteenth. I was to be TL again, with Rucker as my ATL. The AO was astraddle the major ridgeline paralleling the Perfume River, west of Leech Island. I had been up there once before, maybe six months ago. We had found an old trail and a small ammo cache. We had taken an M-2 carbine and left the ammo and grenades booby-trapped.

The terrain was steep. The ridgetop couldn't have been more than twenty meters across at its widest. The cover was all triple-canopy. Lush, green ferns and broadleaf plants were everywhere. I remembered that we could only see a few meters ahead. It was the kind of cover Rangers loved to patrol in.

Gillette, Kilburn, Hillman, and Groff made up the rest of the team. Not a lot of experience among the four of them, but they had been around long enough to know what was happening.

We were only going in for three days. Division wanted to know what was going on in the area. The Roung-Roung Valley was just to the southwest and no one had been back in there since we had gotten our shit blown away last November 20. Pure unadulterated recon! No ambushes, no screwing around trying to nab a prisoner. They just wanted us to cover the crest of the ridge and find out if Charlie was active in the area. The AO was unusually small—three square klicks in a straight line, right down the spine of the ridge. Unless we found something, we wouldn't even have to do any climbing.

April 14, 1969

We went in by rope ladder at first light. I hated ladder insertions. Too damn much time over the LZ! But it couldn't be helped. We had three or four bomb craters in our entire AO, so good LZs were not at a premium. On the overflight, I had spotted just one crater that appeared big enough to handle a Huey. It was at the north end of our RZ, and I wanted to save it to come out on. Ladder extractions were even tougher than ladder insertions.

It took us longer than I liked to get in. The chopper kept rising and falling while we were descending. The pilot was trying his best to get us in as close as possible, but the LZ just wasn't as wide as it had appeared when we had buzzed it on the thirteenth. Every time he dropped, his rotors tore the hell out of the treetops encircling the LZ. We each had to drop the final six feet into the crater. We should have played it safe and rappeled in. We had spent much too long a time on the insertion. Any gooks in the area had plenty of opportunity to get a fix on our infiltration.

We climbed out of the crater and ran fifty feet to the north, before diving into a large cluster of ferns just off the crest of the ridge. We laid dog for an hour. I wanted to be absolutely sure that we hadn't attracted attention on our insertion. Rucker signaled me that our commo was fine. It would be, as long as we remained on top. Whatever happened, we had to avoid going down the west side of the ridge. We didn't have an X-ray team anywhere. We were on a line-of-sight basis with Camp Eagle. The back side of the ridge would put us in a dead zone, and we'd be without commo.

Artillery was also a problem. Firebase Brick was just south of us, but unoccupied at the time. Our support was to come from Firebase Rifle, southeast of us. They couldn't reach us if we got off on the back side of the ridge. I told the team that if we had to E & E, our rendezvous point would be the west bank of the Perfume, directly opposite the north end of Leech Island.

Rucker led us out, moving slowly but deliberately through the lush jungle. I was enthralled at being back in this type of cover. The greens were much richer in triple-canopy. The plant life dominated the environment. It was so thick that, at times, we covered fifty meters or more without being able to see the ground. We seemed to be wading through a knee-deep layer of vegetation.

We made no noise. The damp earth absorbed all sound. There was nothing dry enough to snap underfoot. I looked back over my shoulder from my slack position and was amazed at the effect of the camouflaged Rangers moving slowly behind me. They would have been invisible if I had not known they were there. I hoped the enemy would find them just as difficult to spot.

We patrolled until 1600 hours, covering a good thousand meters. I moved up and tapped Mother on the shoulder and signaled him to look for a place to spend the night. He angled over to the east side of the ridge and dropped just over the crest into a jumble of large boulders sitting in a nest of huge elephant-eared plants. Perfect! Cover and concealment, and excellent commo to boot!

We set out four claymores, three pointing uphill and the remaining one aimed down our E & E route to the east. I felt confident that we had made it in without being spotted.

It got dark early in the jungle. By 1730 hours, I could barely make out the Rangers hidden around the perimeter. We had all spread our poncho liners out on the ground, after clearing the area of any rocks or small sticks. I kept everyone in tight, since the heavy foliage made keeping track of each man almost impossible.

The night passed uneventfully. I think I slept as well before and after my guard shift as I had ever slept on a mission.

April 15, 1969

We ate breakfast quickly and moved out. I was anxious to cover another klick on the second day.

Rucker stopped the team one hundred meters from our NDP. He was standing on the edge of a high-speed trail that appeared to cross the ridge on an angle, from southwest to northeast. It wasn't an old trail, but it had not been used in quite a while. The moss-covered rocks showed no sign of recent passage.

We followed it to the northeast for about fifty meters, until it began to drop down the side of the ridge toward the Perfume River. I motioned for Rucker to let it be and head back up toward the crest of the ridge. Following it down the side of the mountain would have quickly taken us out of our RZ. Besides, I knew where the trail came out. It had to lead to the river crossing we had discovered a couple of months back.

We found nothing else crisscrossing the ridgetop and moved into another thicket late in the day. We had picked up a few land leeches sometime during our patrol. Each of us took turns stripping in the waning light of day, to dab each bloated parasite with a shot of insect repellent. It was great to watch the bastards react to the sting of the bug juice. Gillette won the honors as top producer by coming up with thirteen of them. I only had six on me, but two of the sons of bitches had made a home on my scrotum.

April 16, 1969

We covered the final klick by 1400 hours and found no indication that the enemy had ever been on the ridgeline. The trail, crossing the ridge 1500 meters back, was the only thing that kept our AO from being just another pristine piece of Asian jungle.

We found the crater and moved into heavy cover on the far side, while I called the company for extraction. They came back immediately and told us the choppers would be over us in thirty mikes.

I broke my own rules and lit up a cigarette. For some unknown reason, I had suddenly craved the taste of one right after we were told the birds were on the way. I drew deep, letting the smoke fill my lungs. A couple of more puffs, and I passed it on to the next man hiding in the bushes.

The Huey was right on time. Groff popped a yellow smoke and tossed it out into the crater. The pilot spotted it and moved in over the opening. For a minute, I thought that I had misjudged this one, too, but changed my mind as he eased the slick down through the trees to come to a low hover next to the lip of the crater.

We piled in quickly, anxious to get the hell out of there. It hadn't been an exciting mission, but, like most of them, it had kept the adrenaline pumping until we were on our way back to Camp Eagle. I would miss all of this when I got back home. I knew it sounded dumb, but this kind of life grew on you. There wasn't anything back in the World to compare to it. And the bonding . . . it was unlike any type of emotional or social experience I had ever felt. Yes, I would indeed miss it.

April 17, 1969

It rained the entire day. Not the hard, driving rains of
the monsoon season; but a slow, steady downpour that
knocked the dust down and cooled the temperature a few
degrees. For the first time since I had been in Nam, I took
the time to take a good look at my surroundings. I was
almost at the end of my tour, and I had never really taken
the opportunity to appreciate the countryside. Sure, I had
taken a ton of pictures and over twenty rolls of Super-8
movie film, but what had I observed on my own? Not a
damned thing!

I had gone through ten months of survival in a country
known for its simple beauty and had nearly missed the
experience. I had taken too much for granted and had left
nothing of myself in passing. I had disliked and mistrusted
its people, not because they were physically unattractive
or dishonest by nature, but because I feared and didn't
understand them. Since I couldn't tell who the enemy was,
I tossed them all into that classification because it was
easier on me. My survival instincts had thrown up a wall
between myself and the people of Vietnam that had prevented me from learning anything about them, their culture, or their history.

My conservative, white, middle-class upbringing had
taught me that America was the best, and if it wasn't made
or grown in the U.S. of A., it just wasn't any good.

Now, with just forty-nine days and a wake-up remaining
in-country, I realized what an experience I had missed.
Oh, I had had my share of experiences, but I had lost my
one great opportunity to discover the wondrous things
about an alien culture, much older than my own, that had
sustained these people for thousands of years. Why hadn't
someone taught us to appreciate and recognize the culture

of the people of Vietnam? We had been trying so hard to force our culture on them that we had overlooked the simple, innocent beauty of theirs. It was no wonder they looked upon us as they did. I had given them nothing of myself, and then had questioned why they mistrusted us. The ugly American was never more ugly than he was at that moment.

April 18, 1969

A Korean salesman came through the company area today, peddling Bibles, of all things. They were beautiful! Full of color paintings illustrating many of the religious stories from my youth. I hadn't been religious in years, yet something inside told me to order one of the leather-covered editions and have it sent home directly to Barbara. She would understand why I had spent the thirty-nine dollars. It was a lot of money, but I felt good ordering it. If anything happened to me now, the Bible would . . . well, sort of answer some questions and make some statements for my loved ones back home, that I could just never seem to put in a letter.

Jesus, was it melancholy or what? I couldn't understand what was going on inside me. I seemed full of remorse and misgivings. It seemed to be my week for reflection and deep thought. I should have been happy about my R & R in nine more days, or my DEROS in forty-nine. God, I was really short! No shit! I was no longer just saying it because it sounded good. I was finally short. I used to envy guys who weren't as short as I was now. I couldn't even remember what I had felt like when I had arrived in-country. Then why was I feeling so damned bad?

April 19, 1969

I just received a letter from my mom and another one
from my dad. They had just moved into their brand-new
six-bedroom, five-bath, two-story home. It had taken them
two long years of hard work and unfulfilled dreams to
accomplish what had been their lifelong goal. They had
raised eight children on a low middle-class income and
had done a good job. Times had been rough for us. Old,
rundown homes and ten-year-old cars had not dampened
our spirits. My brothers and sisters had learned to make
the best of a bad situation. My mom and dad had given
what little they had to us kids, trying to help us maintain
a sense of dignity among our classmates who were more
fortunate than we. They must have done a good job, because none of us grew up feeling underprivileged.

Now, they were getting that new home. Their letters
described it in detail and ended with the statement that I
no longer had to be ashamed to bring my friends home.
My God! Is that what they thought? I had unknowingly
made my parents suffer all those years, letting them think
that I was ashamed of my heritage.

I had a wonderful family and a beautiful woman I would
be marrying in two short months, and I had survived a
year in Vietnam. I had everything a twenty-two-year-old
man could ever ask for. Why did I feel so perplexed?

April 20, 1969

At 0900 hours, my world came tumbling down around me. Closson walked into my hootch and announced the incredible news. He had just received a warning order for a mission at last light. The team was to consist of himself, Hillman, Sours, Rucker, Chambers, and me.

I couldn't believe I had heard him right. "Chambers! No way, man. There had to be some mistake. Not Chambers! Chambers and I never went out on the same team." And Closson, Sours, and Rucker, too. "No man, not me," I said. "I'm not going out on this mission. My God, Closson, don't you know about my dream? Jesus, Larry—*the* dream. You remember, goddamn it, the prophesy! Tell me you're only jokin'. That's it, isn't it? A joke! Chambers put you up to it. That son of a bitch! I'll kill him when I catch him. I should have known. You aren't kidding, are you?"

Closson dropped his head and stared at the floor. It was for real. We were going out together on the same team. Well, so what! Hell, don't mean nothin'. At least we weren't going into the A Shau. None of our teams had been going anywhere near the A Shau . . . "Closson, where are we going?" Nothing! "Dammit, Closson! *Where are we going?*"

He looked up and shrugged his shoulders, then shaking his head slowly muttered, "The A Shau. Yeah, we're going into the A Shau."

I stood up from where I was sitting at the end of my footlocker. I couldn't say anything. Words just wouldn't come. Closson wanted to say something, too, but he finally just turned on his heels and walked slowly out of the hootch. It was several minutes before I could even think.

I finally cleared my mind enough to realize the ramifications of what Closson had just said. The nightmare I had had back in March was coming true. I wasn't going to make it after all. I was going to die in the A Shau Valley just like I had dreamed. Suddenly I understood why I had been feeling so melancholy the past few days. I had known! Somehow—someway—I had subconsciously realized that I was going to die. I would never see my beloved Barbara or my family again. How could it happen like this?

A sense of dreadful acceptance swept over me like a heavy shroud. I felt tremendous grief and self-pity, but also some morbid kind of relief. Everything was falling into place. It was a shame it had to happen, but it was all beyond my control—or anybody else's. In Vietnam, shit happens! Don't mean nothin'.

I ran into Sours, Rucker, and Chambers as I stepped out of the claustrophobic barracks and into the sunshine. The looks on their faces told me that they had already run into Closson. I couldn't believe they were also taking my premonition seriously, but I was strangely relieved that they had. Chambers grinned, halfheartedly, and said, "You really don't . . ." He couldn't finish the sentence.

We turned to go down to Closson's hootch to get the rest of the details and find out about the overflight. First Sergeant Cardin ran into us on the way. He stopped me as we passed and held me up while the rest of the team continued on to the team leader's hootch.

When we were alone, he said, "Linderer, I know about your dream. I didn't do this on purpose. Every other team is out in the field or understrength. I realize that you, Sours, and Rucker are short, but I can't send Closson out into the A Shau with a team full of cherries." He grabbed my arm and looked up into my face. "You going to be able to do it?"

I nodded, afraid my voice would betray my feelings if I answered him verbally. I swallowed hard and muttered, "I'll be okay, Top. We all will. Dumb-ass dream don't mean nothin'." He grimaced as I turned to follow the rest of the team. He hadn't believed my bullshit anymore than I had.

Sours was to be Closson's ATL and would walk slack. Chambers would be up front at point. Rucker would be handling our commo as senior RTO. Hillman was assigned to hump the other radio. I would be bringing up the rear at drag position. It was a good team. Except for Hillman, everyone had over fifteen missions. It was my twenty-eighth. Three of us had served team leaders, two others had served as assistant team leaders. Sours, Chambers, and Closson had been through Recondo school at Nha Trang. Sours had even been the honor graduate of his class, while Chambers had been a runner-up. If we didn't survive the mission, it wouldn't be for lack of experience.

While Closson was on the overflight, the rest of us packed our gear. For most of us, it involved little more than stowing rations, water, and special equipment among the items we kept stored in our rucks. I picked up a willie pete and a concussion grenade and put them in the side pouches on my rucksack. When I finished packing, I set a claymore across the top of my gear and pulled the top flap down over it. Sours strapped a LAW to the side of his ruck. There was intelligence on NVA armor operating on the Laotian side of the A Shau.

A quiet, somber resolve had taken the place of the usual excitement and bravado that preceded a normal mission. None of us said anything to each other as we worked on in silence.

Hillman seemed totally baffled by it all. He hadn't been a party to my dream and, at that moment, was unaware of what was causing the serious lack of morale in the rest of us. The youthful, black Ranger had only been out on a few missions and hadn't run into that type of problem before. It must have been tougher on him than it was on the rest of us. We were, more or less, resigned to our fates. He still believed we were just going out on another ordinary mission.

Closson returned from the overflight at noon. He told us that there was one hell of a big mountain on the western edge of our AO. The Laotian border cut across the back side of it. Our mission was to recon the area and try to locate some of the major trails coming from across the border into South Vietnam. The Ho Chi Minh Trail crossed into the A Shau all along the border. There was never a shortage of fresh trails. Or enemy troops.

When we left the briefing and returned to our hootches, I noticed the looks of concern and support on the faces of our fellow Rangers. The word had traveled fast. Several of them stopped by later, trying to cheer us up. Some even went so far as to make light of the whole thing, but stopped short when they realized that their effort wasn't achieving the desired effect. It seemed that my premonition was hurting the whole company, but there was nothing I could do about it.

I felt empty inside. Nothing made any sense anymore. I knew that I was a dead man. It didn't make any difference when it happened. All that mattered was that I wouldn't be coming back from the mission. I had to write some letters, and time was running out. I grabbed a writing tablet and a pen and ran down to the perimeter bunker. I knew that no one would be there.

It was almost cool inside. There was just enough light coming through the firing ports to let me see what I was doing. The first letter was to my parents. I started it three different times but couldn't really find the right approach. Finally, I settled for the coward's way out. I told them that I knew that my tour was almost over, and that I appreciated all the love and support I had received from both of them, and the kids, too. It had made my year in Vietnam bearable. If anything happened to me so late in the game, I wanted them to know that I had always been proud of who I was and what I had done with my life. I owed everything to them. They had taught me the difference between right and wrong, and had given me a set of moral standards to live by that I would never be ashamed of.

The second letter was to one of my best friends from my high school days. John Meese was a hunting buddy and school chum who had written to me often over the past few months. He had been a cutup in class and was one of those guys who never took anything seriously. Yet, when my orders came for Vietnam, it was John who seemed to understand the emotions I was going through.

It was John who offered to look after my girl and to stop by and see how my folks were doing.

I told him about the mission, and about my misgivings over it. I had decided to try to ship home the .45-cal. automatic I had taken off the NVA major I had killed back in November. It was a U.S.-manufactured weapon, so sending it back to the States was prohibited. At that stage of the game, I didn't care anymore. I had captured it, and it was mine. John would know what to do with it. I told him that I was going to break it down into about four different parcels and have a couple of my comrades ship it to him over the next couple of days. I had been carrying it with me on missions. Now, I didn't want the gooks to get it back.

Finally, I told John that I was enclosing another letter with this one. It was for Barb, and to be given to her only if something should happen to me. If I made it home all right, he was to burn it.

When I finished John's letter, I wrote the letter to my girl. Surprisingly, it wasn't a difficult letter to write.

My Darling:

God, I am so sorry for what has happened. Please forgive me! I had hoped that you would never have to read this, but it appears that even my great love for you was not enough to bring me back. Barbara, sweet Barbara, I loved you so much. The pain that you are going through now must become the memorial to the love we had for each other. Memories! They are all that I can leave you. Memories of the good times . . . and the bad. Of our relationship over the past seven years, I have no regrets. I have remembered only the happiness . . . the tenderness of your touch! Your thoughtfulness . . . your laughter at my silly jokes. I never deserved you. I was never worth the pain that I caused you over the years, nor the pain I am causing you now.

Promise me only that you'll remember me. That is where I'll always be for you. Don't grieve for me. What has happened to me was ordained long before we met. You and I . . . we . . . were never meant to be. But I thank God for the time we had together.

You go on without me now. There will be someone else to love you and to be loved by you. It is what I would have wanted for you.

Good-bye, my love! You will always be with me. All my love, all my life,

Gary

I sealed the letter without rereading it. I knew that if I did, I would never send it. I folded it and tucked it in the envelope containing the letter to John. Quickly addressing it and printing FREE in the upper right-hand corner of the envelope, I put it aside and started another letter to Barb. It was short and evasive. I told her I was getting ready to go out on my last mission. I wasn't real crazy about the area we were going into, but at least the team was made up of some of the best men in L Company. I made no mention of the premonition that seemed well on its way to being fulfilled. If it came to pass, she would learn of it soon enough anyway. In closing, I asked her to say an extra prayer for me. When I finished, I hurried up to the orderly room and dropped the three letters into the mail slot. It was 1530 hours and time to start getting ready for the mission.

Schwartz stopped me on the way to my hootch. He was jumpy at first, wanting to say something but not knowing where to start. Finally he blurted out that he wanted to go out in my place. Jesus, was he blaming himself for spreading the story of my nightmare? Was this sacrifice because of guilt? What a manifestation of friendship! I was humbled by his offer, but shook my head no, unable even to thank him for this token of friendship. These were the kind of men who served with the Rangers.

Closson came by and told me we had ten minutes to get down to the chopper pad. I looked at the watch strapped to the left side of my LBE harness, hanging above my cot. It was 1650 hours. Lift-off was set for 1715.

I strapped myself into my web gear, grabbed for my rucksack and rifle, and left the hootch for the short walk downhill to the acid pad. The choppers hadn't arrived yet, but the rest of the team were already at the edge of the pad, running last-minute checks on their equipment and doing some final touch-up on their camouflage. The routine was the same as on all the prior missions, only this time, the premission excitement and good-natured bantering was missing.

No one spoke when I joined them. It was like a football team down 45 to 0 at half time during the championship game. A somber, almost fatalistic aura had settled over the team. I noticed that each man avoided even looking at the others. Everyone was quiet, engrossed in his own thoughts. Had I done this to them? Had my stupid nightmare become a self-fulfilling prophesy? The men weren't mentally prepared for the mission. I had unwittingly set into motion a chain reaction that was putting the lives of innocent people in jeopardy. I felt especially sorry for Hillman. He hadn't been one of the characters in my nightmare. If the dream came true, he would be on his own out there.

The sound of helicopters approaching drew my attention. The two Hueys came in from the southwest, circling around over the Cav compound and coming in to land in front of us. We turned our backs to the wind-blown dust and debris as the two ships landed and switched off their engines.

Captain Cardona walked down from the TOC and approached us as we were preparing to board. "Men, we'll be landing on FSB Blaze for a few minutes before we insert you. The gunships are supposed to link up with us there. You'll be going in a good half hour before dusk. It'll give you a chance to look over the area and find a good NDP before dark." Without waiting for any comment from us, he went over to brief the pilots of the change in plans.

Looney and three other Rangers from the commo section joined us at the pad. They would be staying on Firebase Blaze as our radio relay. We made a little small talk, waiting for the choppers to crank up. We lit up a last cigarette and passed it around.

Finally, the whine of the turbines starting up signaled us that it was time to kick off the show. We sat down, backs to our heavy rucks, and slipped our arms through the padded straps. After pulling down on the cinches to adjust the fit, we struggled to our feet and split up into two groups of three each to board the chopper. I noticed

Schwartz at the edge of the pad, taking pictures of us with his Penn double-E camera as we were getting ready to leave.

The long rotor blades began to turn as the big engines built up torque. They soon settled in to the strong, pulsing vibration that indicated lift-off was imminent. The sounds of approaching helicopters drew my attention. The two Hueys came in from the southwest, circling around over the Cav compound and coming in. Then the C & C ship was airborne, heading west toward the mountains. I felt our own bird suddenly lift from the tarmac, anxious to catch up. We gained altitude quickly. I felt the nose drop as we picked up speed and raced after the CO's chopper.

I looked down as we flew across the rolling hills outside Camp Eagle. We crossed the Perfume River and passed by Bald Mountain. Nui Ke loomed up behind Banana Mountain. I thought about all the missions I had pulled back there. It had seemed so long ago.

We flew by Firebase Birmingham, following the red slash of Highway 547 out toward Bastogne. Then we crossed over Firebase Veghel. It appeared to be unoccupied. I had no idea how close we were to Blaze. It must have been new. I had never heard of it before.

Our chopper abruptly turned and lost altitude. I looked down to see a firebase below us. It was small, just covering the peak of a high promontory across a small valley southwest of Veghel. I could only see mountains off to the west, but they seemed to stop short of the normal horizon. I knew what lay beyond—the A Shau! The valley seemed almost to beckon us. There was no place on this earth that I would rather have avoided than that valley. But it was there, just beyond those mountains—waiting for us.

We landed on a new PSP chopper pad. The six of us slid out onto the deck as the pilot torqued down to idle speed. We had a few minutes to kill before the Cobras arrived. The CO's chopper had set down ahead of us and dropped off the X-ray team, and then had lifted off, heading east again to pick up the gunships.

We milled around, waiting for the word to saddle up. We saw the relay team setting up operations in a bunker on the southwest side of the perimeter. Looney flashed us a thumbs up, as a small mechanized ammo carrier drove by with a load of 155mm rounds for the howitzers in the center of the firebase.

A young artillery officer and a pair of staff sergeants came over and introduced themselves. The officer was the FO for the 155s; the NCOs were in charge of the guns. They laid out a map of our AO and pointed out to us that if we happened to get around on the back side of Dong Ap Bia, the mountain that dominated our RZ, we would be outside the artillery fan. They would be unable to support us. I wanted to tell them that we would also be in Laos. That fact seemed to have entirely eluded them.

We thanked them for the info. As I saw it, we would have artillery support if we stayed in the eastern half of our AO. In the western half, we would be more likely to get a fire mission from NVA batteries out of Laos!

Fifteen minutes later, our pilot signaled that it was time to saddle up. We broke off into two groups and boarded the chopper from both sides.

We lifted off, climbing away from the lonely firebase that guarded the eastern approaches to the A Shau Valley. The soldiers defending it would be our closest friendly support. If the weather soured, and we had to E & E, we would have to come through a range of mountains, cross the floor of the valley, and then cross another series of high ridgelines to reach it. Twenty kilometers through impossible terrain swarming with thousands of hard-core NVA soldiers!

Our chopper swung around and headed west. I could see the C & C ship and the two Cobras high overhead. Our pilot was contour flying, nap-of-the-earth, over the mountaintops and down the spines of the never-ending ridgelines. Then we were out over the valley. Its pock-marked floor seemed to mock us as we passed over it. I felt as if thousands of eyes watched as we headed toward the range of hills commanding the west side of the valley. They were massive—and menacing. Laos, with its countless NVA base camps, was less than three klicks away.

The chopper unexpectedly dropped as it flared over a brushy clearing on the crest of a secondary ridge above the valley floor. False insertion! I had been daydreaming and not paying attention. We lifted up again, only to drop down the reverse slope of the ridge. I could see a grass-covered clearing at the base of Dong Ap Bia coming up below us. Closson was nodding. This was the real thing. No false insertion this time.

I scooted to the edge of the cabin deck and slid out on the skid next to Sours. The two of us and Hillman would be exiting the chopper from the port side. The other three Rangers would be going out the right door.

The LZ was larger than I expected. The grass seemed sparse and barely knee high, as I pushed off from the skid and landed hard on the level ground. I started to run toward the tree line thirty meters away, but saw Closson and Sours both go down in front of me. Thinking we were under fire, I turned to the rear and hit the ground facing out, ready to defend their backs.

The Huey was already climbing out, the sounds of its engine fading in the distance. I heard Closson whisper, "Mines!" I didn't understand what he meant until I saw him pointing to the pressure plate of a large antipersonnel mine exposed by erosion just to the front of the team leader.

Oh shit! Not already! We weren't even going to live long enough to get off the LZ. Rucker called in for a commo check and reported the problem we had encountered. He was told to "wait one" while control did some double-checking. Two minutes later, the radio crackled back to life. Rucker listened, signed off, then in turn whispered that we were on the wrong LZ. We were on the edge of an old 1st Cav mine field.

There was a washout a few feet in front of Closson. The rains had eroded a shallow ditch that ran in the direction of Dong Ap Bia, looming high above us to the west. The team leader signaled for us to follow him in single file down the wash to the tree line on the other side of the LZ.

We covered the fifteen meters in seconds, diving into the thick vegetation bordering the clearing. Funny, but the

danger from the mine field we had just escaped didn't
seem to faze anyone but Hillman. His eyes were wide,
full of terror. The rest of the Rangers on the team were
acting like it was nothing more than a training mission. It
was almost as if they knew it wasn't the right time to
worry yet.

Rucker called in a new sitrep while Closson pulled out
his map to figure out where we had inserted. It didn't take
him long to discover that we had come in about three
hundred meters northwest of our primary LZ. Not as bad
as it could have been, but we were less than five hundred
meters from Laos—if the map was correct.

Just ahead of us, to the southwest, we could see where
the ground began to rise in a steady slope that ran up the
north flank of Dong Ap Bia. Somewhere, about half way
up, the map showed that the slope veered sharply upward
and merged with the steep sides of the mountain that continued on to the crest.

Our present location actually put us in a better overall
position to conduct our patrol plan than our primary LZ
would have. We had only to move first to the southeast,
then swing back around in an arc to the southwest, and
we would have scouted the entire base of Dong Ap Bia
that lay in South Vietnam.

We had less than fifteen minutes to find some heavy
cover for an overnight halt. We were uncomfortably close
to the LZ, and our commo was a lot weaker than we
would have liked. Closson decided that, rather than set
up an NDP at the same elevation that we had infiltrated
into, we would be better off moving up the slope in front
of us and finding some cover on the side of it. The higher
ground would give us better commo, and we would have
more options in case the NVA tried to flush us out during
the night.

We formed up, with Chambers at point, and moved
quickly up the slope. We hit a fresh high-speed trail before
we had covered twenty meters. It came up from somewhere near where we had inserted and seemed to follow
the contour of the ridge we were on.

Chambers led us quickly over the right side of the ridge
and into the double-canopy foliage covering its flanks. Less
than twenty meters from the crest, it began to drop off sharply

toward the valley below. It was getting too dark to continue moving with the high-speed trail above us and a sharp incline below. Chambers found a level spot between three large trees and led us into it. It was less than eight feet in diameter, but it would be better than trying to set up an NDP on a hillside.

Rucker called for a commo check, as Sours, Chambers, and I set out claymores. The trail running up the spine of the ridge was less than twenty meters away. We kept the claymores in close, pointing uphill. If they came for us, it would be from that direction.

When we returned, Rucker was rigging a field-expedient antenna in the trees above our NDP. He motioned that he could barely pick up the relay team on Blaze with the pole antenna, so he was attempting to get a little higher with the jerry-rigged wire antenna. After he had finished, he called Blaze again. His smile indicated that he was now getting a stronger signal.

Darkness settled over us ten minutes later. Closson called in some preplots on the trail above us and on the LZ we had come in on. If we had to get out quickly during the night, a fire mission on the Cavmine field should make it safe enough to get a chopper in to us.

It was a little after 2100 hours when we heard the first NVA go by. They were on the trail, moving uphill. There were twenty to thirty enemy soldiers, strung out about three meters apart. They didn't seem to be looking for us, but they weren't making a lot of noise, either. Closson put us on fifty percent alert for the rest of the night.

An hour and a half later, another group about the same size passed, moving toward the crest of Dong Ap Bia. There had to be something up there. The NVA weren't ambitious enough to climb a mountain as tall as this one just to get to the other side. No, something was up there.

A little after midnight, the sound of a gasoline engine broke the night's silence. No one would be cutting grass in the jungle after dark, so the engine noise had to be coming from a power generator. It seemed to come from somewhere four or five hundred meters up the mountain, close to where our slope turned sharply upward. None of us were sure. The jungle distorted the sound.

We moved together in the center of the perimeter. Closson, Sours, and I draped a couple of poncho liners around us and squatted beneath them to try to determine where the generator was located on the map. The red lens of Closson's flashlight cast an eerie reflection on the acetate covering his topo map. The team leader wanted to walk an artillery barrage back and forth across the site we thought the noise was coming from, but Sours and I told him that it would alert the NVA to our presence. They would know someone was in the area directing the fire. Since it was pretty obvious we weren't above them, their first reaction would be to sweep the slope below them. We had six hours to go until daylight, and none of us wanted to play tag in the jungle with a bunch of pissed-off gooks.

He finally decided to just call in and report our sound contact and wait and see what developed. The enemy had a base camp up there, we were sure of that.

I was on the first guard shift with Rucker and Hillman. We had security watch until 0330. It was pitch black in the jungle. Water droplets from afternoon thunderstorms were just finding their way through the thick double-canopy above us. The generator ran continuously until around 0300, then shut down for the rest of the night. I lay there for a while after my shift was over, wondering if the next day would be my last one.

April 21, 1969

The sun came up across the A Shau. Closson shook me awake and held a finger to his lips. I rubbed the sleep from my eyes and moved next to him. He whispered that another bunch of gooks had just moved past our position, heading uphill. He could just see their heads over the crest of the ridge above us. There were more than twenty of them.

I reached quietly for the canteen on the right rear of my web belt, popping the Velcro strips holding the cover in place. Taking a swig of the cool, plastic-tasting water, I swished it around in my mouth to wash out the stale film of dried mucus that had accumulated while I slept. I leaned over close to the ground and let it dribble silently into the leaves. Spitting would have made too much noise.

Closson motioned for Sours and me to move in close. He whispered that he thought we should move farther up the ridge and find a good spot to set up a patrol base. I asked him how far up he felt we needed to go. He said, "Maybe another two hundred meters." Sours and I both nodded. We were too damn close to the trail to set up a patrol base where we were. Maybe we could find a better place farther up. Besides, it would improve our commo. None of us liked having a field-expedient antenna stretched out through the branches above us while we were set up so close to a major trail.

We took turns eating cold LRRP rations, taking every precaution to bury our trash and sterilize our perimeter. When we finished, we gathered in the claymores as Rucker called in our scheduled sitrep. He was taking the antenna down as we returned to the perimeter.

We moved out cautiously, staying low to the ground as we paralleled the trail. We moved uphill, being careful to stay just over the crest of the finger we were ascending. It took us better than an hour to cover just 150 meters. Chambers stopped us in some thick vegetation while we decided on our next step. Closson wanted to cross the trail and get on the east side of the ridge. It was almost too steep to maneuver on the west side, and if we crossed over, we would almost have line-of-sight commo with Blaze.

Sours and Chambers moved up to check out the trail. They returned ten minutes later and motioned for us to follow them up to the crest. We moved out silently, five meters apart, and were soon in some thick cover at the edge of the trail. Closson signaled for us to cross it, two

at a time, and move twenty meters beyond before we
stopped.

Sours and Chambers crossed first, moving rapidly but
quietly into the cover on the far side of the trail. Closson
and Rucker followed them a couple of minutes later. Hillman and I moved into position a meter back from the trail.
I could see it in front of me as I crouched, peering through
the bushes. It wasn't what I had imagined. There was no
high-speed trail running up the spine of the ridgeline. It
was no more than a narrow, dirt footpath meandering
through the jungle. It was dark, almost black, nothing like
the red clay trails that were so common on the other side
of the A Shau. I cupped my hands to my ears, listening
intently in both directions. Hearing nothing but sounds of
the jungle, I stood up in the brush to look first uphill, then
downhill, for any sign of approaching enemy soldiers. It
was clear. I looked back over my shoulder at Hillman,
crouched next to a large mahogany tree, and jerked my
head toward the trail for him to follow me. I moved forward quickly, turning sideways at the last minute to ease
through the brush bordering the trail. I cleared the path in
one giant stride, careful not to damage any of the vegetation. When I reached the spot where the rest of the team
lay huddled in a perimeter, I looked back for Hillman. He
was right on my heels.

The two of us dropped into our security positions on
the hasty perimeter thrown up by the team. We laid dog
for almost fifteen minutes, listening for any sign that we
had been spotted. When we were relatively certain our
crossing had gone undetected, we moved farther back away
from the trail toward the eastern flank of the ridge. We
dropped over the crest and set up again, amid a cluster of
thick vegetation.

Closson seemed pleased with the move. We were farther back from the trail than we had been before. The new
location would give us some breathing room and serve as
an excellent patrol base. He told us to set out three claymores on the side of the perimeter facing the trail, with
another one covering each flank.

Chambers told me there were fresh footprints all over
the trail. I hadn't stopped to look when I had stepped
across it.

We spent the remainder of the day in hiding, listening for movement on the trail thirty meters away. If the NVA were using it during daylight hours, they weren't making any noise.

Around 1530 we heard chopping up the ridge from us. It sounded closer to us than the location of the generator. We called in and reported probable bunker construction at the estimated coordinates.

At 1600 hours, dark clouds began moving in from the west. Within minutes we had lightning flashing all around us. The floor of the A Shau Valley was nearly two thousand feet above sea level. When the afternoon thunderstorm moved in around us, we were right up in the clouds with it.

Thunder and lightning continued for thirty minutes. A heavy rain started up and quickly soaked us to the bone. Our visibility during the storm was reduced to less than ten meters. The thinner double-canopy on this side of the ridge provided little protection from the elements. We pulled our camouflaged poncho liners from our rucksacks and draped them over our heads. They didn't keep us dry, but they prevented the heavy drops of rain from hitting us full force.

It was over as quickly as it started. We hung our rain-soaked blankets over some low shrubs downhill from our perimeter. If we could dry them a little before dark, our night would be a lot less miserable. It would be dark in three hours, and the chill of the evening would be upon us.

We took turns eating our last meal of the day. The spaghetti LRRP ration tasted like shit. The cold water I had mixed with it right after the storm had passed had only partially re-hydrated the meal. Crunchy pasta with cold tomato sauce was not at all appetizing.

Darkness descended over us like a moist blanket. It was our second night in the bush, and I was convinced that the NVA up on Dong Ap Bia had no idea we were in the area. If we could avoid stumbling into one of their patrols during the next two days, I honestly felt we could survive the mission and prove my premonition false.

We heard movement on the trail again around 2245 hours. Someone slipping and falling out on the damp trail, then muttering in Vietnamese, alerted us that more enemy soldiers were climbing toward the high ground to our south.

The generator kicked in again a few minutes after midnight. This time, it ran only for an hour before being shut down.

April 22, 1969

We had survived another day. I was beginning to feel like maybe we would make it through this, when Closson announced that he wanted to move up the ridge to find out what the enemy was doing there. He should have shot me on the spot. Something inside me snapped! I looked at him like he was nuts. "Closson, there ain't no fuckin' way I'm going up that ridge. What the hell do you want, man? You know what's going on up there."

He honestly looked hurt at my rejection of his idea. He got up in my face and said, "Our mission is to find out what the enemy is doing out here, and that's what I intend to do."

He was serious! "Look, Closson, you go ahead and go. I'm staying right here. Man, if we go up there now, I'll guarantee you my dream'll come true. I'm not going."

I could see he was getting upset. He was losing control of the situation, and he had to do something quickly. "Linderer, I'll court-martial you if you refuse to follow orders." I could tell he didn't mean it when he said it, but he was in too deep to stop now. "I mean it, I'll file the charges as soon as we get back."

I had to be alive to be court-martialed! "Go ahead, Larry. You do what you got to do. All I know is I'm too damn short to go up that ridge with you. John and Mother are too short, too, and Chambers won't go if the rest of us don't. You and Hillman go ahead and go. You guys can be the heroes. I'm staying right here until we get extracted tomorrow afternoon.'' I had called his bluff and had drawn the rest of the team into it behind me. If they didn't back me now, I was screwed.

I glanced over at Rucker and Sours. They looked at each other, then turned toward Closson and announced they weren't going, either. Sours was down to twenty-eight days, and Rucker had thirty-five days left in-country. Chambers popped up and announced that you didn't have to be short to have common sense. He, too, wasn't going to get himself killed just to verify what we already knew.

Closson was flabbergasted. He couldn't believe what was happening any more than we could believe he wanted to climb that damn mountain. He would have to court-martial all of us when we returned to Camp Eagle. I looked over at Hillman. He was stunned. The poor kid didn't know if we were all playing a big joke, or if he was witnessing a remake of *Mutiny on the Bounty*.

Finally, Closson gave in. He must have realized we were dead serious. Besides, we weren't in the best place to debate the merits of our arguments, but under the guidelines of a democratic society, he had just been plain out-voted.

We spent the rest of the day straining to listen for enemy traffic up on the trail. It was becoming apparent they were only using it at night.

At 1600 hours, another massive thunderstorm moved in around us and tried to turn us into Navy SEALs. It dropped a heavy volume of moisture on us, while scaring the hell out of us with volley after volley of streak lightning. I was beginning to understand where the phrase Arc Light came from.

When it ended thirty minutes later, Closson said he wanted to move to another location. It was bad policy to spend two nights in the same location. I probably pushed my luck when I thoughtlessly told him, ''You go ahead. I'm staying here till pickup.'' But by then, all my intentions of going out as a true Ranger had been forgotten.

Survival was now the only thing on my mind. In just over twenty-four hours, a helicopter was going to come and get us out of there. If Closson wanted to go, he was more than welcome.

Again, he didn't argue the point. But this time he was right. We should have moved. It was foolish staying in one place too long.

Our last night passed quickly. The generator came on again around midnight, and ran damn near to daylight. But we didn't hear any movement on the trail. I began to feel a little guilty for the way I had treated Closson. He had only tried to do his job. If it wasn't for that damn dream and the fact that I was so short, I would have gone up that ridge with him in a minute. It struck me at that instant that I was finished as a Ranger. My nerves were gone. I had seen it happen before. On four other occasions, LRPs and Rangers I had served with had just suddenly decided they weren't going out anymore. They had been good men and good soldiers, but had reached a point where they realized they had just had enough. No one had thought any less of them. It was company policy never to force anyone to go out on a mission. A man out there who didn't belong could jeopardize the entire team. Maybe they would understand my situation.

I finally drifted off to sleep wondering where I had misplaced my guts. I couldn't justify my actions earlier that day. I felt ashamed and knew that no one would ever understand.

April 23, 1969

I awoke chilled but relieved to be facing my last day in the bush. All we had to do was get through the next eleven hours without making contact, and a Huey would pick us up at our primary LZ.

I skipped breakfast. The chicken with rice LRRP I had premixed and then slept with just didn't seem very appetizing. My stomach was in no mood for that type of invasion.

Closson was avoiding me. I couldn't tell if he was still pissed or just hurt over my refusal to follow him up the mountain. There was a change in the air. All of us were beginning to react like death row inmates who had just been given a last-minute commutation of sentence.

We took turns napping and monitoring the trail for the rest of the day. No more groups of enemy soldiers passed our position, but we heard the faint sounds of hammering on two different occasions.

Closson called in our scheduled sitrep at 1500. When he passed the handset back to Rucker, he whispered that we would be extracted at 1800 hours from the same LZ we were supposed to have inserted into. We would move out right after the usual afternoon storm hit and try to reach the PZ fifteen minutes before the scheduled pickup. According to our topo map, the LZ was only three hundred meters west-southwest of us, at the base of the ridge we were on.

Less than three more hours and we would be out of this place. The premonition would become a bad memory, and I would be packing to leave for my R & R in four days. When I got back to the company around the seventh of May, I would be down to twenty-nine and a wake-up. Chances were I wouldn't pull another mission.

We could see the clouds gathering over and around Dong
Ap Bia a few minutes before 1600. I marveled at the odd-
ity of the phenomenon. Did this happen every day? Surely
it changed with the seasons.

At 1600 hours, right on the money, the clouds started
moving over us. We could hear the rumbling of the thunder as it swept toward us. Streaks of lightning tore the
gray sky apart, unzipping the bulging, low-hanging clouds
and forcing them to self-destruct in sheets of torrential
downpour. It rained so hard I could barely make out
Chambers sitting across the perimeter from me, eight feet
away. He sat huddled against his rucksack, wrapped in the
oilskin NVA poncho he always carried with him. He liked
it because it wasn't as noisy in a rainstorm as the U.S.-
issue heavy plastic ponchos. None of us ever used them
in the field for that very reason. Our nylon poncho liners
protected us for a little while. If the rain continued, we
just got wet. Unless it was during the monsoon season,
you knew the boiling sun would eventually return and bake
you dry.

About ten minutes after the storm hit, the rain let up a
little, only to give way to hail. No kidding! Hailstones in
Vietnam. Actual ice balls in the middle of this steamy blast
furnace of a country. What would they think of next?
Maybe the guys would have snow this Christmas. Too bad
I wasn't going to be here!

Closson was sitting in the center of the perimeter with
his back to me. I had set my rucksack up against a sapling
and was using it for a seat. At least it kept my ass out of
the mud. I looked down at Closson sitting at my feet. I
couldn't resist the temptation. Reaching down and picking
up a couple of hailstones, I dropped them down the back
of his neck. He reacted like he had been shot as the
marble-size ice cubes slid along his spine. Sours pulled
out his Penn double-E camera and started taking pictures
of my antics. The team leader finally figured out what was
going on and good-naturedly leaned back against my knees
to profile for the next shot. The famous Closson grin was
plastered all over his face. I sensed that I had been forgiven and things were back to normal.

Sours dropped his camera back into the clear plastic

battery cover and stuck it back into the pouch on the side of his ruck.

Closson drove an elbow back into my knee, a signal that the fun and games were over. It was almost time to move down to the PZ. He signaled for Rucker to contact the X-ray team across the valley on Firebase Blaze and tell them that we were heading out for the pickup point.

I saw Mom turn and pick up the handset tucked under the top flap on his indigenous rucksack. He had a plastic battery wrapper around it to keep it dry. Hillman had let the handset for the other radio get wet the second day out, and it had not worked since.

Rucker hunched over his codebook, constructing the message that would alert the relay team that we would be on the move. When he was done, he put the headset to his ear and keyed the ''talk'' button.

A blinding flash of light erupted around us, followed by a tremendous explosion that seemed to compress my ears together somewhere near the center of my skull. I opened my eyes just in time to see a black tidal wave of smoke and flying debris engulf us. Chambers disappeared in it as it rolled over him from behind. I remember flying up through the air and hitting something hard before crashing back to the earth . . . then nothing.

Something was dripping on my cheek . . . running down across my lips. Couldn't remember . . . where was I? Must be night. Can't see anything. Wait! I see something . . . like looking through wax paper. Ringing in my ears . . . they hurt. Everything's so quiet, only the sound of the rain. What's happened? Where am I? My God, why can't I move my legs?

Panic swept over me. The dream . . . the dream . . . it was happening now! I'm dying—maybe already dead. I don't feel anything, just the water running down my face. My arms . . . have to move them . . . feel my face. Yes— God yes—I can move my arms.

I brought my right hand up to my cheek, then to my eyes. I could see! Mud! My hand had come away covered in mud. My eyes darted left and right. Nothing looked familiar. The rest of the team was nowhere in sight. Everything looked different . . . brighter. I realized that all the overhead cover was gone. I tried to turn my head to look to my left. It hurt, but it was moving. I opened my eyes to see the trunk of a large teak inches from my face. Where was I? Nothing was familiar. Where was the rest of the team?

I had to get up . . . find out what had happened. The last thing I remembered was Rucker calling in the sitrep. The flash . . . explosion . . . smoke. Jesus, we had been hit. Why wasn't I dead? Got to move . . . find my weapon. No—nooo! My legs . . . nothing. Can't feel them. Got to look. No! Feel them.

I slid my right hand down along my side, past my hip, to the back of my leg. I slowly rolled the palm around the shape of something that was occupying the spot where my right thigh should have been. My touch told me it was there, but no message reached my brain from my right leg. I squeezed the object behind me. It had the substance of jello, not flesh. If it wasn't my leg, what was it? I turned my head, letting my eyes retrace the path my arm had taken. Oh God, *no*! It was my leg that my hand was grasping. But I couldn't feel it. The leg wasn't part of me anymore. The shock of it overwhelmed me. I was paralyzed! My legs were shattered. I couldn't feel anything from midchest down. Was this how I was to die—alone in the jungle, unable to move?

I wanted to scream. I was dying . . . wanted to die. I had always known that I would prefer death to a life sentence trapped inside a prison of unresponsive flesh and bone. My survival was no longer the question. I would not bring what was left of me back to the girl I loved. I could almost see the look of pity and sorrow on her pretty face, and realized that I could never condemn her to a life of a twenty-four-hour-a-day nursemaid to a cripple. She deserved a hell of a lot more than that.

An inner peace came over me. I had made my decision. I would die where I had fallen. If the enemy didn't find me soon, I knew I could will my own death. There was nothing more to live for. I felt no pain, but I knew the damage had to be severe. Surely I was bleeding somewhere. Bleeding to death was painless, like falling asleep. I turned my face toward the ground and closed my eyes to await the final moment. I saw Barb's face. She was crying. It wouldn't be long now. Just let go . . . let it happen.

I heard a voice, off in the distance. Couldn't make out what it was saying. It was in my mind. . . . No, I heard it again. Getting closer. I could hear brush breaking, someone breathing hard. The enemy was coming . . . looking for me. It would be over soon.

"Linderer! Linderer, you cocksucker . . . answer me." It was Chambers. He was behind me, downhill. "How bad are you hurt?"

I felt him at my shoulder, trying to roll me over. "Hang on, man. We'll get some help in for you. Just hang on."

I turned my head back to the right. "Leave me alone, Larry. Let me die. I'm not going back like this. My legs are gone. It's just like in the dream, dammit. Just go away."

He wouldn't give up. "Your ass! Your legs are all right. What the hell's the matter with you?"

I didn't answer. Let him ramble. I knew how bad it was. I was going to die right here, and there was no way Chambers could stop me.

"I'll be back. Hang on. I'll get help." I could hear him moving off to the rear. Good! Now I can die in peace.

Minutes later he was back. He had Sours with him. It was only then I realized that Chambers couldn't walk. He was crawling, unable to move his legs. Sours stood there holding his left arm. He was stunned, unable to understand what had happened. Chambers told him to help drag me back into the perimeter. I felt them grab me under the armpits and begin tugging.

I must have lost consciousness, because when I awoke, I was on my back surrounded by my teammates. Sours was still holding his left arm at the elbow. I heard him muttering, "Where's my arm? Where's my arm? It's got to be around here someplace."

Rucker was on his knees next to the radio, staring at his blackened hand and crying.

Closson was standing near the edge of the perimeter, left arm dangling clumsily by his side, looking like his mind was a long way off . . . a very, very long way.

Hillman was a little higher up the slope, still holding his weapon. His eyes flashed wide in the handsome black face. He couldn't begin to understand what had happened to the rest of his teammates.

I heard Chambers talking to Sours. "It wasn't the gooks, I'm telling you. It was lightning that hit us. Rucker's hand-set melted. It blew out the side of the radio. All our clay-mores exploded. Where's all our gear . . . our weapons?"

Rucker seemed to be recovering from the traumatic shock he had been suffering. I heard him say, "Got to get the other radio working. We need help quick." Hillman brought it over to him and set it down in front of him. He picked up the handset, switched frequencies, and called the relay team. The radio hadn't worked in two days, but Looney's voice came back, loud and clear as a bell. Rucker turned the volume down, then reported that we had five injured and requested dust offs for the entire team. Looney confirmed the message and told us to hang on, help was on the way.

Less than twenty minutes later, the radio crackled to life. It was a medevac asking us to pop smoke. Hillman pitched a yellow smoke canister down the slope from our position, as the Huey circled overhead. It swung in above us, hovering just over the tops of the trees. I watched as a steel body basket was lowered at the end of a wire cable. It hung up in the top of a six-inch-thick tree, jutting up from the edge of our perimeter. I could see the crew chief trying to maneuver it out of the branches, but he seemed unable to pull it clear of the vegetation. Sours moved over to the base of the tree and began pushing on it, trying to snap it off. Suddenly, Closson staggered down the slope and threw his weight onto it. The tree began bending, arching away from the opening in the overhead cover above us. It started to fall as the team leader forced his body higher up the trunk.

Free of the obstruction, the basket continued its down-ward path, finally coming to rest on the ground five feet from where I lay. Chambers grabbed it and slid it next to me. With the help of Sours and Hillman, he rolled me into it and secured the safety straps. I couldn't believe this was happening. Why couldn't they just let me die? But I no longer had the strength or the desire to protest.

I felt the cable grow taut, then lift me clear of the ground. Sours swung it away from the trees and guided it clear of the brush until I swung out of his reach. I saw the trees dropping beneath me, as the undercarriage of the Huey grew ever closer. Soon I could see the helmeted head of the crew chief looking down at me. He reached out and grabbed the cable, pulling me into the chopper. Tears came to my eyes as he slid the basket up against the rear wall of the cabin and disconnected the cable. I felt myself going under, losing consciousness . . . drifting away. Finally! I wouldn't fight it. I let myself go, welcoming the darkness that was settling over me. . . .

I was dreaming that I was on a soft white cloud. I must be in heaven. It couldn't be hell. I had just left hell. It was green and wet. A bright, blinding light . . . off in the distance . . . voices, muted and unintelligible. Faces, human faces, were swimming in and out of focus around me. They were looking down at me. Hands were reaching out . . . touching me . . . pulling on me. I could hear scissors snipping through cloth. I was in a hospital. I wasn't dead. "Let's get some X rays on him." Someone was wiping my face. Several people in surgical garb surrounded me. The light was so bright . . . giving me a headache. Why couldn't they turn it off . . . get it out of my eyes?

The faces disappeared. I felt a jerk. I was moving away from the light. Somebody was talking, telling me I was okay. "Concussion probably. No wounds." They couldn't have been talking about me! My legs were gone.

I was wheeled into another room. The lights weren't as bright. Two guys slid me onto a table. It felt cold under my back. Why couldn't I feel it anywhere else.

Someone said, "Hold it, don't move." They surely didn't mean me. I couldn't move if I wanted to.

I looked up to see the gray machinery of an X-ray unit over me. I heard the click and whir off to the side as the technician snapped his first exposure. He quickly changed plates and took a second shot. He came out from behind the leaded screen and shifted the boom from over my legs to a spot above my midsection. He disappeared back behind his shield and took another exposure of my spine.

They left me lying there for what seemed like hours while they developed the X rays. Finally, a couple of black medics came out and moved me back onto a gurney, then wheeled me down a long hallway to a recovery ward. I raised my head and saw that someone had been decent enough to cover my nakedness with a clean white sheet.

A doctor came in a few minutes later, a clipboard cocked over his arm, and asked me how I felt. I told him I didn't feel anything. He smiled and told me not to worry. It was trauma that was causing my paralysis and loss of sensation. He had talked to four of my teammates who were on another ward and had reconstructed what had happened. The lightning had hit our radio when the RTO had keyed the handset to call in that final sitrep. The electricity had exploded our claymores and detonated the concussion grenade in the side pocket of my rucksack. He said that since I had been injured the worst, and all of the hair had been singed off my legs, it had probably been the concussion grenade that had caused most of the damage. What he couldn't understand was why the lightning hadn't detonated our other grenades or the LAW that Sours had strapped to his rucksack. I didn't want to think about the willie pete that was in the opposite side pocket on my ruck. Somebody up there had been watching over us. He went on to tell me that the X-rays hadn't revealed any skeletal damage. With a little luck and some time, he didn't see why I wouldn't make a full recovery.

I couldn't believe his prognosis. And just a few hours ago, I had wanted to die! I asked him how the others were doing. He smiled and said they were all suffering from various degrees of concussion and shock, but were in better shape than I.

I drifted off to sleep, wondering if I should write and tell Barb and my family what had happened to me or wait to see if and how I recovered. Finally realizing that the army would probably be sending another wire, I wrote a short note to Barb telling her I was doing fine and was recovering quickly. I just hoped the doctor was right.

April 24, 1969

A nurse woke me at 0300 to give me a shot in the hip and a couple of pills. First time I ever got a shot that didn't sting. I noticed that my pillow was full of grit and tiny pieces of bark. When I ran my hands through my hair, I felt enough crap in there to root a houseplant. I wondered how long it would be before someone decided it was time to clean the jungle out of me.

They brought breakfast to me at 0700. I hadn't eaten in over thirty-six hours. The food was good, better than the standard army fare. They had to prop me up in bed to eat. The lower part of my body wouldn't function on its own. The sudden realization that I could easily be spending the rest of my days like this brought more tears. I couldn't accept the fact that the dead limbs lying under the sheet on the other end of my bed belonged to me.

Toward evening, a pretty brunette nurse stopped at the side of my bed and told me that Sergeant Sours and Sergeant Closson were being discharged. Except for a ringing in their ears and some numbness, they had made a full recovery. She said they had related the story of what had happened to us, and that we were all very lucky young men. I said, "Yes, ma'am, I sure am lucky all right." If she knew how lucky I was feeling right about then, she would have put a pistol in my mouth and pulled the trigger. "That's right, sergeant! In two or three days, you should be back on your feet again. The shock you suffered should begin to wear off anytime. Oh, you may experience some numbness and tingling in your legs, but you should make a full recovery. By the way, Sergeant Sours told me that you are getting married in a couple of months. Good luck to you." She turned and walked quickly out of the ward.

I looked up at the ceiling, as a feeling of relief swept over me. "My God, am I really going to survive this in one piece? Was the dream only a dream after all?" I suddenly realized my war was over. When I recovered, I still had an R & R coming. By the time I got back to the company, I would be under four weeks.

April 25, 1969

I awoke anxiously on the morning of the twenty-fifth, hoping that the feeling had returned to my useless limbs. Nothing! I fought back the wave of anxiety that surged up from my bowels, trying to grip my heart in its icy clutch. Oh, God, how I wanted to believe I would recover. They had promised me, assured me, that the feeling would return. When? When?

The same pretty nurse came back around supper time and told me Rucker and Chambers were regaining sensation in their limbs. They would be returning to L Company on the twenty-sixth. She asked me if I felt anything yet. I could only shake my head and respond, "Nothing!"

April 26, 1969

A doctor and a couple of nurses came in right after breakfast and said they wanted to run a few tests on me if I felt up to it. I said, "Yeah, go ahead."

They pulled the sheet down below my feet, exposing

my legs. I couldn't help but notice that someone had cleaned me up. I just couldn't remember when.

They ran a series of tests that checked for reflex, surface sensation, and muscle response to stimulation, temperature, and pain. I flunked them all. It was as if I were lying there watching them poking, prodding, and punching on someone in the next bed. When they finished, they smiled and tried to act like I was really coming along nicely, but I sensed a feeling of concern among them that belied their actions. I wasn't coming along nicely!

Right after lunch, I was propped up in bed, attempting to write a letter to my fiancée, telling her the truth about my condition. One of the bloods at the end of the ward was playing Little Richard music on a jam box—too loud. I was having a hard time concentrating. As I lay there pondering on a way to say what I needed to say, I looked down at my lifeless feet. They were the same feet I had taken for granted for twenty-two years, and it had never occurred to me that there would come a time when they would no longer serve me. In my hazy state of self-pity, I almost missed the movement. Matter of fact, I wasn't even sure it was movement. But something had caught my attention. I looked around quickly. No one was there! I glanced back at my feet. They were still at parade rest. Dammit, something had moved! I looked at them again . . . willing life into them. Move, you bastards! Move! The toes on my left foot flexed. I couldn't say that it was in response to my command, but they moved. I was ecstatic! I called for the nurse—anybody.

A black medic hurried over from the nurse's station in response to my shouting. He grinned when he saw me pointing at my toes. They were waving back excitedly. He quickly left the ward and returned a short time later with my doctor and the pretty brunette nurse. They were all smiling as they stood around the bed and watched me work out.

I couldn't believe how quickly total muscle control returned to my legs. By 1500 hours, I was walking up and down the ward. I wasn't going to win any races for a while, but, by God, I wasn't going home in a wheelchair, either.

The doctor tested me again three hours later. Except for

some residual numbness and poor epidermal sensation, he pronounced me as good as new. He would discharge me the following day. I thought for a moment, then asked him to discharge me right then and there. I was due to leave for R & R the next day. If I didn't get back to my unit, I would miss my flight. He laughed! "Soldier, three days ago you told me you were a dead man. Now you're worried about missing your R & R. Damned if I'll stand in your way!"

An hour later, I was standing outside the front door of the surgical hospital in a set of used OD jungle fatigues, waiting for a Jeep from L Company. I felt like I was returning from the dead. My legs had regained their strength to the point where I could walk again without holding on to something.

When I got back to the Ranger Compound and reported in, First Sergeant Cardon told me that S.Sgt. Dedman from the 1st Platoon had been killed six klicks away from where we had been hit by lightning. The slick he had been flying bellyman on took an RPG round going into an LZ.

April 27, 1969

I was back down at Phu Bai 1100 hours the next morning waiting for a C-130 flight to Bien Hoa. It looked like I would be in Hawaii a day or two before the letter I wrote the night before even reached my girl. I had rushed it off telling her that I would be in Honolulu on the thirtieth. I had already written to her on the twenty-fifth saying that, because of my injury, I wouldn't be going on R & R. I planned to call her the day I arrived to let her know what had happened. She would be confused—but elated.

The C-130 flew nonstop to the busy airport at Bien Hoa. I arrived at 1430 and reported to the R & R departure center with a copy of my orders. They sent me over to a

dispensary to get a couple of shots and to have myself
checked over for any sign of infectious disease. The medic
wanted to know what happened to the hair on my legs. I
don't think he believed the story I pitched him.

When I finished the physical, I hurried to the supply
area to reclaim the Class A uniform and civilian clothes I
had left there for safekeeping. Someone had gotten into
my duffel bag and removed the Levi's, sport shirts, and
deck shoes I had hidden at the bottom. I found my khakis
and my cunt cap wadded up under my jump boots. The
REMF son of a bitch that got into my gear even took my
civilian underwear. Well, I would just have to replace everything once I got to Hawaii.

I hurried over to the Korean laundry and dropped my
khakis off to be laundered and to have my E-5 stripes sewn
on. Then I ran over to the PX to pick up my ribbons. The
National Defense ribbon I had worn over from the States
had acquired some company. I picked up a Vietnamese
Campaign ribbon, a Vietnamese Service ribbon, a Bronze
Star with V device, a Purple Heart, and a Silver Star. The
CIB I bought next would look good with the two rows of
ribbons and my jump wings. At least no one would mistake me for a goddamned cherry.

April 29, 1969

After spending two days in a swimming suit soaking up
some rays, I boarded a Pan Am 707 for the twelve-hour
flight to sunny Hawaii. There were 126 of us on board,
most of whom were officers. Rank seemed forgotten as
we partied hard, trying to make the most of this break
from war.

April 30, 1969

When we landed at Honolulu International Airport, I could see scores of women waiting for us on the balcony of the terminal building. I had heard such stories about Sydney, Australia, but no one who had come back from Hawaii had reported this phenomenon. I prepared to fight them off as we disembarked from the plane. After all, I had avoided the disease-ridden dens of sex and sin in exotic Vietnam for nearly eleven months. I had made up my mind to leave it alone for the last month of my tour, so I could enjoy that much more the pleasure of making love to the woman who had waited so loyally for my return. It sounded corny at the time, but it fit the noble returning soldier image I was trying to build.

I held back as we walked across the concrete apron to the terminal. At least I wouldn't have to fight through all of them. The ladies began waving madly as we approached. There were some real beauties in the cluster of milling females. My resolve was about to be tested.

They were waiting for us when we cleared customs. I was amazed to see how they seemed to know exactly which soldier they wanted. When the mad rush was over, I looked around to see that only myself and a Marine lance corporal were left behind. Now, I may not be the best-lookin' guy in the world, but I was a damn long way from being the ugliest. I couldn't believe that out of 126 soldiers, I tied for last place—and with a bald-headed Marine to boot. The elastic garters, blousing my pants, were the only thing that prevented my ego from sliding down my leg and out onto the floor of the terminal.

I noticed the jar-head was looking over at me. Knowing that they hung queers in the Corps, I figured that he was only trying to be friendly. I smiled, and he moved over to

273

where I was standing alongside my duffel. "Makes you kinda wish you were married, too, doesn't it?"

I guess the surprised look on my face pushed him to elaborate. "Yeah, all those females are here from the States to meet their husbands. Married men are about the only ones who ever come here. This was my second choice. I wanted Sydney, but you got to be halfway through your second tour or suck some general's ass to get Australia. I guess you ain't married, huh?"

I shook my head. "No, but dammit I oughta be!" We went outside and caught a cab to downtown Honolulu. I sure in the hell didn't want to go out to Fort DeRoussie and let the army show me how to enjoy my R & R. My plans were to eat at every restaurant in Honolulu over the next six days. For exercise between feeds, I would soak up rays on Waikiki Beach. That was my idea of rest and relaxation.

May 5, 1969

It was tough going back to Vietnam. Civilization had made a valiant effort to reclaim me. I threw myself into the almost carnal pleasures of exquisite repasts and copious libation—I ate and drank my guts out.

A $300, two-and-a-half-hour call to my fiancée fulfilled every sexual fantasy I could imagine. She was as anxious to be married as I was. I promised her that, come June 20, a lust-driven LRP/Ranger would make her wedding night a most memorable one indeed.

Throughout my R & R, I was plagued with guilt about having left my comrades in the field. How could I enjoy myself while they were back in the Nam suffering and dying out in the mountainous jungles? Man, if six lousy days could bring on this type of survivor's guilt—what was DEROS going to do to me?

May 9, 1969

The C-130 touched down lightly on the airstrip at Phu Bai. I felt like I was back home again. I had been gone almost two weeks, and it had felt like years. I wondered if we had lost anyone while I was gone. Every one of those Rangers was a brother to me, and the loss of any one of them would leave a permanent scar on my very soul. A panic set in as I walked across the hot, sticky tarmac to the terminal. I felt a sense of foreboding. I didn't take the time to call the company for a Jeep, but hitched a ride with a truckload of engineers heading for the 326th.

They dropped me off outside the entrance to the company area. I nodded my thanks and walked quickly up the road toward the TOC.

I dropped my bag outside the entrance to the orderly room and entered through the screen door. Tim Long was sitting behind his desk reading the latest issue of *Stars & Stripes*. He looked up and smiled, then took the paperwork I held out to him. He asked how my R & R had gone, and I told him I had probably gained fifty pounds.

I stepped back into the bright sunlight and headed past the line of hootches toward the second to last one, housing Teams 22 and 24. I ran into Kenn Miller crossing the road, coming from the supply tent. He waved when he saw me, so I stopped to wait for him to catch up.

"Did you hear about Hammond and Reynolds?" he asked as he climbed the embankment in front of me.

"No! What happened?" I queried, not really wanting to hear what I knew had to be bad news.

"Hammond got killed on a mission four days ago. The stupid son of a bitch just had to go out on one mission before he DEROSed. Couldn't stand being the CO's driver and watching the rest of us go out all the time. Talked me

into taking him out with my team. Never should have
agreed.'' Miller had tears in his eyes as he started to tell
the story.

"We got a warning order on the first for a mission in
an RZ just southeast of the A Shau. They told us during
the briefing that two Special Forces recon teams, one from
FOB 1 and the other from Project Delta, had disappeared
without a trace in the same area during the past twelve
months. Both teams had failed to make scheduled sitreps.
Neither team had reported any movement or sightings prior
to its disappearance. We were given the locations of their
last reported positions, but not any information on the
proposed routes of march they'd prepared before their insertion.

"The terrain was mountainous, with a dogleg valley
containing a fairly wide stream that was visible from the
air during our overflight. The stream was just east of our
RZ. There was a lot of double-canopy, but some fairly
open areas with high grass and clumps of trees on the
slopes and ridges. The north-south section of the valley
was all triple-canopy, but the northwest-southeast segment
of the dogleg was nearly all elephant grass, with a few
stands of trees.

"My ATL, Dearing, thought there must have been one
hell of a fire in that part of the valley a few years back.
What seemed strange to me was the complete lack of bomb
craters anywhere in the RZ, except up on the ridge where
we were inserting.

"We were to go in on the morning of the third. Hammond begged to go out on the mission with us. He was
scheduled to ETS in ten fuckin' days and wanted to be
able to tell one real war story when he got home. He had
been running the Ranger lounge since you left for R & R.
I shouldn't have agreed. I had a bad feeling about this
mission, but shook it off as my first case of short-timers
nerves.

"A major from G-2 came down and told us we'd get a
pallet of beer and a case of whatever kinda whiskey we
wanted if we brought back a prisoner. He also wanted us
to look for any sign of those two Special Forces teams that
had vanished. They even gave us a new mini-size starlight
scope, about the size of a soda bottle. He issued us a

recently developed collapsible gas mask that was only good for CS gas, and recommended we use CS canisters during any attempt to grab a prisoner. It struck me as a load of shit, but I filed it away, just in case.

"Our 'first light' insertion ended up getting us in at about 1000 hours. We went in on the ridge full of craters and laid dog for quite a while. I got this big fuckin' leech on my arm while we were hiding. The prick exploded like a firecracker when I touched a match to him.

"We moved down the slope and found a whole network of trails, paralleling each other along the ridge. There wasn't much cover between them to hide in. A couple of hundred meters off our LZ, we found a complex of five or six abandoned hootches that hadn't been used in a few months. They were at a junction of three trails. We got some photos, then moved on down the side of the ridge.

"We hadn't gone very far, when we found another trail that had some fresh sign on it. We pulled off into some heavy cover, while Hammond and Dearing went out on a point recon. They returned a few minutes later, saying they had found a fresh cache.

"I took the whole team back to the site and set up security around it. We dug in the fresh dirt and came up with an old log coffin. You should have seen it! The damn thing looked like it had just been buried, but the coffin was old. I checked it for booby traps, then slowly lifted the lid. There was a skeleton inside, laying in a bed of black mud. There was nothing else in the grave. We took a picture of it, then reburied the whole thing.

"We spent the rest of the day monitoring trails farther down the side of the ridge. We were still under double-canopy, but could tell that there was only grass and shrubs below us. We had discovered several places where the cover had been cleared away next to the trails. The sites were big enough for a full platoon to laager overnight in. We found some heavy cover nearby and spent the night listening for the gooks to come back.

"Around noon the next day, we moved farther down the side of the ridge where the grass started. We found a wide, hard-packed high-speed trail and set up an OP to monitor it. It looked like a good place to snatch a prisoner and get out quick, so we set up some CS grenades along the trail with electric detonators and sat back to wait.

"An hour later, we heard someone singing and spotted this gook dressed in fatigues coming down the trail. He didn't have a weapon, but he was carrying a big canvas satchel. We blew our CS when he was right in front of us. Dearing and Doc Glasser jumped out to grab the dude while he was disoriented, but he took off down the trail, screaming and shouting for help. Dearing and Glasser realized they weren't going to catch him, so they opened up on him. They hit him, but it didn't slow him down a bit. Man, that CS never even fazed the bastard.

"We heard someone hollering back from farther down the trail, so we skied up and booked out of there—muy pronto! We covered a couple hundred meters, and I pulled the team up into some heavy cover. It looked like our good weather was about ready to come to an end. The clouds were really coming in from the west. Knowing we had been compromised, I called for an extraction on our alternate insertion LZ. The X-ray team passed it back to the CO, and I heard the bastard radio back and tell the relay team that we could forget it. He wanted us to stay in and develop the situation.

"I wasn't developing nothin'. We busted ass in the direction of our alternate LZ anyway. The weather broke before we even got there. It was the worst goddamned rainstorm I had ever seen. It got dark, and the rain was coming down so hard that we couldn't hear anything. I didn't know whether to shit or give thanks.

"We spent the night in a tight wagon-wheel perimeter, in the middle of the thickest patch of vegetation we could find. It was right between two trails, with another one just below us. We lost our commo and spent the rest of the night freezing our asses off, while gooks walked all around us with flashlights looking for us. A couple of the guys even thought they heard dogs. Nobody slept a wink.

"The next morning, the rain let up. We had commo again, and I reported what had gone on around us during the night. The CO told us to move to the LZ for pickup.

"We moved out immediately and found boot prints in the mud everywhere. We didn't see anyone, and I don't think anyone saw us, but you never know.

"When the chopper got there, we could see Miner, flying belly-man, ready to kick out the rope ladder. I hate those fuckin' ladders. The damn rungs are too far apart.

"The brush was whipping all around us as we started to climb. Dearing was anchoring the ladder. I could hear firing as the first four guys went up. I started up and motioned for Dearing to come up behind me. Just as I started to scramble into the cabin, I saw the door gunner signaling me to get off the ladder. I thought he was out of his fucking gourd.

"Suddenly the ship began turning beneath its rotors, and I knew we were going to die. We bounced a couple of times, then started rolling down the hillside. I remember trees snapping as we kept turning over. Then I must have fallen out of the ship. I was downslope—alone—without my rucksack or my weapon. I felt a pain in my hand, and when I looked down, there was a piece of metal sticking through it.

"I spotted the wreckage of the chopper uphill from me and headed toward it. I found my rucksack and that piece-of-shit starlight scope right away, but I couldn't find my CAR-15 anywhere. I stopped to wash the dirt off my face in a little stream that was trickling down the slope, then realized it was chopper fuel.

"I thought Dearing had been crushed on that first bounce. The Huey must have landed right on top of him. Then I saw him up near the PZ. I was fifty meters from where the chopper had tried to pick us up. We linked up and headed for the wreckage.

"We found Hammond's body on the way. The top of his head had been chopped off, slick as shit. I couldn't believe it—one fucking mission and he gets it like that. His rucksack and weapon weren't anywhere around.

"We moved up to the top of a little box draw. The pilot, a captain, was running around blaming us for his ship getting shot down and snapping orders that didn't make sense. I had to pull my pistol out and shove it in his face to get him to calm down. I told him I was in command on the ground, not him. He finally settled down. We pulled the SOIs, the M-60s, and the radios from the wreckage, while the door gunners sat there dazed.

"I knew that the gooks would be moving in on us at

any moment. I looked up, and we got a Cobra overhead, making gun runs around us. We picked up Captain Cardona on the radio, and he tells us there was no other ship in all of I Corp rigged with ladders or McGuires. It's going to be a while before we get any help.

"The Cobra fires up his ammo and has to go back to rearm and refuel. The CO follows him back in the C & C ship. All we got left for company is the relay team—and the gooks. By this time, we can hear them moving around above us. For some unknown reason they never come down for us.

"We retrieved Hammond's body just before the CO gets back out to us. I ask for permission to destroy the chopper before they come in to get us out. He tells me that he can't accept my word or the pilot's that the ship is beyond salvage. He has to get permission from a general officer to authorize us to destroy it. I ain't believin' it. We either blow it or the gooks get it.

"Finally, a dust off comes out and hovers over us. I got to go through the relay team to talk to him because of a 'hot' mike. When I inform him that I can see him taking rounds in his belly, he relays back and tells me that it's okay—he wants to get our friend's body out. God, I wish he'd have been flying our extraction! He radios back and wants to know if we have anymore casualties. I told him 'negative' and sent him away. I had already pulled the piece of metal out of my hand and wrapped a bandage around it. I was cowardly tempted to go out as wounded, but the temptation passed as quickly as it came. I'm still ashamed I even thought about it.

"Finally, after an hour and a half, a ladder-rigged ship with Chambers flying belly-man arrives on the scene. I had to make the chopper crew of the downed Huey get up on the nose of their ship and leap for the bottom rung of the ladder. Man, I never thought they would make it. Funny what a little adrenaline can do for you!

"Each of them got part way up and crapped out. Chambers had to come out on the skid, then halfway down the ladder to help them up. The pilot is holding the chopper in as close as he can get, and Chambers is all over the outside of the ship directing the pilot and helping people up the ladder. The chopper was really boxed in. I kept thinking that it was going to put a rotor into the slope above it.

"The Cobra shows up again, takes some fire and makes a few gun runs, and then has to leave.

"I never saw the C & C ship again. I could hear the CO on the radio, but he managed to stay out of sight. The extraction ship gets the chopper crew on board along with three of our guys and heads back to the nearest firebase.

"Finally, five or six hours after we go down, only McCann and I are left on the ground. I got a pistol, an M-79, and somebody's 16. McCann and I each have a radio. I look up and see black storm clouds coming back in. I just knew they wouldn't make it back in time.

"Then we see the chopper coming back, just a tiny dot running ahead of the cloud front. It's over the top of us quick, and Chambers gets us aboard just as the storm hits. Man, a few more minutes and we would still be in there.

"As we're flying out, a fast mover comes tearing in to destroy the wreckage of the Huey. Some general somewhere must have given the CO permission. I guess that's where he'd been all that time!

"Boy, was I relieved to get out of there. When we got back to Eagle, Chambers says the pilot thought we were going down just as we were lifting out. He looked down and saw gooks swarming all over the slope we had just come out of. It was almost like they had been waiting for us to leave. I hope the F-4 got 'em all."

I stood there, still trying to rationalize Hammond's death. He had been a neat guy, older than the rest of us and highly educated. He had a master's degree from some ritzy east coast university. He had been a Ranger, but didn't belong out on a mission like that. I could only hope that my friend, Miller, would not blame himself for Hammond's death. He seemed very upset that the army hadn't listed Hammond as killed by hostile action. They had listed him as killed by accident.

I shook my head, then asked Miller what had happened to Reynolds. He told me that he hadn't gotten all of the facts yet, but that Reynolds's team had been on a mission out near the game preserve the previous day. They were following a trail out of the jungle, with Reynolds walking his own point. When they came out into the open, the gooks were waiting. They opened up on the team, killing Reynolds immediately. The team recovered his body and pulled back for an emergency extraction. They had to call in artillery on the enemy positions to keep the gooks at bay until they were airborne.

Reynolds had been a tall, good-looking E-6 who had graduated from the NCO program back at Benning. He had won the Gerber dagger at MACV Recondo School just a month before. He'd been one hell of a team leader before he had gotten himself greased.

Miller and I walked on past the hootches. The loss of two more Rangers weighed heavily on each of us. We sat on top of the last bunker chain-smoking a half pack of Winstons and talked about what it would be like going home. He was scheduled to leave in a couple of days to spend his final month recruiting replacements for the company down in Bien Hoa. I was down to twenty-seven days and a wake-up and just wanted to survive for four more weeks.

May 12, 1969

Somebody was out to get the first sergeant. Last night, he found a claymore under his bunk pointing straight up where his head would have been. The electrical wire was running out under his hootch and up toward the rear of our compound. He seemed to be a little shook up by the experience and had scheduled guards to patrol around the lifer's hootch during the hours of darkness.

Word came down through the grapevine that the 3/187th had stepped into some shit out in the A Shau. Colonel "Blackjack" Honeycutt's Rakkasans had run into some dug-in NVA bunker complexes on the slopes of Dong Ap Bia. We heard that it was pretty close to the area where we had gotten zapped by lightning back on April 23. I didn't envy them a bit. The very name of the place now evoked a fear in me that was more than I wanted to deal with at the time.

May 14, 1969

We had some trouble with a bunch of bloods from 501st Signal. They tried to come into the company area after dark and ran into one of our guys down near the entrance to our compound. When he informed them that the Ranger compound was off-limits, they jumped him and were giving him a pretty rough time until the first sergeant and a couple of other Rangers heard the noise and came to the rescue. No more blows were thrown, but the bloods made some nasty threats before they finally withdrew. Man, none of us had any idea what was happening over here, but things seemed to be going to hell in a hurry.

May 16, 1969

About 2300 hours, I was sitting on my bunk writing a letter to my fiancée, when all hell broke loose down at the other end of the row of hootches. There had been a dull explosion, followed by a short burst of automatic-weapons fire. I grabbed my M-16 and a bandolier of ammo and ran through the back door of the hootch, intending to come up behind the rear of the bunker between my hootch and the one next door. I figured that we had sappers down in the wire.

As I cleared the hootch, I heard another burst of automatic-weapons fire and saw red tracers ricocheting up toward the 501st Signal battalion's compound. My first thought was that we had gooks behind us, already well inside the base camp.

I locked-'n'-loaded and headed down toward the scene of the action with about fifteen other armed Rangers. When we got to the rear of the lifer's hootch, we found that the Ranger who had been on guard outside the NCO barracks had done all the shooting.

He told us that he had spotted someone standing on the inside of the concertina wire strung across the back of our compound. When he had yelled for the man to stop and identify himself, he heard the *pop* of a lever flying off a grenade, and then the dull thud of something heavy landing on top of the sandbagged blast-wall outside the lifer's hootch—just about where First Sergeant Cardin was sleeping.

The sentry grabbed the grenade before it cooked off and pitched it back over the embankment behind the TOC shed, then turned and fired a burst from his M-16 at the saboteur. As the grenade exploded harmlessly, he emptied the rest of his magazine in the direction of the fleeing figure.

Fortunately, no one had been injured in the affair. The terrified first sergeant quickly doubled the guard around the NCO's barracks and swore that it had to have been the bloods he had run off a couple of days before. They had come back to get even.

The situation in Nam was deteriorating rapidly. News of fraggings and soldiers refusing to follow orders was coming in every week. Not so much in the 101st, but in some of the leg units south of us. The antiwar and racial tensions back home were beginning to be felt among the troops. So far, it seemed to be manifesting itself primarily among the noncombat units. Vietnam was dangerous enough without this kind of shit going on.

May 19, 1969

I took an eight-man ambush team outside the wire the night of the eighteenth. I had to admit that it felt good to be out again. It was a humbug—nothing passed through our kill zone. I would have liked to have had just one last crack at the enemy before I left country. Of course, I had seen enough of my friends killed and wounded in those little humbug missions where nothing was ever supposed to happen.

When we came back in at first light, I discovered that my bridge-playing buddy, Bill Marcy, had been killed on a mission the night before. His team had been inserted at last light on a mountaintop near Firebase Rakkassan west of Camp Evans. They had laid dog until after dark, then had started to move off the crest. Twenty meters over the side, they heard movement below them, and Marcy moved the team back up onto the LZ.

Soon, they had movement all around them. Marcy called in and reported that they had been compromised on their LZ and asked for an extraction.

As the choppers were approaching, Bill moved outside the perimeter and turned on his strobe light. He radioed for the chopper to land twenty-five meters away from the strobe, close to where the rest of the team lay hidden. The Gooks moved up to the edge of the perimeter and began to mass for an assault. Marcy took off in a dead sprint for the Teams perimeter. A burst of AK-47 fire caught him in the back, killing him instantly.

Frank Anderson took over the team and went out on the LZ to recover Marcy's body and the primary radio. Fortunately, the NVA withdrew until the team was extracted.

It was a sad day in L Company. Bill had been popular. He had come from Massachusetts and had been the son of a navy admiral. His father had disowned him for turning down a chance to go to the U.S. Naval Academy and enlisting in the army instead. Tragic! Marcy had been another excellent team leader whose loss we could ill afford. We had suffered four dead in less than four weeks. Three of them had been team leaders. May had already become the second-worst month for casualties the company had ever experienced.

Sours left to go home on the eighteenth. He had promised me that he would be in my wedding on the twentieth of June. Tim Long, Jim Schwartz, and John Looney all swore they would be there, too—just to make sure that I went through with it. If they only knew!

I couldn't help but think about Terry Clifton. Terry would have been there if he hadn't been killed last November. I had avoided thinking about his death, but as I got closer and closer to DEROS, it was constantly on my mind. My guilt over his death, always there just under the surface, was beginning to build into an emotional crisis for me. He would be alive today, if he had not volunteered to switch places with another teammate just to go out with me. I was responsible for his death.

May 23, 1969

The action out near Dong Ap Bia ended a couple of days ago. It was called Operation APACHE SNOW. The 3/187th ran head on into the 29th NVA Regiment entrenched on a mountaintop out in the A Shau. Before it was over, eleven days later, the 1/506th and 2/506th, the rest of the 3d Brigade of the 101st, and two battalions of the ARVN 1st Infantry Division were fed into the battle. We destroyed the NVA regiment but suffered heavy losses doing it. The operation centered around the capture of the NVA regimental base camp on a high mountain on the western end of the A Shau. We had known the moutain as Dong Ap Bia four weeks ago, when we had watched over two hundred NVA soldiers move past our OP on their way up its side. A month later, the survivors of the 3d Brigade would call it "Hamburger Hill."

May 24, 1969

Only twelve more days and a wake-up, and I'm out of here. I received my orders assigning me to the 82d Airborne back at Fort Bragg. The wound in my right leg and the injury to my back from the concussion grenade would probably keep me from jumping again. If the army put me on a physical profile, I made up my mind that I would 1049 to another duty station closer to my home. I would not serve in the 82d and not be able to jump. Besides, it would be easier on my future bride if I could get stationed closer to home. I owed her that much, at least.

May 27, 1969

The realization that I was now a single-digit midget was just beginning to hit home. Somewhere, back in the States, some commercial pilot had already received his flight schedule authorizing him to bring my freedom bird over to pick me up and take me back to the World. You couldn't get much shorter than that!

May 29, 1969

In the afternoon, I was to catch a flight out of Phu Bai for the rear. A week of processing out and waiting for my flight, and Vietnam would become nothing more than a memory. I realized just how much I was going to miss these guys. Most of them had already gone. John Sours, Jim Schwartz, Dave Biedron, Joe Bielesch, Kenn Miller, and Mother Rucker had already departed for the rear. John Looney, John Mezaros, Claymore Owens, and Boom Boom Evans would be leaving for Bien Hoa around the same time as me.

The company held an awards ceremony late in the morning. I was presented with another Silver Star. The orders stated that it was for my actions during the ambush we initiated on the morning of November 20, 1968. It didn't make any sense to me. They had already given me a Silver Star as an impact award for the action that day. Now they were trying to distinguish between the ambush we initiated and the subsequent ambush we got caught in. I'll never figure the army out.

They also gave me another Purple Heart. That did make sense! I got hit two times in the same firefight. That should be worth a couple of Purple Hearts. Besides, Hillman and I were the only two Rangers on the team who didn't get Purple Hearts after we got hit by lightning a month before. Colonel DeLoach also pinned above my left pocket a Bronze Star for meritorious service, an Army Commendation Medal with V (for the Firebase Jack mission), and an Air Medal with an oak-leaf cluster. Well, at least I would not be going home bare-chested.

I felt a deep sense of pride, not because of the medals, but for the recognition for a job well done. Decorations and awards for valor have a way of never quite telling the true story. But because of the heroic men I had served with, my medals became a symbol to me that I had been one of them. Those people back home who had sat out the war would never know the feeling that clutched my heart at that moment.

June 5, 1969

The big Tiger Airlines 707 gained speed as it raced down the runway at the Bien Hoa Airbase. I closed my eyes and held my breath as the nose of the plane tilted back and lifted off the tarmac, plunging up through the superheated air over the world's busiest airport. The pressure in my ears convinced me we were airborne. I opened my eyes and looked up at the top of the bulkhead. I had made it! I had survived my year in hell.

Suddenly, I found myself screaming like a banshee with the rest of the homeward-bound GIs. The war was over for us. The hurt, the pain, the suffering, the nightmares, the dead comrades, were all back there behind us. We were on our way back home to resume the lives that Vietnam had interrupted. At least that's what we believed at the moment.

Tears filled my eyes as I took one last look at Vietnam. The green and brown grids of rice paddies and jungle, crisscrossed by meandering ribbons of silvered waterways, slid from view as the plane flew out over the South China Sea. Vietnam would always be a part of me.

EPILOGUE

The Vietnam War ended in 1975. For me, it ended fifteen years later, in 1990. I had spent twenty-one long years thinking I had left my war in those steamy, verdant jungles of Southeast Asia. I hadn't. It had followed me back to the World. It had lurked behind me on dark nights. It had reopened old wounds every time I watched a movie about Vietnam. It had prevented me from loving my wife and children as a husband and father should. It had forced me to avoid making deep commitments to others, and made me fear any type of emotional bonding that could result in my being hurt again.

Its vivid nightmares had come so often that I could no longer sleep like a normal human being. I forced myself to remain awake each night until, finally, utter exhaustion sent me into an unconscious state where dreams did not exist.

Its memories, both good and bad, were never far away. I was proud to have served, but ashamed to have survived. I lost a lot of good friends and buddies whose faces plague me to this day—not in a haunting way, but in a way that keeps them constantly in my thoughts and in my prayers. The bonding—welded in fire, fear, and blood—had lain dormant over all those years since the Nam, but its absence had left a gaping void in me that had prevented me from feeling whole again.

In 1986, the first reunion of the men who had served in 1/101 LRRP, F Company, 58th Inf. (LRP), and L Company, 75th Inf. (Ranger), took place at Fort Campbell, Kentucky. Nearly two hundred of us now-middle-aged recon men gathered there to once again re-establish and reaffirm that sense of camaraderie that had tied us together so closely in our youth; not to recapture that youth, but to rekindle that spirit that we had never forgotten.

Together, we had loved and laughed, played and partied, fought and died. We didn't do it for America. We didn't do it for tradition. We didn't do it out of some archaic sense of patriotic duty. We did it for each other. When it all came down to the final curtain—we were all we had.

Writing the story of my year in Vietnam has helped me to heal the open wounds left by that experience. I have never been bitter, nor placed blame on anyone for the failure of our effort in Vietnam. Yet, a devastating sense of guilt for my share in that failure was always there, just below the surface. But now I realize that our effort was as valiant, and as noble, and as pure, and as sacrificing, as any effort put forth by any soldier who had ever defended our flag. Unfortunately, our endeavors were judged alongside the inept and ignominious performance of our government, under the ignoble and traitorous influence of our media, and by the disloyal and uncaring vocal minority of our countrymen who condemned us.

We sought forgiveness and understanding, and received nothing but contempt and scorn in return. Most of us have borne our wounds quietly, hiding the pain of those memories deep in our subconscious, hopefully never to resurface again. But we have all discovered that the fathomless depths of our subconscious were not deep enough to protect us from the nightmares and the flashbacks of Vietnam.

When those horrible memories resurfaced, as they did on occasion, we tried to make others understand, but no one wanted to listen to our stories. Well, America, it's time to listen now. We have suffered long enough.

The healing balm for our wounds has always been there, waiting for us to find it. It was not in the shame and hurt we have borne for the duty we fulfilled. It was not in the advice and counsel of well-meaning professionals. It was not in the business end of a loaded revolver. No, my friends, the medicine we needed to heal those old wounds was in each of us—helping each other to restore those old bonds of friendship and devotion that were forged in the flames of war. Make the effort to locate those old comrades. Attend the reunions. Put to rest those demons that come to haunt us in the night. The good-byes that were never said were never really meant to be good-byes. We survived Vietnam by supporting each other. We can survive post-Vietnam the same way.

CASUALTIES
1st Brigade LRRPs, F Co. (LRP),
L Co. (Rangers)
Killed in Action

Date	Rank	Name	Unit
05/15/67	Sp4c.	David Allen Dixon	1/101
09/15/67	Sp4c.	John Lester Hines	1/101
11/01/67	Pfc.	George Buster Sullens Jr.	1/101
12/19/67	Sgt.	Patrick Lee Henshaw	1/101
01/23/68	Sp4c.	John T. McChesney	1/101
03/22/68	Sp4c.	Thomas John Sturgal	F Co.
04/23/68	Pvt.	Ashton Hayward Prindle	F Co.
06/02/68	Sgt.	Thomas Eugene Riley	F Co.
11/20/68	Sp4c.	Terry W. Clifton	F Co.
11/20/68	Sgt.	Albert D. Contreros Jr.	F Co.
11/20/68	Sp4c.	Arthur J. Heringhausen Jr.	F Co.
11/20/68	Sgt.	Michael Dean Reiff	F Co.
04/01/69	Sp4c.	Barry Leigh Golden	F Co.
04/23/69	S. Sgt.	Dean Julian Dedman	L Co.
05/05/69	Sgt.	Keith Tait Hammond	L Co.
05/08/69	S. Sgt.	Ronald Burns Reynolds	L Co.
05/20/69	Sgt.	William Lincoln Marcy	L Co.
10/26/69	Pfc.	Michael Linn Lytle	L Co.
01/11/70	S. Sgt.	James William Salter	L Co.
01/11/70	Sgt.	Ronald Wayne Jones	L Co.
04/08/70	Sp4c.	Rob George McSorley	L Co.
05/11/70	Sgt.	Gary Paul Baker	L Co.
05/11/70	S. Sgt.	Raymond Dean Ellis	L Co.
05/11/70	S. Sgt.	Robert Lee O'Conner	L Co.
05/11/70	Cpl.	George Edward Fogleman	L Co.
05/11/70	Pfc.	Bryan Theotis Knight	L Co.
05/11/70	Sgt.	David Munoz	L Co.
05/19/70	S. Sgt.	Roger Thomas Lagodzinski	L Co.
05/22/70	S. Sgt.	John Thomas Donahue	L Co.
08/25/70	Sp4c.	Jack Moss Jr.	L Co.
08/29/70	Sp4c.	Lawrence Elwood Scheib Jr.	L Co.
08/29/70	Pfc.	Harry Thomas Henthorn	L Co.
01/11/72	Sp4c.	Hershel Duane Cude Jr.	L Co.
09/25/70	Sgt.	Lloyd Harold Grimes II	L Co.
11/16/70	S. Sgt.	Norman R. Stoddard Jr.	L Co.
11/16/70	Sgt.	Robert George Drapp	L Co.

02/15/71	Sgt.	Steven Glenn England	L Co.
02/15/71	Lt.(jg)	James Leroy Smith	L Co.
02/15/71	Sgt.	Gabriel Trujillo	L Co.
02/21/71	Sp4c.	Richard Lee Martin	L Co.
03/22/71	Sp4c.	David Roy Hayward	L Co.
03/26/71	Cpl.	Joël Richard Hankins	L Co.
04/06/71	S. Sgt.	Leonard James Trumblay	L Co.
04/16/71	Capt.	Paul Coburn Sawtelle	L Co.
04/16/71	Sgt.	James Bruce McLaughlin	L Co.
04/24/71	Sp4c.	Johnnie Rae Sly	L Co.
05/08/71	Sgt.	Gary Duane Ellis	L Co.
06/12/71	Lt.(jg)	Ralph Lee Church	L Co.
06/13/71	Pfc.	Steven John Ellis	L Co.
06/13/71	Cpl.	Charles Anthony Sanchez	L Co.
08/20/71	Cpl.	Johnny Howard Chapman	L Co.
01/20/72	Sp4c.	Harry Jerome Edwards	L Co.

Honorary LRP/Ranger

03/09/69	CWO	David Allen Poley	2/17 Cav.

Missing In Action

04/24/71	S. Sgt.	James Albert Champion	L Co.

Died

1968	John James Quick	F Co.
1969	Donald L. Brickle	L Co.
	Terry N. Thayer	F & L Co.
1971	Vern W. Kirkland	F & L Co.
1972	William R. Kirby	L Co.
	Raymond P. Zoschak	F & L Co.
1975	Kenneth D. Steimel	L Co.
1976	Steve Kosimides	L Co.
	James M. Meiners	F Co.
1978	James L. Walker	F & L Co.
1979	Clarence J. Cardin	L Co.
1980	Nick Caberra	F Co.
	Edward I. James	L Co.
	Charles Wilkes	L Co.
1981	Peter Pirdavri	L Co.
	Joseph R. Rivera	L Co.
1982	Russel J. Brocker	L Co.
1983	Dave Clark	L Co.
1984	Stephen M. Ubel	L Co.
1985	Jarvis L. Dail	L Co.
1989	Albert T. Bartz	L Co.

1990	Richard R. Butler	L Co.
1990	Neal R. Gentry	L Co.
1990	Ronald H. Bowman	F/L Cos.

Rest in peace.

GLOSSARY

(A)

AA—anti-aircraft.

AC—aircraft commander, pilot.

acid pad—flat, hard-surfaced area designed to accommodate helicopter landings and take-offs.

AFVN—Armed Forces radio and TV network-Vietnam.

air burst—an explosive device, such as a grenade, a bomb, an artillery round, or a mine, rigged to detonate above the ground to inflict maximum damage by expanding the range of shrapnel.

air-conditioning—an artificial temperature control device, widely used by army rear echelon and air force personnel, said to establish and maintain living conditions similar to those found in civilian life in the continental United States.

airstrike—surface attack by fixed-wing fighter/bomber aircraft.

AIT—Advanced Individual Training following Basic Combat Training.

AK-47—Communist made 7.62 cal. automatic assault rifle. It was the primary individual weapon used by the NVA/VC forces.

AO—Area of Operations. A defined geographical area where military operations are conducted for a specific period of time.

ao dai—traditional Vietnamese female dress, split up the sides and worn over pants.

ARA—Air Rocket Artillery. Military description of Huey gunships.

Arc Light—B-52 bombing mission.

Article 15—Punishment under the Uniform Code of Military Justice. Less severe than general courts-martial.

artillery fan—Area within range of supporting artillery.

ARVN (Arvin)—Army of the Republic of Vietnam.

ATL—Assistant Team Leader. Second in command on a LRP or Ranger team.

AWOL—Absent Without Leave.

(B)

BCT—Basic Combat Training. Initial course of training upon entry into the United States Army.

BDA—Bomb Damage Assessment. A special operations mission for the purpose of verifying results of an aerial bombing attack.

beaucoup—derived from the French word for "very many."

berm—high, earthen levee surrounding most large, permanent U.S. military installations as part of the perimeter defense system.

black box—Sensor devices planted along trails, roads, rivers, and at intersections and junctions to detect body heat, perspiration, or sound given off by passing enemy troops.

blasting cap—the detonator inserted into claymore mines, grenades, satchel charges, and other explosive devices, which initiates the actual detonation.

blood trail—spoor sign left by the passage or removal of enemy wounded and dead.

blue line—Designation on maps of streams, rivers, and other natural waterways.

body bag—rubberized canvas or plastic bags used to remove dead U.S. casualties from the field to Graves Registration locations.

body basket—a wire litter lowered by cable from a medevac helicopter to aid in the evacuation of critically wounded personnel, where landing is impossible because of terrain conditions.

boonies—informal term for unsecured areas outside U.S. military control.

boozers—slang term for military personnel who frequently indulge in heavy alcoholic consumption.

bush—informal term for the jungle, also called boonies, boondocks, Indian country, or the field.

butter bar—second lieutenant.

(C)

CA—Combat Assault.

CAR-15—commando version of the M-16 assault rifle.

C-3 or C-4—plastique explosives.

Cs or C rats—canned individual rations.

C & C—Command and Control.

CG—Commanding General.

CIB—Combat Infantry Badge.

CID—Criminal Investigation Division.

CO—commanding officer.

COSVN—Commanding Officer, South Vietnam.

CS—riot-control gas.

cammies—camouflaged jungle fatigues—blouses, pants, hand hats or berets.

cammo-stick—dual-colored camouflage greasepaint in a metal tube.

canister round—M-79 round containing numerous double-O BB shot.

Cav—short for Cavalry.

cheiu hoi—an enemy soldier who has rallied to the South Vietnamese government.

cherry—new, inexperienced soldier recently arrived in a combat zone.

Chi-Com—designation for Chinese Communist or an item of Chinese Communist manufacture or origin.

chopper—informal term for any helicopter.

chopper pad—designated landing or takeoff platform for one or more helicopters.

Chuck—informal term describing the enemy, also Charlie, Mr. Charles, Victor Charles, or VC.

clacker—informal term describing the electric firing device for a claymore mine or a phoo gas barrel.

claymore mine—command-detonated, antipersonnel mine designed to saturate an area 6'–8' above the ground and over an area of 60 degrees across its front, with 750 steel ball bearings.

cockadau—Vietnamese slang derivative meaning "kill."

cold—term describing an area of operations or a landing zone that is devoid of any enemy sign or activity.

commo—communication.

commo check—radio operator's request to verify the reception of his transmissions.

compromise—enemy discovery of the presence of a LRP/Ranger in its vicinity, thereby resulting in the termination of the mission and the extraction of the team.

concertina—coiled barbed-wire strung for perimeter defense.

contact—firing on or being fired on by the enemy.

contour flying—low-level, high-speed, daring helicopter flight adjusting altitude only for terrain features.

crapper or shitter—slang terms describing single-hole or multi-hole latrines.

CONEX—large steel container used to transport and store U.S. military supplies and equipment.

(D)

daisy-chain—more than one claymore mine wired together det cord, to effect simultaneous detonation.

DEROS—Date of Estimated Return From Overseas.

det cord—detonator cord, demolition cord: timed-burn fuse used with plastique explosives or to daisy-chain claymores together.

dex tabs—dexadrine tablets: an aid to prevent sleep; could cause hallucinations or wild, uncontrolled behavior if taken to excess.

di di or *di di mau*—Vietnamese phrase meaning "get out" or "go."

diddly bopping or diddy boppin'—slang term meaning "to move about foolishly and without taking security measures."

dopers—slang term for soldiers who use drugs.

double canopy—phrase used to describe primary jungle with a lower layer of undergrowth.

dragging ass—slang term to describe a condition of physical exhaustion.

deuce and a half—two-and-one-half-ton military transport truck.

dust off—helicopter conducting a medical evacuation.

(E)

early out—termination of military service prior to normal ETS.

E & E—Escape and Evasion.

EM—Enlisted man.

ETS—Estimated Termination of Service.

exfiltration—the procedure of departing a recon zone after completion of a mission.

extending—prolonging one's tour of combat duty beyond the normal DEROS date.

extraction—the removal of troops from the field, usually by helicopter.

(F)

F-4 (Phantom)—McDonnell-Douglas fighter/bombers that saw heavy use in Vietnam.

FAC—Forward Air Controller.

FNG—Fucking New Guy, slang term meaning an inexperienced soldier newly arrived in a combat zone.

FO—Forward Observer.

FOB—Forward Operating Base.

fast mover—U.S. fighter-bomber.

firebase or fire support base—forward artillery base.

firefly—LOH scout helicopter, mounting a searchlight and capable of dropping aerial flares.

firefight—small arms battle.

fire mission—directed artillery barrage.

flak jackets—vests worn by U.S. soldiers to lessen the severity of torso wounds caused by shrapnel.

foo gas or phoo gas—a mixture of JP-4 aviation fuel and naphtha, which performed like napalm when detonated. It was placed in fifty-five gallon drums and buried outside military perimeters as part of the frontline defense. Very effective against massed troops.

frag—fragmentation grenade.

Freedom Bird—name given to any military or commercial aircraft that took troops out of Vietnam.

free-fire zone—an area declared off-limits to all personnel. Anyone encountered within its confines was assumed to be hostile and could be fired on without verification or authorization.

(G)

G-2—Division Intelligence section.

G-3—Division Operations section.

goofy grape—slang for purple.

gook—derogatory slang term for any oriental person, especially Vietcong or NVA. Also dink, slope, slant, or zipperhead.

go to cover—move into heavy concealment.

Graves Registration—section of the military service charged with reception, identification, and disposition of U.S. military dead.

grunt—U.S. infantryman.

gunship—heavily armed helicopter used to support infantry troops or to independently attack enemy units or positions.

(H)

HE—high explosive.

H & I—harassment and interdiction, pre-plotted artillery fire designed to keep the enemy on edge and possibly catch him off balance.

HQ—Headquarters.

halazone tabs—halazone tablets, used to purify water before consumption.

heads—slang term for soldiers who smoke marijuana.

heat tabs—heating tablets, small blue chemical discs that burned slowly and gave off an intense, smokeless heat when ignited. Used for heating rations and boiling water.

heavy team—a LRP or Ranger team of 10 or more personnel.

helipad—(see acid pad or chopper pad)

Ho Chi Minh Trail—a vast network of roads and trails, running from southern North Vietnam, down through Laos, Cambodia, and South Vietnam and terminating just to the northwest of Saigon. It made up the transportation system that enabled the North Vietnamese Army to replace its losses of manpower, arms, and equipment.

Ho Chi Minhs—a slang name for the sandals worn by the Vietnamese made from discarded automobile tires and inner tubes.

hootch—slang term for any small civilian family or military shelters in Vietnam.

horn—term used to describe radio communication.

hot—term describing an area of operations or a landing zone where contact has been made with enemy troops.

Huey—UH1 helicopter, the primary helicopter troop transport in Vietnam.

hump (the)—the midpoint in a soldier's overseas combat tour, usually the 183rd day.

hump (to)—to walk on patrol, usually heavily laden and heavily armed: to perform any difficult task.

(I)

I Corps—northernmost military district in South Vietnam.

II Corps—central military district in South Vietnam.

III Corps—southernmost military district in South Vietnam.

IG—Inspector General.

in-country—term used to refer to American troops serving in Vietnam.

Indian country—the jungle, also known as the bush, boonies, boondocks, the field.

infiltration—the procedure of entering a recon zone without detection by the enemy.

insertion—the placement of combat or recon forces in the field, usually by helicopter.

instant NCO or Shake 'n Bake—derogatory informal terms used to describe soldiers who received their rank as noncommissioned officers, not by time in service and time in grade, but by graduation from the NCO school in Ft. Benning, Georgia.

(J)

Jody—universal name for the guy back home who tries to steal the GI's girl while he is overseas.

jungle penetrator—a metal cylinder with fold-out legs, attached by steel cable to a helicopter-mounted hoist, used to medically evacuate wounded soldiers from thick, jungle terrain.

(K)

K-bar—type of military combat knife used primarily by the Marines, LRPs, and Rangers.

KIA—Killed In Action.

killer team—a LRP or Ranger team with the primary mission of inflicting casualties upon the enemy through the use of ambush or raid.

kill zone—the target area of an ambush.

Kit Carson scout—former VC/NVA soldier, repatriated to serve as a scout for U.S. combat forces.

klick—one thousand meters, a kilometer.

(L)

LAW—Light Antitank Weapon: a single shot, disposable rocket launcher.

LBE—Load Bearing Equipment.

LOH or Loach—Light Observation Helicopter.

LP—listening post.

LRP—Long Range Patrol.

LRRP—Long Range Reconnaissance Patrol: also a dehydrated ration used by special operations units.

LZ—Landing Zone.

land line or lima-lima—ground telephone communications between two points.

lay dog—going to cover after insertion to wait and listen for any sign of enemy movement or presence in the area.

lifer—a career soldier.

Lima Charlie—the phonetic military designation for the letters "L" and "C" which is used as a reply to the radio commo request, "How do you read me?" It means "loud and clear!"

lister bag—a waterproof canvas bag, suspended from a beam or a tripod, providing potable drinking water to troops in bivouac.

lock 'n' load—to chamber a round in one's weapon.

(M)

M-16—lightweight automatic assault rifle used by U.S. forces in Vietnam: 5.56 cal.

M-60—light 7.62 cal. belt-fed, machine gun used by U.S. forces in Vietnam.

M-79—single shot, 40mm grenade launcher: also called a blooper or a thumper.

MACV—Military Advisory Command, Vietnam.

MIA—Missing In Action.

MP—Military Police.

MPC—Military Payment Certificate: funny money or script issued to U.S. military personnel in Vietnam.

mag—ammunition magazine.

McGuire rig—a nylon sling or seat attached to a 120-foot rope, used to extract special operations personnel from dense jungle under extreme conditions.

meal-on-wheels—mobile snack trucks found at major U.S. military bases.

medevac—helicopter conducting a medical evacuation.

mikes—phonetic military designation for the letter *M*: usually means minutes or meters.

monsoon—the rainy season in the Orient.

(N)

NCO—Noncommissioned Officer: ranks E-5 thru E-9.

NCOIC—Noncommissioned Officer in Charge.

NDP—Night Defense Position.

NVA—North Vietnamese Army.

Nam, or the Nam—short for Vietnam.

nouc mam—rotten-smelling fish sauce use by the Vietnamese.

number one—slang, means the very best.

number ten—slang, means the very worst.

(O)

OCS—Officer Candidate School.

OP—observation post.

one-oh-five—105mm howitzer.

one-five-five—155mm artillery.

one-seven-five—175mm artillery.

op order—operations order, a notice of an impending operation.

overflight—pre-mission aerial scout of a recon zone for the purpose of selecting primary and secondary landing zones and extraction points, determining route of march, and locating possible trails and enemy supply depots, structures and emplacements; usually conducted by the team leader and his assistant team leader. The inserting helicopter crew flies the overflight.

(P)

PAVN—People's Army of Vietnam.

PF—Popular Forces: South Vietnamese irregular forces.

PFC—Private First Class.

PLF—Parachute Landing Fall.

POW—Prisoner of War.

PRC-25 or Prick-25—portable radio used by American combat troops in the field.

PSP—perforated steel plating, used for airstrips, helicopter pads, bunker construction, and bridge matting.

PT—Physical Training.

PX—Post Exchange.

PZ—Pick-up Zone.

peter pilot—copilot of a helicopter.

piastres, or Ps—Vietnamese currency.

pig—affectionate slang nickname for the M-60 machine gun.

pink team—airborne hunter-killer team consisting of one or more LOH scout helicopters, a Huey C & C helicopter, and two or more Cobra gunships.

piss tube—a 12-inch pipe or the shipping case for an 8-inch artillery round, with one end buried at a 60 degree angle and the other end projecting 30 inches above ground and covered with screen wire mesh. It served as a semipermanent urinal for U.S. troops in bivouac.

point—a unit's advance man in line of march, or the scout in a combat patrol.

Psy Ops—Psychological Operations unit.

pull pitch—term used by helicopter pilots that means they are taking off.

punji stakes—sharpened bamboo stakes, hidden in grass, vegetation, in covered pits, or underwater, to penetrate the feet and lower legs of unwary troops. They were often dipped in feces to cause infection to the wound.

(R)

REMF—Rear Echelon Mother Fucker; slang derogatory term of endearment that combat troops called noncombat administrative and support troops.

RPD—Communist-made, drum-fed, light machine gun used by the VC/NVA forces in Vietnam.

RPG—Communist-made rocket launcher, firing a B-40 rocket: used by both the VC and the NVA, it was effective against U.S. armor, fixed emplacements, helicopters, patrol boats, and infantry.

R & R—Rest and Recreation: five to six day out-of-country furloughs given to U.S. military personnel serving in a combat zone.

RTO—Radio Telephone Operator.

RZ—Recon or Reconnaissance Zone.

radio relay, or X-ray—a communications unit, usually set up on a firebase, with the mission of relaying transmissions from units in the field to their rear commands.

rappel—the controlled descent, by means of a rope, from a tall structure or a hovering helicopter.

reaction force—a military unit established to respond quickly and determinedly to another unit's request for rescue or reinforcement; also called "blues."

rear seat—the gunner in a Cobra gunship, and in certain dual-seat fighter-bombers.

Recondo School—an exclusive training program, conducted by 5th Special Forces personnel in Nha Trang, which taught small unit special operations techniques to members of U.S., South Vietnamese, Korean, Thai, and Australian special operations units.

redlegs—informal name given to artillerymen.

revetment—sandbagged or earthen blast wall erected to protect aircraft and helicopters from shrapnel and blast caused by hostile mortars, artillery, rockets, thrown satchel charges, or demolitions.

rock 'n' roll—a slang term used to describe the firing of a weapon on full automatic, as opposed to semi-automatic.

ruck or rucksack—infantryman's backpack.

(S)

SAR—Search & Rescue.

SERTS—Screaming Eagle Replacement Training School, orientation course given to all new replacements in the 101st Airborne Division upon their arrival in Vietnam.

SFC—Sergeant First Class: E-7.

SKS—Communist-made 7.62 cal. semiautomatic assault rifle used by the VC and the NVA in Vietnam.

SOG (MACV)—Special Observation Group; specialized in deep-penetration patrols across the borders into South Vietnam's neighboring countries.

SOI—Signal Operating Instructions; the booklet that contained the call signs and radio frequencies of all units in Vietnam.

SOP—Standard Operating Procedure.

sapper—specially trained enemy soldier, with the mission to penetrate the perimeters of U.S. and allied military installations by stealth, and then to cause as much damage as possible to aircraft, vehicles, supply depots, communication centers, command centers, and hard defense positions. He would utilize satchel charges, grenades, demolition charges, and RPGs to accomplish his mission; sapper attacks often preceded mass infantry assaults and took place under heavy shelling by their own mortar and rocket crews.

selector switch—a three-position device on the M-16 and CAR-15 assault rifles, enabling the operator to chose safe, semi-automatic, or automatic fire merely by thumbing it in ninety-degree increments.

shit-burning detail—the most detested extra duty in Vietnam; it involved the disposal of raw human waste by burning it in half fifty-five-gallon drums; diesel fuel was poured into the barrels and ignited; the mixture was allowed to burn until a layer of ash accumulated on the surface, then it was stirred back into the raw sewage by means of large paddles and reignited; this procedure continued until only dry ash remained.

short, or short timer—a term to describe a soldier whose time remaining in country is less than sixty days.

single canopy—phrase used to describe low, dense jungle or forest growth, with no overhead cover from mature trees.

sitrep—situation report; regularly scheduled communication check between a unit in the field and its rear command element, to inform it of their present status.

Six—radio call sign for a unit's commander.

slack—the second position in a line of march or in patrol formation; also means "go easy on."

slack jump—a rappel involving a short free-fall before the commencing of a standard rappel.

slick—informal name for a Huey troop transport helicopter.

smoke—informal name for a smoke grenade; they came in a variety of colors, and were used to signal others, to mark positions, to determine wind direction, and to provide concealment.

Snake—informal name for the Cobra gunship.

snatch—to capture a prisoner.

spider hole—a one-man camouflaged enemy fighting position, often connected to other positions by means of a tunnel.

spotter round—artillery or mortar shell producing a dense cloud of white smoke; they were used to mark targets or to assist units in establishing their correct locations.

stand down—an infantry unit's return from the field to a firebase or base camp for rest and resupply.

starlight scope—a night vision device utilizing any ambient light source, such as stars, the moon, electric lights, distant flares, etc., to artificially illuminate the area within its range of view.

Stars and Stripes—U.S. military newspaper.

strack—a term used to describe or designate the ideal in military dress, demeanor, and bearing.

(T)

TAOR—Tactical Area of Responsibility.

TDY—Temporary Duty.

TL—Team Leader.

TOC—Tactical Operations Center.

Tac Air—fighter-bomber capability of the Air Force, Navy, and Marine air wings; as opposed to the strategic bombing capacity of the Air Force's B-52s.

tanglefoot—fields of barbed wire stretched tightly over a grid of metal stakes, approximately twelve inches above the ground; it was part of a perimeter's static defense, and was designed to discourage rapid and uninterrupted penetration.

tarmac—a term describing the hard-surfaced coating used to construct permanent airstrips, helicopter pads, and roads; the word comes from "tar" and "macadam."

ten-forty-nine, or 1049—the U.S. military form for requesting a transfer to another unit.

toe popper—a small, plastic U.S.-made anti-personnel mine, designed to cripple rather than kill.

tracer—ammunition containing a chemical composition to mark the flight of projectiles by a trail of smoke or fire.

triple canopy—phrase used to describe mature jungle or forest, with a third layer of ancient trees, often reaching heights two hundred feet or more, and blocking out the sun.

typhoon—an Asian hurricane.

(U)

Uncle Ho—familiar title for Ho Chi Minh, the leader of North Vietnam.

(V)

VC, Vietcong, Victor Charles—slang names describing members of the People's Army of Vietnam.

(W)

WIA—Wounded In Action.

WP, willie peter, willie pete, or willie papa—white phosphorus grenades, mortar rounds, or artillery rounds that exploded into a spray of chemical fire, which ignited on contact with air, and could only be doused by removal of the source of oxygen.

wait-a-minute vines—strong, barbed ground creepers that caught at the boots and clothing of American soldiers, and retarded their forward movement.

warning order—a directive that gives final approval for an upcoming mission.

"white mice"—a derogatory slang term for the military police of the South Vietnamese government.

World (the)—the States, USA, home.

(X)

XO—Executive Officer.

X-ray team—(see radio relay team)

(Z)

zapped—killed, slain in combat.

zipperhead—derogatory name for the Vietnamese, or any Oriental.

About the Author

Gary Linderer served with the LRP (later Ranger) Company attached to the 101st Airborne Division in Vietnam from June, 1968 to June, 1969. Among his decorations are two Silver Stars, a Bronze Star with V device, an Army Commendation Medal with V device, and two Purple Hearts.

He lives today with his wife, Barbara, and their four sons in Festus, Missouri. He works in the field of investment, risk, and debt management. This is his second book and a sequel to *Eye of the Eagle* (Ivy Books), which describes the first half of his tour in Vietnam.